DATE DUE

GAYLORD   PRINTED IN U.S.A.

Reclaiming
a
Scientific Anthropology

Lawrence A. Kuznar

ALTAMIRA
PRESS

A Division of Sage Publications, Inc.
Walnut Creek • London • New Delhi

For information address:

AltaMira Press
A Division of Sage Publications, Inc.
1630 North Main Street, Suite 367
Walnut Creek, CA 94596 U.S.A.

SAGE Publications Ltd.
6 Bonhill Street
London EC2A 4PU
United Kingdom

SAGE Publications India Pvt. Ltd.
M-32 Market
Greater Kailash 1
New Delhi, 110 048 India

#35574521
70822
GN
42
·K89
1997

PRINTED IN THE UNITED STATES OF AMERICA

Library of Congress Cataloging-in-Publication Data

Kuznar, Lawrence A.
  Reclaiming a Scientific Anthropology / Lawrence A. Kuznar.
    p. cm.
  Includes bibliographical references and index.
  ISBN 0-7619-9113-1 (cloth: acid-free paper)
  ISBN 0-7619-9114-X (pbk: acid-free paper)
    1. Anthropology–Research. 2. Anthropology–Methodology.
    3. Science–Methodology. 4. Observation (Scientific method).
    I. Title.
  GN42.K89 1996
  301'.0723–dc20   97-35699

97 98 99 10 9 8 7 6 5 4 3 2

Production and Editorial Services: David Featherstone
Editorial Management: Jennifer Collier, Nicole Fountain
Cover Design: Ravi Balasuriya
Text Design: Denise Santoro

Contents

About the Author

Lawrence A. Kuznar was born in Wilkes-Barre, Pennsylvania, in 1963. He earned his bachelor's degree in anthropology at the Pennsylvania State University, where he found that his interests in ecology and human social behavior complemented one another in an anthropological perspective. He went on to do graduate studies at Northwestern University. His initial interest was the early domestication of camelids in the Andes, and he began his graduate career conducting archaeological research to address this issue. In time, his interests shifted toward ethnographic and ethnoarcheological studies of contemporary indigenous Andean herders. He combined his research on the prehistory, material culture, and ethnography of Andean herding in his dissertation, and in 1990 he was graduated from Northwestern with a doctorate in anthropology and a master's of science degree in mathematical methods in the social sciences. Dr. Kuznar has published articles on the ecology and economics of herding, on ecological symbioses among plants, animals, and humans, and on the economics of the Inca Empire. His work appears in journals such as *Human Ecology, Mountain Research and Development, Nomadic Peoples, Journal of Quantitative Anthropology, Chungara, Diálogo Andino*, and *Journal of World Systems Research*, as well as in edited symposium volumes. He is also the author of *Awatimarka: The Ethnoarchaeology of an Andean Herding Community* (Harcourt Brace, 1995). Dr. Kuznar is currently conducting ethnobotanical and ecological research among traditional Navajo sheepherders and ranchers in Arizona.

Preface and Acknowledgments

This book reflects my concern that when contemporary anthropologists analyze and evaluate accounts they are abandoning the basic tools of scientific analysis—logic and empirical data. Instead the emotional impact of rhetoric is becoming the standard for the evaluation of claims. This concerns me because anthropologists have made tremendous strides in building more objective knowledge using empirical data and logic. Should anthropologists abandon these operating principles, they will continue to generate knowledge, but the knowledge will be more partial, more biased, and more easily used in political power plays. I have one bias that permeates the pages of this book—I don't like politics. The politics that concern me involve a priori admissions that only certain truths are permissible. Anthropological research has always had an impact on people's politics as anthropologists gathered scientific data that refuted political prejudices. However, this research has primarily been aimed at uncovering the truth about matters (e.g., debunking untrue racial and gender stereotypes, describing the complex social structures and ideologies of so-called primitive savages, etc.). I perceive a shift in our focus today. It is no longer enough that we generate more objective knowledge; we are being told that our knowledge must, first and foremost, "do good." As the prime purpose of anthropology shifts away from generating more objective knowledge to producing morally good knowledge, there is a shift from dealing with representative data to the rhetoric of good and evil. If one's goal is to effect political change, the truth is no longer necessary to one's argument. I am concerned that in this political shift in focus, anthropologists will increasingly abandon even the tentative and partial truths created through science. Perhaps this book can serve as a corrective to this trend.

I have written this book with a particular audience in mind. One reviewer thought that I wrote this book to get the "big boys'" attention. It would be nice if the main players in the science debate regarded this book, resolved their differences, and forged a more robustly scientific anthropology, but I suspect that many of the big boys *and* girls have probably already made up their minds. However, their students hopefully have not already made up *their* minds. I have written this book for the benefit of anthropology students (graduate and otherwise) so that they may be informed on all sides of this debate, and then may make their own decisions about the usefulness of science for anthropology. I present basic issues of science that, according to undergraduates that I send to graduate school, are no longer necessarily taught. This book can be used as a primer for anyone (pro or con) concerned with science in anthropology. I present basic scientific methods as formulated by anthropologists, the basic arguments against science, and my own arguments in favor of a scientific approach. Readers will then be able to judge the merits of these various arguments and, if they want, use the bibliography as a guide to the literature. If this book is useful to students as they formulate their own anthropological approaches, that is great; if students are convinced that scientific methods should be retained in anthropology, that is even better. If professionals can be humble enough to reflect on their own positions, and I sincerely hope they can, that would be great, too.

In conclusion, I wrote this book because I do not want us to throw away more than a century of progressively better knowledge about the human condition. Anthropology is a unique discipline that offers all people a better, more complete, more objective understanding of humanity. Scientific knowledge is always partial, and never exempt from political, cultural and ethical biases. The question we face is whether we want to go in a direction that will increase the partialness and bias of our accounts, or whether we wish to continue to struggle against these distorting influences and honestly confront the world. I hope we choose the latter.

Many people played a part in this book's production, some supportive, some adversarial, and all helping me to do better work. My undergraduate education was a truly formative experience for a naive kid from rural Pennsylvania. Had James Hatch not mentored a budding anthropologist, my career might never have happened. Joseph Michaels taught an archaeological method and theory course in those years that gave me my first important taste of the philosophy of science. William Irons continued my formal methods and theory education in graduate school and built upon the foundations laid by my undergraduate mentors.

A very special thanks must go out to my colleagues in the Department of Sociology-Anthropology at Indiana-Purdue University at Fort Wayne. I am fortunate to be not only in a department where people get along, but in a department where there is an active intellectual interchange among us all. I have spent hundreds of hours discussing this book with my colleagues, and hundreds more discussing the general issues that inform this book. My anthropologist colleagues Robert Jeske, Paul Provost, and Alan Sandstrom all have had a major impact on my thinking and, in turn, this book. Bob Jeske and Alan Sandstrom made especially important contributions by reading early versions of the manuscript, as well as by discussing and debating the issues with me incessantly. I am indebted to Dr. Jeske for the Hopewell example and for informing me of its significance as an example of anthropological science. Alan Sandstrom and Pamela Sandstrom provided other useful examples.

My sociology colleagues also graciously put up with my writing this book. Anson Shupe provided essential materials on the IQ and race controversy as well as on creation science. Judith DiIorio exposed me to feminist philosophies of science and gave me opportunities to explore them more fully. Peter Iadicola, Pat Ashton, and Michael Nusbaumer each provided me with useful examples of neo-Marxist critiques of postmodernism. Bronek Mistal, now of Catholic University, in Washington, D. C., introduced me to current European thinking on postmodernism. Collectively, my sociology colleagues offered me many chances for lively debate on the issues that I address in this book.

Numerous people read the book manuscript, and I am greatly indebted to them for all of their efforts. As far as anthropologists go, I thank Oswald Werner, Roy D'Andrade, Marvin Harris, and Barry Lewis, and an anonymous reviewer for their constructive criticism. They all had useful comments, and I did my best to incorporate their insights into the final version of this book. I also want to acknowledge Steven Beckerman, Mark Aldenderfer, James Brown, Lee Cronk, and Lawrence Keeley for having made contributions through discussions. Two other people who read this book were not anthropologists, but philosophers; and I also am greatly in their debt. Richard Watson and Clyde Holler both spent much time and effort providing detailed and unforgiving criticism of the manuscript. They helped me realize that anthropologists do not necessarily need to take on the issues that consume philosophers, although I maintain that we anthropologists should not be unaware of philosophical issues, and that we can make contributions to them. The result of their criticism was a more anthropologically relevant argument, and a better written book.

I thank Mitch Allen for his support of the book throughout the editorial process. Not only did he lend his editorial expertise, but he also was able to understand why such a book would be written because of his own anthropological background. I also want to thank Cornell University Press for its permission to quote extensively from Sandra Harding's 1991 *Whose Science? Whose Knowledge?*

Finally, a great debt of gratitude goes to my family. I thank my wife, Christine, for putting up with me as I wrestled with epistemology and at times lost my normally rosy outlook on life. My children, Shannon and Eric, played a vital role in the production of this book. Through their frequent injuries, their occasional illnesses, our nighttime readings, our gardening, and our adventurous fishing trips, they served as a constant reminder that no matter what the philosophers say, there is a reality.

Lawrence A. Kuznar
July 4, 1996
Warren, Pennsylvania

Introduction

How many a dispute could have been deflated into a single paragraph if the disputants had dared to define their terms.

Aristotle

Either they [analysts of science] *went on being relativists even about the settled parts of science—which made them look ludicrous; or they continued being realists even about the warm uncertain parts—and they made fools of themselves*

Bruno Latour

This book originated, in a way, from a class I once had on anthropological method and theory. I was sitting in a class that, over the weeks, had degenerated into a constant battle between a professor trying teach scientific methods and students who wanted no part of what he was covering, and especially no part of him. Every class had become the same. He would enter and say something regarding hypothesis testing, and a group of students would erupt, lock-step, in a chorus of "Sociobiology!" "How can you say that!" or "What about Marx!" The students were reacting to the professor's examples, which were from sociobiology, rather than to the topic he was teaching. The course never went anywhere. A verbal battle ensued, students huffed off in moral indignation, and we all remained as ignorant as the day class began.

1

The professor eventually refused to teach that course, and it was replaced by a lecture seminar in which each professor of the department gave a lecture on his or her latest research—a little theory, a little data, much too much opinion, and no method.

I am, in retrospect, grateful to my radical peers for more than their companionship, intellectual stimulation, and the excellent potlucks we shared. One day, after the usual debacle, I was feeling cheated. I understood the political aspects of my peers' arguments, in fact, we all were able to spout off the various ills of society and their causes in a neat, formulaic fashion. I did not, however, share the confidence of my peers in having all the right answers for anthropology, let alone for the world. I still (naively, perhaps) wanted to learn something, and I felt that my peers were cheating me of the chance to learn. So I stormed off in my own little huff one day, marched down the street to the funky little academic book store (every major university has one, with its disheveled piles of books, faded spines, and burnt-out graduate student behind the counter), stepped up to the philosophy section, pulled Popper, Kuhn, and Nagel off the shelf, forked over my eighty dollars plus (I still remember the amount, it hurt to spend it in those impoverished student days), and set out to read what had my peers so up in arms. That was, unbeknownst to me, the birth of this book.

This book is about scientific methods in anthropology and the contentious issues that have arisen around their application. The discipline of anthropology is arguably in a state of crisis over these issues that concern the very foundations of anthropological knowledge. As Rubel and Rosman note, "the epistemological differences about which anthropologists are arguing today threaten to tear the discipline apart" (1994:342). The issues involve the status of reality, the evaluation of competing claims, and the politics of research. These issues are not only relevant to today's anthropology, but to many other disciplines as well, and to society at large. Postmodernists and critical theorists have attacked the notion that there is a real, knowable world, that researchers can strive to be more objective in evaluating theories; and they have levelled allegations that science is nothing more than a politically motivated scheme to provide capitalists with power and to deny it to others. The thesis of this book is that these criticisms are far overblown, they do not obviate the use of the scientific method in anthropology, and furthermore, that postmodern (and other) approaches are likely to subvert the very values that their proponents advance. I will not only criticize these propositions, but I will also point out how anthropologists may use them to improve the scientific generation of knowledge in anthropology. If we anthropologists can find a way of incorporating what is useful from these criticisms, then perhaps we can find a way out of our present state of crisis.

Marxist and postmodernist critics represent most of the contemporary critiques of anthropological science, while conservative intellectual and ideological positions come from creationists and some racialists. Most of these critics share the same basic skepticism about science, and they use surprisingly similar lines of argumentation. I will review these varied critiques and evaluate their significance for the practice of science in anthropology. Critics of anthropological science are motivated both by their own biased agendas and by failures in the practice of science, and those of us who wish to retain an essentially scientific perspective in anthropology have much to learn about our own shortcomings by reviewing challenges to scientific anthropology. Hopefully, I will not only successfully defend scientific methods, but also expose ways in which to make the practice of science even more robust.

I aim to clarify points made in the various texts reviewed. I hope that some conciliation is achieved by exposing similarities between some views (e.g., practice of interpretation and science) and by demonstrating that some issues (e.g., science and morality) are not necessarily connected. A major contention of mine is that, on many practical issues, scientific and non-scientific anthropologists actually agree, despite the different language in which they couch their practice. As Aristotle noted, many raging debates are caused by ambiguity, not real difference. Identifying such similarities will enable anthropologists to dispose of much of the current debate and also of much of the acrimony. While this may clarify and reconcile views, there will be certain principles and ideas that are incommensurable. Those principles that are a matter of style will remain unresolved. Other principles will be superior (or less inferior) to others, and I would expect anthropologists to retain them and discard the less efficacious or defensible. In the end, I will leave a lot of gray areas behind, but hopefully fewer than when I started.

We live in very contentious times, and the issues discussed in this book are nothing if they are not contentious. The issues include the nature of religion, the question of reality, and the role of morality and ethics in the sciences. Much of the acrimony we now experience in academia and elsewhere over these contentious issues is the result of misunderstandings and miscommunications. These arise not from regarding what people say, but from inventing straw-man opponents who say what people want them to say. I am determined to avoid this weak and misleading form of argumentation, and I will make liberal use of quotes and do my utmost to present views in their intended context. If I at all fail to do this, it is a sin of omission, not commission. Following Marcus and Fischer's (1986:viii) disclaimer, I apologize to those I did not cite and I beg the indulgence of those I have cited.

I have chosen foundational works that represent the core arguments of each of the positions I treat. The work of Marvin Harris (1979), H. Russell Bernard (1994a), Roy D'Andrade (1995a,b), Patty Jo Watson (1992, and others 1971, 1984) and Lewis Binford (1977, 1982, 1983) are among the main works representing scientific anthropology. The work of applied philosophers of science (Richard Watson, Alison Wylie, Merrilee Salmon, James Bell), and historical philosophers of science (Sir Francis Bacon, David Hume, Auguste Comte, Bertrand Russell, Karl Popper, Carl Hempel, Imre Lakatos, Thomas Kuhn) are also important as reflections of what, in the abstract, scientists do and should be doing. However, I will focus on science as it is described and practiced by anthropologists, as this is what is at issue in anthropology today. The work of the Creation Science Institute in San Diego (Morris, ed. 1974), and the writings of its director Henry Morris (1984), represent creationist attacks on scientific anthropology, although I also address the somewhat competing views of Phillip Johnson (1991). I concentrate my discussion of race upon the most recent presentation of race-oriented research found in Herrnstein and Murray (1994) and Rushton (1995). While postmodernists cringe at the thought of foundations, there have emerged such works in this anti-canonical, anti-foundational movement as well (Rabinow 1986:244). The foundations of postmodernism upon which I focus include Jacques Derrida (1976), Pierre Bourdieu (1977, 1990, 1991), Michel Foucault (1972, 1977, 1978, 1980, 1984), Jean Francois Lyotard (1984), Jean Baudrillard (1983a,b,

1987) and Barry Smart (1994). I also discuss briefly the philosophy of Martin Heidegger (1962) and Jürgen Habermas (1968). Cultural anthropologists who pioneered postmodern and critical approaches include Dell Hymes (1974), Talal Asad (1973), James Clifford (1986a,b), George Marcus and Michael Fischer (1986), Paul Rabinow (1986), and Steven Tyler (1986, 1991). Finally, postmodern archaeologists have also produced foundational works, namely those by Michael Shanks and Christopher Tilly (1987a,b), and Ian Hodder (1991a,b).

While I am in a disclaiming mood, I want to make a note about politics. This book is not intended to be a political work. This is a hard claim to make, since the issues contained herein are contentious primarily because people have perceived (correctly or not) them as political issues. While admittedly, politics and biases permeate much of what anthropologists do professionally and otherwise, every act is not necessarily part of some concerted political agenda, nor is this book part of some such agenda. I recognize the role of the reader in the life of this text, and I recognize that I have no control over how a reader takes this book for his or her own political purposes. When possible, I will spell out where I think this book has a lack of political relevance, but ultimately, the reader will determine that. My intent here is simply to clarify various authors' positions and to point out their strengths and weaknesses. There are statements concerning the best political environment for science, but this is not a moral argument for a particular politic, simply a logical argument for what works best for generating maximally objective, scientific knowledge.

Science seems to be a lightning rod in today's debates, with some writers touting it as a crowning achievement of Western civilization (Gellner 1992; Gross and Levitt 1994; Kuhn 1970; Harris 1979), and others as the last dying gasps of a failed Enlightenment project (Smart 1993; Hollinger 1994; Marcus and Fischer 1986; Tyler 1991). Which shall it be? Most analysts of science, pro or con, would at this point launch into arguments favoring their point without defining the very phenomenon that concerns them— science. This is true of many science studies such as Thomas Kuhn's famous *The Structure of Scientific Revolutions* and Gross and Levitt's *Higher Superstition* as well as criticisms of science such as Harding's *Whose Science? Whose Knowledge?* and Foucault's *Archaeology of Knowledge*. Works like Nagel's *Structure of Science*, Hempel's *Aspects of Scientific Explanation*, and Popper's *Logic of Scientific Inquiry* are written for philosophers and remain inaccessible to non-scientists, and barely accessible to scientists. In the interest of clarity and in an attempt to avoid Aristotle's condemnation, I will provide a definition of science that hopefully will be true to anthropologists' and philosophers' ideals. This will be a very terse definition of science, upon which I will expand in part 1.

Science is a method of generating knowledge about the experienced world based on the evaluation of logical theories with empirical data. There are many other important details, but the notion of testing an idea against data and the requirement that theories must adhere to the rules of logic are indispensable and distinctive elements of scientific practice. Other forms of knowledge generally are based on inviolate truths that are more than mere assumptions; they must be accepted on faith, and they are never permitted to be scrutinized fully. The ability to test ideas thoroughly is inherently limited in these other forms of knowledge. For instance, a Christian theologian may have latitude in musing on the nature of God and existence. However, a theologian is not permitted to test the notion that God exists and especially is not permitted to falsify the concept of God. Likewise, a Marxist culture critic has much latitude in describing how capitalists exploit laborers, but most Marxist analysts would be loath to fail to find exploitation; a Marxist assumes that exploitation is an inviolate truth of capitalism. Similarly, economists in our business colleges nearly always interpret evidence that contradicts their basic assumptions (like utility maximization) as excessive government interference in the free market, not as evidence that refutes economic theory. In true scientific inquiry, all ideas are subject to scrutiny and eventual falsification. This makes science the only systematically self-correcting means of generating knowledge. Despite contemporary criticisms of the alleged scientific monolith by historical and cultural revisionists, science is the ultimate in revisionism.

Current debates regarding science are debates concerning different ways of knowing, or epistemologies. Epistemology, the study of how we know what we know, traditionally deals primarily with logical problems. People do not commonly ask this question of their knowledge, although it is an important question that could clarify one's personal thinking on many matters from daily concerns (How do I know that my toothpaste fights cavities better than brand X?) to profound thoughts (Does God exist?). There are different rules for knowing, or epistemologies, and most epistemologies have rather narrow applications. Since epistemologies are limited and science is based on certain epistemological principles, science is likewise limited. It is important to realize this fact. Just because science has certain limits hardly condemns science; it actually helps people appreciate just how useful science is when applied to appropriate questions. Likewise, by understanding the limits of other epistemologies, one gains an appreciation of why they are inappropriate when addressing questions best addressed with scientific methods.

What kinds of questions are appropriately addressed with scientific epistemology? Basically any question that concerns a statement that one is willing to disprove, that is logical, and that can be addressed by looking at real-world (measurable, experienced) observations. Scientists can address the mutation of DNA or the exchange of nutrients in an ecosystem. People can measure and observe these phenomena, and scientists are ultimately willing to abandon their theories about these phenomena should data contradict them. Science cannot address the existence of things metaphysical, aesthetic, and supernatural such as God, the beauty of a sunset, or poltergeists. Until these phenomena can be measured in a way that all people can recognize using their natural powers of observation (perhaps technologically aided), these phenomena remain outside of the purview of science; religion, ethics and morality are simply not the concerns of scientists. Scientists cannot disprove the truth or falsity of moral issues, nor can they verify them. If this concept was widely appreciated by scientists and non-scientists, this book and the many other books written on science (both pro and con) would be unnecessary. So why is this book necessary?

I am writing this book because both the fluorescence of science and perhaps its most biting criticisms have emerged in this century. My perception is that the tide, especially within anthropology, is turning against science as an epistemological approach (Smart 1993; Holinger 1994; Clifford 1986a,b; Rabinow 1986; Tyler 1991), and I am concerned that anthropologists may abandon methods that have yielded much sound knowledge in favor of other epistemologies that will turn out to be arbitrary, unreliable, and subject to political fiat. Such a shift will result in the generation of less objective knowledge. Anti-science challenges come in different forms and certainly from across the political/ideological spectrum. Despite their specific differences, they share the same basic feature; these challenges are based on metaphysical assumptions about morality and ethics that ultimately people cannot test empirically. These epistemologies, then, are essentially religious. One does not have to thump a Bible to be religious; one can just as well thump Marx's *Das Kapital*, Foucault's *Discipline and Punish*, or Adam Smith's *Wealth of Nations*. The central argument in this book is not against religion, but against assertions that religious epistemologies are science and assertions that science is not possible, or is, itself, just another set of unquestioned beliefs.

What are these twentieth-century challenges to science? There are many, but contrasting creationism and the panoply of views that come under the rubric of postmodernism demonstrates a common thread to all of these challenges. Creationists and postmodernists appear on the surface to be diametrically opposed. Creationism is founded on fundamentalist Christian precepts, especially on a literal interpretation of Genesis. Creationists argue that moral absolutes exist. In the United States, creationism is associated with socially conservative political views. Creationists have a certain degree of respect for and awe of Western European civilization, especially its religious and economic institutions (see Morris 1984). Postmodern arguments, while diverse, share several fundamental characteristics. Postmodernists are blatantly critical of Western civilization, and most especially of capitalism. Postmodernism is most often associated with leftist and liberal political perspectives in the United States (see Gross and Levitt 1994; Rosenau 1992). Some postmodernists adopt a version of radical relativism in which all views are considered incommensurable. Many postmodernists would hold that Christianity has been a totalizing and repressive force in Western history that has served the needs of ruling classes, oppressed underclasses, and destroyed non-Western peoples. How, then, can these two seemingly diametrically opposed perspectives be similar?

They are similar on an epistemological level. Proponents of both perspectives make similar assumptions about how the world works, adopt idiosyncratic language and modes of analysis, make implicit and explicit notions of ethical right and wrong (despite some postmodernists' call for moral relativism), are intolerant of other epistemologies, and most importantly, prevent finding fault with their most fundamental assumptions. It is no accident that some postmodern writers have drawn parallels between their own New Age world view, Christian and Islamic fundamentalism, and medieval mysticism (Smart 1993:29). I will describe these aspects of each movement in subsequent chapters. In the process, I will demonstrate that science is an epistemology that is useful for answering questions about the empirical world and, because of its limits, cannot be used to address metaphysical issues. Scientists, therefore, can be unconcerned with and thus tolerant of other epistemologies; scientists can live with other world views. The question is whether proponents of other world views will live with science.

My reason for writing this book is a concern that anthropologists will abandon the quest for increasingly objective knowledge, and that this discipline will loose its synthetic, holistic qualities. Anthropology is an extremely broad discipline that includes studies of language, religion, culture, social organization, primatology, genetics, human evolution, and prehistory. Anthropologists' traditional aim was to achieve a holistic understanding of the human condition by integrating the varied aspects of human existence mentioned above, and anthropologists have long advanced a scientific approach. The American Anthropology Association prescribed such an approach in its Articles of Incorporation in 1902. One benefit of science is that it is not necessarily culture-specific. As Gross and Levitt (1994:131) point out, people from varied societies and ethnic groups have joined the ranks of Western science's esteemed without contributing anything more than their profound intellects. On the other hand, should someone from a particular cultural background expose a Western assumption as arbitrary, or provide a new perspective that can advance knowledge, then scientific anthropologists are uniquely capable of revising their faulty assumptions and theories and incorporating the new perspective. Indeed, this is a potential benefit of both anthropological fieldwork and the integration of persons of varied backgrounds into the sciences (Harding 1991). The important point to remember is that weakening adherence to faulty assumptions and abandoning them is hardly damning of science, it is science.

Anthropologists, for these reasons, are capable of being particularly sensitive to the benefits of the scientific method. Unfortunately, there is a growing movement within anthropology to abandon the scientific approach in favor of varied postmodern epistemologies and critical theory (Clifford 1983; Marcus 1994; Tyler 1991). Scientists in fields such as physics and chemistry have not yet directly encountered anti-science challenges within their disciplines. They have, however, encountered persons outside of their discipline who are now attacking all of the sciences as being limited in scope and totalizing in practice, and this has alarmed some scientists to speak out against postmodernism. Gross and Levitt's 1994 *Higher Superstition* is an analysis of some of these arguments. However, Gross and Levitt have not witnessed the advance of postmodernist projects and other anti-scientific challenges within their disciplines (biology and mathematics) to the extent that this has happened in anthropology. The popularity of anti-scientific arguments in anthropology makes our discipline a canary in the mine, and what befalls anthropology will eventually hit the physical sciences. This gives an anthropologist both an appreciation of how conditions within a discipline can give rise to an anti-science movement and a first-hand look at the effects of such movements.

Finally, I think that the arguments within this book are ones with which scientists of all disciplines as well as non-scientists should become versed, because anti-science movements will always exist and threaten scientific research. Anti-science movements exist for a reason. Science, because of its limits, can be very disillusioning to people if scientists sell science as something it is not. If scientists promise peace, harmony, prosperity, and happiness, while science is inherently limited in its ability to address these moral/ethical issues, non-scientists rightfully will feel cheated and let down when scientists fail to deliver. In fact, much of the postmodern criticism of science addresses the failure of an alleged modernist project to create a better world through science. Scientists must appreciate their limits in generating knowledge as well as their strengths, and they must convey these limits and strengths to non-scientific communities. As most scientists realize, science is a very particular and special way of knowing about the world, and it has certain limits that we are obliged to respect. This book will highlight those limits as well as the strengths of the scientific method in anthropology.

I present my argument in three parts. Part 1 contains a presentation of scientific anthropology. Within part 1, chapter 1 contains a presentation of how anthropologists have conceived and justified their science. The work of philosophers, contemporary and historical, is not ignored; and I make use of their insights about what scientists do and should do, as well as note some major dilemmas with which philosophers of science have grappled. I do not intend to engage these philosophical issues since I am an anthropologist concerned with the scientific practice of anthropology, not with resolving the issues that concern philosophers. My intent is rather to present a basic description of what anthropologists as practicing scientists are taught in graduate school, and what scientific anthropologists actually try to do in their research. This is really the crux of the debate over science—what do scientists do and how does that relate to the norms of scientific evaluation?

Science is not simply a mechanistic application of a set of abstract rules. Scientists are people, and there is a human, sociological dimension to the practice of science that I shall not overlook. In chapter 2, I consider this poorly understood dimension. One central concern in that chapter is the role of paradigms—the set of background assumptions and questions that influence more explicit scientific work—in scientific inquiry. Do paradigm shifts represent a progressive improvement in knowledge? I will argue that, even though paradigm shifts may not have much to do with old scientific problems, they nonetheless can be regarded as progress within a scientific discipline, and that paradigm shifts are not capricious or necessarily irrational. While the discussions of chapter 2 intrude upon the work of historians and philosophers of science, they do address issues of human behavior, thought, and interaction, and therefore warrant anthropological treatment.

Abstract statements by anthropologists, philosophers, and historians on what science is and what scientists do are fruitless if they do not have some bearing on actual scientific practice. I try to place examples of anthropological science throughout the book to illustrate my points, but in chapter 3 I provide two extended examples. One example is from cultural anthropology, research on the role of hunting in forager society; the other example is from archaeology, the history of research on Hopewell culture in the American midwest. These examples permit me to demonstrate how anthropological research generally does conform to the scientific principles anthropologists advocate. Also, through these examples, I demonstrate the strengths of using a scientific approach, as well as the weaknesses of abandoning it. Finally, these examples provide a realistic view of how anthropologists apply scientific principles.

Part 2 contains descriptions of specific challenges to scientific anthropology. In chapter 4, I deal with traditional critiques of scientific anthropology such as the creationism debate, with special reference to what is called creation science. I will demonstrate that creation science is not science, but rather a form of religious inductivism akin to medieval Scholasticism. While it has a place for those who wish to believe in its tenets, religious inductivism cannot qualify as a scientific understanding of the past since its central tenets must be immune to testing at all times. Next, I deal with the extremely contentious issue of race and intelligence. I will review the most recent incarnation of this debate, especially Herrnstein and Murray's 1994 tome, *The Bell Curve*. This is a useful example since it illustrates that science must involve much more than simple data; it must concern itself with relevant, valid data and, most importantly, with theory. Their work, because of its controversial nature, has received much publicity and criticism, with critics mostly attacking their work on moral grounds. I do not wish to get into these issues, but rather to address whether or not Herrnstein and Murray's work really conforms to anthropological scientific standards.

After considering these traditional, conservative critiques, I deal with the varied Marxist and postmodern critiques of science and anthropology in chapters 5 through 7. Chapter 5 contains a discussion of postmodernism and general criticisms of science. This is important because critical and postmodern anthropologists hail from these more general social movements. I will critique these approaches, but also point out what I see as their usefulness to scientists. In chapter 6, I examine postmodern cultural anthropology, its dictates for the future of anthropological practice, and its weaknesses. Similarly, in chapter 7 I consider the case of postmodern influences in archaeology, and the especially contentious issue of the mutability of the past. While this part of the book contains specific analyses of the varied criticisms of scientific anthropology, the final part contains a comparison of these critiques. Comparing the similarities among them enables me to address more general issues in the practice of anthropology.

Part 3 begins with chapter 8, which contains a comparison/contrast of the different anti-science arguments levelled at scientific anthropology. I will draw similarities in argumentation among the different contemporary critiques of science, and I will demonstrate their basis in dogmatic adherence to ethical, political, and metaphysical principles. Chapter 9 is a discussion of the problem of advocacy in anthropological science. I will demonstrate that, ironically, the only way in which to use information for emancipatory purposes (both a modernist and a postmodern tenet) is to adhere strictly to scientific methods. First, scientific methods produce arguably the only type of knowledge that can transcend cultural boundaries. Second, scientific knowledge has a tremendous pragmatic appeal. Third, the exposure of bias is a sword that cuts both ways. Advocacy implies bias; and bias in one direction does not invalidate bias in another direction (Rabinow 1986:241), it simply adds another invalid and irreconcilable perspective to a debate. The problem with critical theory and advocacy is that, in the end, researchers utilizing such advocacy-based epistemology can rely on only one thing for validation—the exercise of power in silencing criticism. Of course, once people set this precedent, those that can monopolize power get to promote the valid theories. I think that most postmodern and critical theorists would wish to avoid such a situation.

In chapter 10, I consider the wider implications of today's debates. I will discuss what I think is the logically proper relationship between science and society, and what I think the future could hold for a scientific anthropology. This final chapter concludes with a recap of the basic anthropological scientific method and its practice. This is an argument *of* science, but the chapter also contains an argument *for* science. As pointed out in chapter 9, a science in which scientists attempt to be blind to bias and advocacy is the very system of knowledge that unwittingly may be the best form of emancipatory knowledge. Furthermore, as a practical note, few people would genuinely wish to return to a pre-scientific world, a world without modern creature comforts, without life-saving medicines, and without the regularity in food supply that many of us enjoy. Therefore, scientists must be doing something right. The less people interfere with the process, perhaps the better.

In the end, this book is about reconciliation, understanding, and a degree of epistemological tolerance. We all evaluate theories about the experienced world we share in light of our observations upon that world, and therefore we should be capable of appreciating the scientific method. We often seek deeper meanings for these observations and theories, and therefore appeal to religious and ethical types of knowledge. Finally, we all should be able to realize new perspectives through ethnographies, reflect upon how our idiosyncratic perspectives and use of language impinge upon our science, or appreciate the meanings in a work of art, and we therefore should appreciate postmodern perspectives.

Science
in
Anthropology

Chapter 1

Anthropological Science

False facts are highly injurious to the progress of science, for they often endure long; but false views, if supported by some evidence, do little harm, for everyone takes a salutary pleasure in proving their falseness; and when this is done, one path towards error is closed and the road to truth is often at the same time opened.

Charles Darwin
The Descent of Man

Scientific anthropology is under attack from a variety of political and academic positions, both left and right. Postmodernists and critical theorists allege that "neither the experience nor the interpretive activity of the scientific researcher can be considered innocent" (Clifford 1983:133), and describe science in terms of "fascism" and "hegemonic discourse" (Tyler 1991:82, 91). Creationists accuse scientists of complicity in a conspiracy to foist evolutionary thought upon the world in an attempt to defeat Christianity (Morris, ed. 1976). Critics in both camps also allege that science largely developed to advance the arbitrary political projects of secular, Enlightenment elitists (Johnson 1991:150; Tyler 1991:81). Before engaging these accusations, I want to establish just what anthropological science is by examining what scientific anthropologists say they do, how they justify their science, and how anthropological science is part of the larger scientific tradition of skeptical thought. I will demonstrate that anthropologists have developed a more-or-less coherent scientific approach during this century that has the following central features: an assumption that there exists an external, knowable world; a realization that theories are humanly constructed and therefore require evaluation; and the adoption of the procedural rule that a theory's fit to all relevant data is the most important criterion for acceptance or rejection of a particular theoretical position. Anthropologists have stated and justified these basic tenets of anthropological science in a number of publications and public debates, and I will detail these views of anthropological science in this chapter.

My focus is on the scientific anthropology of today, but this scientific anthropology did not develop in an historical vacuum; it is part of an intellectual tradition of skeptical, empirical, and theoretical thought that began during the Enlightenment four hundred years ago. It is beyond the scope of my present treatment to detail the history of this scientific thinking, and I recommend Harris (1979: 6–27), and Bernard (1994a:4–14) for brief anthropological overviews of this history, and Harris (1968), Russell (1972), or Losee (1972) for more in-depth historical and philosophical analyses of the scientific tradition.

My sources' scientific position statements include various journal articles and books, as well as the public position statements and debates published in the October 1995 through May 1996 *Anthropology Newsletter* editions. The *Newsletter* statements are particularly interesting, since the editors of the *Newsletter* called for such submissions in order to address the current epistemological crisis in anthropology. I also use philosophical sources, although this can be particularly difficult as the issues that concern philosophers are not always relevant to the practice of scientists and it is often difficult to decide what scientists should or should not heed from philosophical discourse. The relevance of philosophy to scientific practice is of great concern to philosophers who, on one hand, think that they have useful insights about science, but on the other hand are cautious about uncritical and superficial borrowing from their field. A review of how the borrowing of philosophical issues has been manifest in archaeological debates illustrates the point.

Archaeologists have borrowed rather directly from philosophers over the past thirty years, whether it be the scientific philosophy of Carl Hempel, or the humanistic, historical philosophy of R. G. Collingwood (see analysis of this phenomenon by M. Salmon 1992). In addition to practicing archaeologists, several applied philosophers, trained in philosophy and using archaeological practice as a subject for addressing their own intellectual concerns, have published statements regarding what archaeology should or should not be. Such a situation is ripe for misinterpretation, turf squabbles, and accusations, none of which aid the development of better research methods (see P. J. Watson 1992 for a candid and humorous reflection upon her philosophical writings as an archaeologist).

Richard Watson, a philosopher, is very troubled by the borrowing of archaeologists. "In short, they [archaeologists] are not philosophers concerned with foundational problems of epistemology and ontology" (R. Watson 1991:279). "Archaeologists do not have to take stands on or try to answer questions in formal logic, any more than they have to answer metaphysical questions" (R. Watson 1992:265). He goes on to assert that much of philosophy is irrelevant to the practice of science anyway. The "results of philosophy strictly speaking need not affect science at all" (R. Watson 1991:278), and "a lot of results in formal logic have no practical influence at all in scientific practice" (R. Watson 1992:265). In a similar vein, Alison Wylie, another philosopher, has lamented that unsystematic borrowing of philosophical concepts by archaeologists has led to a bricolage philosophy that lacks coherence and consistency (cited in P. J. Watson 1992:128).

Practicing archaeologists have defended their delving into philosophy. Patty Jo Watson, defending archaeologists against Wylie's charge of philosophical incoherence, states,

> I submit that *bricolage* is somewhere near the core of science, if not its behavioral essence. Pragmatic concerns about the most efficient way to obtain answers to research questions are what drive working scientists. There are and must be serious attention to conceptual issues, but only in so far as those are relevant to the effective progress of the enterprise, which is not philosophy after all but archaeology, an empirical discipline. (1992:128)

Other archaeologists (Preucel 1991; Riley 1991) have defended an archaeological awareness of philosophical issues of ontology and the epistemic status of concepts precisely because archaeologists must use concepts in doing their science. Assuming that philsosphers can lend particularly insightful and rigorous analyses of how anthropologists can do this, I do not see how we can afford not to familiarize ourselves with philosophy.

What follows is an examination of such attempts at bridging the philosophy of science with the practice of scientific anthropology. Because critics contest the use of scientific methods in anthropology, I will focus most of my attention on what practicing scientific anthropologists have to say about their science. I will invoke the work of philosophers, contemporary applied philosophers as well as historical figures in philosophy, when their insights are relevant to the concerns of practicing scientific anthropologists. The result will be a definition of scientific anthropology, a working definition of what scientific anthropologists try to do rather than a work of philosophy. I will begin by looking at common definitions of science that anthropologists offer, then examine the underlying assumptions of such science, as well as its goals and the methods that scientific anthropologists advocate.

DEFINITIONS

How do scientific anthropologists define their science? Interestingly, in no critique of anthropological science, no matter from what camp it originates, does any critic ever employ an actual definition of science given by a scientific anthropologist. One may very well ask the critics of science whose science they are criticizing, a science that exists, or a construct of their minds? In order to set the record straight, I will quote some of the definitions of science offered by scientific anthropologists.

> [Empirical science is] systematic description and classification of objects, events, [and] processes, and the explanation of those events and processes by theories that employ lawful regularities, all of the descriptive and explanatory statements employed being testable against publicly observable data. (O'Meara 1989:354)

> Anthropology as a social science may be defined as that discipline whose practitioners are interested in formulating and testing hypothetical laws

enabling explanations and prediction of human cultural behavior. (Watson et al. 1971:161)

There is general agreement that doing science is (1) trying to find out about the world by making observations, (2) checking to see of these observations are reliable, (3) developing a general model or account that explains these observations, (4) checking this model or account against new observations, and (5) comparing it to other models and accounts to see which model fits the observations best. Science is simply a systematic way of trying to find out about the world....The most important thing about science is that it involves continuous checking. (D'Andrade 1995b:1)

A number of anthropologists offered definitions of science in an e-mail discussion on the nature of science in anthropology published in the *Anthropology Newsletter* in March 1996, some of which follow.

"Science" is being done whenever one is willing to admit the possibility of bias regarding relationship(s) between variables. (Ralph Holloway)

"Science" is most usefully defined by its *purposes* and *methods*...insights generalizable as theory...emphasis on some shared criteria of confirmation or falsifiability; one has to constantly ask oneself why a particular conclusion is warranted, and try to discipline oneself to change one's mind. (George L. Cowgill)

Here are the properties of science-like activity I think important. *Questioning*: Science-like activity is inquisitive. *Explanation*: Important objectives include proposing answers to "why" and "how" questions. *Generalization*: You hope that your explanations will apply to more than one instance. *Explicitness*: Logical coherence...changeability. (George L. Cowgill)

These definitions, intended to be concise and not all encompassing, share a number of features and contain a number of assumptions, shared goals, and methodological issues. The obvious features of these definitions include an empirical focus, explicitness, logic, theoretical explanation, self-criticism, and open, public debate. I will address each of these features.

Science Is Empirical

Science involves making observations about the world. Anthropological scientists are not evaluating whether or not this world actually exists. They accept that we all share experiences from the world and that science addresses these phenomena. As I will detail in the section on assumptions, this is hardly a naive realism, and in fact it represents an acceptance of human limitations of knowing. Scientific anthropologists realize that data are influenced by theoretical perspectives as well as by the instruments used to observe the world.

Science Should Be Systematic and Explicit

Being systematic and explicit involves how scientists make observations and generate data, as well as how they formulate ideas about what is going on in the world. Explicitness aids scrutiny of any particular scientific theory, or even scrutiny of the validity of anthropological data. Anthropologists should make observations on all relevant phenomena to a theory and should limit the biases in their observations.

Science Is Logical

Ideas about the world should be logical. Given certain conditions and relationships that anthropologists observe between phenomena, they can define expectations about the world that logically follow from these conditions and relationships.

Science Is Theoretical, Explanatory, and Predictive

Scientific anthropologists are not naive about the realism of their theories; all theories are conjectures that anthropologists make up in their minds. The reason why scientific anthropologists maintain that scientific conjectures are especially sound knowledge is because these conjectures receive an unusual amount of scrutiny. Scientific theories furthermore contain statements of cause and effect.

The issue of causality is a tricky one in philosophy. David Hume (1960 [1735]:205) suggested that causality is a psychological phenomenon that occurs when humans perceive a constant conjunction of events. Contemporary philosophers of science continue to grapple with the relationship between probability and cause, failing to reach a consensus (Carnap 1974; W. Salmon 1992). It is useful for anthropologists to note the difficulties with the notion of causation, if only as a reminder that scientists do not discover absolutely true, invariant, necessary causes.

Predictability is one measure of the likelihood of causal connections; if one successfully predicts phenomena with a theory, then the proposed causal connection between the variables has support (R. Watson 1992). A rough-and-ready notion of causality as employed by anthropologists would be that if two events are seen to occur together, one event being antecedent to the other, and the occurrence of the antecedent event seems to be necessary to the occurrence of the subsequent, one has reason to suspect a causal connection.

Scientists aim much research at scrutinizing suspected causal connections in order to exclude spurious correlations and uncover indirect relationships. For instance, research in the contentious area of race and intelligence scrutinizes the empirical fact that people of African descent score lower on IQ tests than do other races, and that IQ appears heritable. Is there a direct, causal connection between IQ and race? Anthropologists, biologists, and psychologists have spent and are spending much effort to determine if other variables, namely social ones, are more valid causal factors in the lower IQ of Africans, and they are assailing the causal connection between race and IQ on a number of other scientific grounds (Gould 1981, 1994; Hunt 1995; MacKenzie 1984; Montagu, ed. 1975; Perkins 1995).

Scientific Activity Is Self-Critical, Limits Bias, and Is Based on Testing

Since scientific theories are just theories, there is a constant need for checking whether these ideas about the world have any reliability and validity. Do researchers regularly and repeatedly observe the same relationships among variables? Can scientists predict phenomena? Are the data biased in some way? Are there other data that contradict a theory? Are there competing theories that better account for the data? Scientists constantly ask these self-critical, reflexive questions about their data and theories. Indeed, a major strength of anthropology is its cross-cultural perspective in which anthropologists, by virtue of their experiences in very different social and environmental settings, come to regard the arbitrariness of their own concepts. Such reflection has led to reconsiderations of nineteenth-century concepts of unilineal evolution (Radcliffe-Brown 1965 [1924]; Steward 1955), the sustainability of land use in the steppes of the southwest United States (Fanale 1982), and re-evaluations of the historical and ecological place of the !Kung of southern Africa (Kuper 1992). This reflection has fueled a long-standing debate over the social, ecological, and material roles of trade in non-market, non-capitalist societies (Malinowski 1984[1922]; Mauss 1967 [1925]; Rosman and Rubel 1986[1971]; Strathern 1971; Suttles 1968). Scientists engage in such self-critique because they recognize the tentative nature of observations and knowledge, and because the social setting of academic science favors the debunking of old theories—it's a great way to make a name for oneself and build a career, as Darwin recognized over a hundred years ago. Because of this reflection and the competitive social setting in which it takes place, science serves as "the best bias destroyer we have" (D'Andrade 1995b:4).

Scientific anthropology is a continuation of the tradition of skeptical and reflexive thinking initiated by Sir Francis Bacon nearly four hundred years ago (R. Watson 1991). Rebelling against the acceptance of received knowledge by scholars, Bacon urged scientists to base their knowledge on experience, not received wisdom (Bacon 1960 [1620]:99). Scientists have regularly rediscovered his powerful methods of inductive theorizing even into the twentieth century, calling them "The method of multiple hypotheses" (Chamberlain 1904), and "strong inference" (Platt 1964). The potential of scientific, skeptical thinking for reducing bias was long ago recognized by positivist philosopher Auguste Comte.

> Our feeble reason may often fail in the application of positive theories; but
> at least they transfer us from the domain of imagination to that of reality,
> and expose us infinitely less than any other kind of doctrine to the danger
> of seeing in facts what is not. (Comte 1974 [1855]:476)

Science Is Public

Science cannot occur without scientists, and scientists interact as a community. Furthermore, this community ideally is open to new ideas and data, and freedom of expression should in no way be curtailed. These democratic and libertarian ethics may or may not appeal to one's political views, but the very workings of scientific activity make these conditions necessary for a robust, active, progressive science. James Bell, a philosopher of archaeological science, prescribes the following social situation for a maximally effective science.

> The importance of a social framework in which ideas can be asserted boldly, but also criticized severely, is best guarded by attitudes implied by refutationist method, attitudes that encourage people to assert bold ideas and yet be open to criticism of those ideas. (Bell 1994:292)

Because theories are best evaluated in light of all relevant data, and because one cannot predict from where new insights and theories may occur, science is best practiced as an open, public activity. Admittedly, sciences become restrictive as their knowledge base grows, as extensive training is required before one can usefully engage the theoretical issues of the discipline, and as the instrumentation required to make observations in a discipline gets more expensive. Anthropology, because of the accessibility of its subjects—people—and the comparatively immature development of its theories, is more open than many other disciplines, such as physics. This is not because anthropology is a "kinder, gentler" discipline or because anthropologists have adopted an official political code favoring open democracy; it is a function of the competitive, public, self-critical nature of the scientific enterprise itself.

These definitions contain the kernel of what scientific anthropologists strive toward in their practice. Theories are regarded as constructs, and data are used as the ultimate arbiters of which theories provide the best explanations. Because anthropologists continually generate new data, and because anthropologists rather actively seek out concepts from other disciplines that may be useful in explaining anthropological phenomena, there is a constant and public checking of theory against data that provides for self-criticism, the limitation of bias, and the improvement of knowledge. While these definitions provide a useful starting point for this exposition of scientific anthropology, there are more complex issues that underlie anthropology's scientific epistemology. These issues involve the assumptions, goals, and methods of anthropological science.

ASSUMPTIONS

Several of the definitions reviewed above contained rhetoric about investigating the world, but what does a scientist mean by that? We all possess a unique viewpoint on the world. How can we, given our idiosyncratic vantage points, determine what the world is in the first place? The issue of the existence of a single world, external to an individual's existence, is one of the foundational issues of philosophy; it is the core issue separating postmodern anthropologists from scientific anthropologists today. I will treat postmodern conceptions of the world in part 2. For now, I will treat what scientific anthropologists assume about the world.

> (1) There is a reality "out there" (or "in there" in the case of ideas and emotions); (2) it can be apprehended, more or less, by human beings through direct experience (or through some proxy for direct experience); (3) all natural phenomena can be explained without recourse to mysterious forces beyond investigation; and (4) though the truth about phenomena is never known, we do better and better as old explanations are knocked down and are replaced by better ones. (Bernard 1994b:168)

> The basic assumption of all science is that there is a real, knowable world. The empirically observable behavior of the entities which make up this real world is orderly and can be predicted and explained.... (Watson et al. 1971:4)

> They [scientific archaeologists] assume that there is a real, knowable (empirically observable), orderly world; in this case, the real, knowable, orderly world is that of past human events and behavior patterns. (Watson et al. 1971:22)

O'Meara (1989:360) and Roscoe (1995:499) in anthropology, and Hammersley (1992:51) in educational ethnography likewise note that scientific ethnographers assume that a real world exists, and furthermore that there is some order to this observed world. For a philosopher, the realism expressed by scientific anthropologists may be somewhat uncomfortable. Immanuel Kant argued two hundred years ago that *noumena*, or reality that may underlie what we experience, is forever beyond empirical grasp; all we can observe is what we perceive—phenomena (Jones 1969:63). Philosophers continue to debate ontology, or the nature of existence, generating various positions such as the phenomenology of Edmund Husserl and Martin Heidegger (Molina 1962), positivism (Schlick 1959), and the realism of falsificationists (Bell 1994:231; Popper 1959). The realization that scientists deal only with phenomena led logical positivist philosophers of science to abandon the question of reality altogether, noting that the lack of empirical tests for reality renders the concept meaningless (Carnap 1959; Schlick 1959). Logical positivists assert that scientists need only accept phenomena as given (Ayer 1959:242; Schlick 1959:83).

Scientific anthropologists tend to be uncomfortable with abandoning the notion that the world exists, while at the same time being very critical of monolithic conceptions of reality. There is a mitigated realism (Wylie 1992b; see Hodder 1991b for guarded objectivism) that surfaces in their work. On the one hand, Bernard, Watson et al., O'Meara, and Roscoe simply state that anthropologists assume that the world is there, observable, and ordered. At the same time, these authors and other scientific anthropologists note that ideas about the world are indeed mental constructs and in need of constant reappraisal. Archaeologist Thomas Riley, criticizing the notion that archaeological facts simply are given, notes that "artifacts, features, settlement systems, etc., exist not as objects but as constructs embedded in a sociocultural matrix" (1991:590). A chipped stone of cryptocrystalline rock, triangular in plan view and narrow in cross-section, does not become an arrowhead until an archaeologist applies theoretical work to infer that the object is an arrowhead. For a scientific anthropologist, a theoretical construct is a representation of reality, mitigated by cultural and theoretical biases, the state of empirical knowledge, and one's powers of observation.

The aim is to limit the influence of these mitigating factors in anthropological theory.

Anthropologists cannot simply accept their data as given. An arrowhead may have, in reality, been used as a knife and not a projectile; the concept of social class that may seem so real in a modern industrial state will have problematic use for explaining wealth differences in a forager band; a curved femur may indicate separation from the human race or simply an intraspecies adaptation to a cold environment; the Kalahari !Kung may be indigenous foragers or marginalized goat thieves. This is why anthropological realism is mitigated. However, the realism is there because chipped stone tools, dead Yanomamö warriors, the !Kung, and bushels of corn seem awfully real to anthropologists gathering data in the field. Anthropologists cannot determine the nature of reality; but they constantly, as part of scientific practice, question the validity of concepts—some things are more real than others. Robert Preucel defends this more philosophical questioning about whether or not anthropologists are getting it right when he says, "the relevance of philosophy [to archaeology] lies in its principled questioning of the nature of reality (ontology), how we know that reality (epistemology), and how we use our knowledge about it (ethics)" (1991:287).

For example, scientific anthropologists are trying to "get it right" in the hotly debated !Kung issue (Kuper 1992). Positions on the existence of the !Kung range from assertions that they are the indigenous people of the Kalahari who have lived there for several thousand years (Solway and Lee 1990) to assertions that the !Kung represent the marginalized dregs of modern pastoral society (Wilmsen and Denbow 1990). Anthropologists hotly contest these positions, and the debate at times becomes acrimonious. However, what ultimately is at stake is the reality of the !Kung—who is getting it right? As Adam Kuper (1992:67) recalls of this debate, "All the ethnographers with whom I corresponded were open to alternative interpretations of their material, eager to ensure that the record was accurate."

Another assumption about the world is that it is ordered and that this order is observable. Scientific concepts of order are very much misunderstood by postmodern critics of science, who assert that scientists artificially impose static classifications and simplistic relations upon the more richly variable and unpredictable world that we experience (Clifford 1986:18;

Marcus and Fischer 1986:32–33; Rosaldo 1991:21; Tyler 1986:130). Scientific anthropologists do not seek to impose some rigid classification and order on the human condition, but simply to understand why certain patterns such as bilateral kinship, a belief in ghosts, comparatively late weaning of infants in forager societies, or the imposition of taxes by bureaucratic state institutions so regularly occur under predictable circumstances. To the extent that classifications and explicit causal relationships do not accurately reflect anthropological phenomena, scientific anthropologists investigate why and attempt to correct for the deficiency.

So scientific anthropologists, like other scientists, assume that there is a knowable, ordered world to investigate. The final basic assumption that scientific anthropologists make is that no supernatural, metaphysical forces need to be invoked in order to explain phenomena. This assumption is one that creationists find very threatening (Morris, ed. 1974; Morris 1984:27), and that humanists decry as denying people their humanity and agency (Shanks and Tilley 1987a:34–35). None of these science critics necessarily must adopt such a defensive stance. Scientists did not concoct this assumption to eliminate Christianity or to enslave and control the proletariat. Because scientists realize that all they can deal with in a public, common, and reliable way are the empirical phenomena that they experience, they therefore cannot conduct scientific tests of the supernatural or metaphysical. It is entirely possible that God created the earth in six days, or that an undifferentiated consciousness pervades the universe, and that these forces actually cause our experiences. However, because these forces are metaphysical in nature, they cannot be reliably, publicly, and empirically studied; there is no scientific, empirical test that can verify or refute the existence of such phenomena. The separation of metaphysics from science is an old position in the philosophy of science.

> The true idea of the nature of the research being thus attained, the next step was to determine the respective offices of observation and reasoning, so as to avoid the danger of empiricism on the one hand, and mysticism on the other. We have accordingly sanctioned, in one relation, the now popular maxim of Bacon, that observed facts are the only basis of sound speculation; so that we agree to what I wrote a quarter of a century ago—that no

proposition that is not finally reducible to the enumeration of a fact, particular or general, can offer any real intelligible meaning. On the other hand, we have repudiated the practice of reducing science to an accumulation of desultory facts, asserting that science, as distinguished from learning, is essentially composed, not of facts, but of laws, so that no separate fact can be incorporated with science till it has been connected with some other, at least by the aid of some justifiable hypothesis. (Comte 1974 [1855]:799)

Philosopher of science Rudolf Carnap (1959:76) describes the meaningful statements that concern scientists in the following way: "They are therefore (true or false) *empirical statements* and belong to the domain of empirical science. Any statement one desires to construct which does not fall within these categories [tautologies, contradictions, empirical statements] becomes automatically meaningless." This necessarily excludes metaphysical phenomena from scientific analysis, since by definition a metaphysical concept is beyond operationalization and common, public experience.

In summary, scientific anthropologists assume that there is a world to know, that it has order on some level that can be observed, and that metaphysical forces need not be invoked to explain the phenomena we experience. Given these assumptions, what can scientists accomplish?

GOALS

Scientific anthropologists share the following goals in common: knowing the empirical world, being able to explain and predict phenomena in the world, and generating progressively more accurate knowledge by proposing theories that can be scrutinized and refined through time.

The aim of scientific research is to formulate explanatory theories which are (1) predictive (or retrodictive), (2) testable (or falsifiable), (3) parsimonious, (4) of broad scope, and (5) integratable or cumulative within a coherent and expanding corpus of theories. (Harris 1994:64)

Central to Hempel's discussion is concern with explanation because successful explanations enable successful predictions and, ultimately, the establishing of laws about the subject matter in question. (P. J. Watson 1992:123)

General laws in archaeology that concern cultural processes can be used to describe, explain, and predict cultural differences and similarities represented in the archaeological record, and thus to further the ultimate goal of anthropology, which is the description, explanation, and prediction of cultural differences and similarities in the present. (Watson et al. 1971:3)

In the e-mail debate published in the March 1996 volume of the *Newsletter*, Eugenie Scott stated that "The *goal* of anthropology is to understand human beings, in all our species' physical, cultural and historical variation," while George Cowgill stressed that scientists strive for "insights generalizable as theory," and Roy D'Andrade stated that science is about "trying to find out about the world." Philosophers of science note the same basic goal for all natural science disciplines, the "goal of science is to put forward and to test theories about the empirical, or experienced and measurable, world" (Popper 1959[1934]:31; 1972:40). A concern with knowing the world, rather than advocating a view of the world because it confirms some political, ideological, or religious project, has always been fundamental to scientific philosophy.

However great may be the services rendered to Industry by science, however true may be the saying Knowledge is Power, we must never forget that the sciences have a higher destination still; and not only higher, but more direct—that of satisfying the craving of our understanding to know the laws of phenomena. (Comte 1974 [1855]:40)

Given that scientific anthropologists assume (or at least act like they assume) the existence of an ordered world external to themselves and that they experience that world through their experience of phenomena, their primary goal is to find out about that world through observation. Because scientific anthropologists do not deal with metaphysical explanations, the only scientific way of knowing the world is by some means of monitoring and measuring it. Monitoring the world is no simple task, and I will address the methodological difficulties in measuring the world in the next section.

Scientific anthropologists, though, all agree that systematically recording the external world is the only scientific means of dealing with it.

Scientific anthropologists are not only concerned with measuring phenomena in the world and describing them, but primarily with generating explanatory theories about the world. Prediction is an important, but hardly final, measure of explanatory power. Harris states that prediction is a goal of science; and P. J. Watson, invoking Hempel, stresses the importance of prediction in science. The ability to generalize theories, or to generate law-like statements, is another measure of a theory's explanatory power. An explanation of a particular phenomenon in a particular place at a particular time may be historically gratifying, but it has limited use in a science. Scientific theories, if they are to be useful, must apply to more than one particularistic case. This is why prediction is so important to scientific research. One cannot test a theory until one can apply that theory, holding relevant variables constant, in another time and place. If the theory provides accurate predictions when generalized, then it has further support as being the best explanation for the phenomena in question. Marcel Mauss's (1967 [1925]) early recognition that gifting activities and prestige economies are not only a systemic social feature of Melanesian societies, but that a similar function and form of gifting was integral to ancient Germanic and contemporary Northwest Coast Indian societies, gave tremendous support to prestige theories of exchange in tribal societies. Much supporting evidence since has corroborated Mauss's findings, although researchers still debate the actual role of prestige within these societies (Rosman and Rubel 1986[1971]; Strathern 1971; Weiner 1976; Peregrine 1992; Jeske 1996).

Progress (i.e., knowing more about the world in more detail) is also a goal of scientific anthropology, as indicated in Harris's statement that theories should be "integratable or cumulative within a coherent and expanding corpus of theories." This does not mean that the activity of scientific anthropologists is to generate supporting arguments for established theories. Sometimes, finding supporting evidence for a theory helps to corroborate it and indicates that it may be the best explanation of a phenomenon. However, scientific anthropologists are just as concerned with finding the shortcomings of established theories in order to modify or reject them. Anthropologists, faced with evidence that hunter-gatherers were not on the brink of starvation and actually were well-fed and in generally good health, revised their scientific understanding of forager life; they thus changed their view of forager lifeways, noting that foragers were more like an "originally affluent" society (Lee and Devore 1968; Sahlins 1972). Research since then, primarily by archaeologists, indicates that the view of peaceful, harmonious, and affluent foragers, while a corrective to older stereotypes, was also not entirely consistent with the empirical record of forager life (Keeley 1996; Price and Brown 1985; Smith 1991). Confronting the growing archaeological, ethnohistoric and ethnographic records of forager life, anthropologists are now generating newer, better descriptions and explanations of forager life (Kuznar 1996; cf. Ingold, et al. 1991a,b; Kelly 1995; Chapter 3).

Some critics may charge that these revisions were motivated by political/moral agendas (feminism, 1960s radicalism, Marxism). These influences did play a role, and I elaborate on them in chapter 3. While agendas influence the science anthropologists do, the reason why people were able to use forager lifestyles to advance an agenda is because the data indicated that old stereotypes were empirically incorrect. Furthermore, the data gathered on foragers has been insensitive to 1960s political agendas, and now anthropologists are revising 1960s views of forager life so as to be more consistent with the ever-emerging empirical record of forager life. Clearly, we know much more about forager lifestyles today than we did one hundred years ago, when Franz Boas exhorted anthropologists to go out and study these societies. Anthropologists now have much more data about what people are really doing and thinking in these societies, and they have improved explanations of why foragers think and behave the way they do.

The criticism integral to scientific anthropology, combined with the progressive nature of the field (we keep learning more), means that the knowledge scientific anthropologists produce is only tentative and partial. This is precisely the goal of scientific anthropology—the creation of knowledge that, for the time being, is the best explanation of phenomena, but that is always open to systematic, scientific revision. This is a crucial point often missed by critics of science (see Johnson 1991; Tyler 1986:123, 1991:80). If scientific anthropologists constructed absolute truths, then once a truth was constructed, the truth could never be revised. If anthropologists really took such a dogmatic approach, then archaeologists would not have refuted

nineteenth-century theories that Native American burial mounds were constructed by ancient Egyptians, anthropologists would still think that forager
life was simply "nasty, brutish and short," they would never have appreciated the different roles played by exchange in non-market societies, and a
host of other revisions of anthropological knowledge never would have taken
place. As Marvin Harris (1995a:67) aptly states, "Constructed and partial
truths are not the nemeses or terminators of science but the defining condition of its existence."

Scientific anthropology is, in this way, consistent with the skeptical traditions of scientific philosophy. David Hume stressed that no amount of
philosophy or empirical research could establish the nature of reality, so
there would always be a need for skepticism among scientists. He also pointed
out that this does not lead to nihilism, but rather to an increased need for
using rational thought to constantly question the status of knowledge.

> Thus the skeptic still continues to reason and believe, even though he as-
> serts that he cannot defend his reason by reason; and by the same rule he
> must assent to the principle concerning the existence of his body, though
> he cannot pretend, by any arguments of philosophy, to maintain its verac-
> ity. Nature has not left this to his choice, and has doubtless esteemed it an
> affair of too great importance to be trusted to our uncertain reasonings and
> speculations. (Hume 1956 [1735]:219)

This realization of science's limitations has been reinforced by scientific
philosophers ever since Hume, including the founder of positive philosophy, Auguste Comte.

> Our intellectual weakness, and the scientific difficulties with which we
> have to cope, will always leave us in the midst of irreducible laws.... (Comte
> 1974 [1855]:799)

A fundamental requirement of scientific anthropological theories is that
they be testable. The notion of testability is the hallmark of scientific enquiry—scientists must always be able to challenge theories on logical and
empirical grounds. Otherwise the progress noted above would not be pos-

sible. However, testability begs the central methodological issues of scientific anthropology, and so I shall now turn to that topic.

METHODOLOGICAL PRINCIPLES

Testing implies evaluation. Tests, even when testing to confirm, can be failed, and so evaluation is central to the notion of scientific methodology. Lewis Binford is explicit about the centrality of evaluation to anthropological science.

> Scientific methods are designed to evaluate ideas....the problem that any scientist must understand is how one moves from ideas to facts or observations, and, in turn, how one may then relate the empirical findings back to ideas in an evaluative manner. (1977:2)

This is aesthetically somewhat unpleasant for some—scientific practice does involve telling some people that their ideas are wrong. However, science is not meant to make people feel good about themselves, it is meant to explore the world; science is not therapy, it is inquiry.

Scientific anthropologists use two primary criteria when judging theories: the extent to which a theory is logically consistent and the extent to which a theory's statements are in agreement with all relevant data. Logical consistency means that a theory cannot contain statements that contradict one another. Logical consistency is important because if a theory is inconsistent, then the theory can entail any possible statement. This would render the theory untestable with empirical data, thereby violating one of the assumptions of science and preventing scientists from determining its falseness (or correctness) (Bell 1994:321). As an hypothetical example, stating that bigmen impoverish themselves while becoming wealthy is, if this is all one has to go on, contradictory. Data that indicate that bigmen are poor will not contradict the theory, just as data that show bigmen gaining wealth will not contradict the theory. Such a theory needs to be made more explicit if anthropologists can evaluate it. For instance, stating that giving away wealth places recipients in debt to the impoverished bigman, and that in time the impoverished bigman collects his debts and more, specifies a temporal order that can be tested empirically. The rules of logic are indispensable to any scientific theory.

The other criterion is empirical consistency. Are a theory's predictions consistent with all relevant data at hand? Or, do these predictions fail? A theory that neither predicts phenomena well, nor holds the promise of predicting new phenomena, is not likely to be highly regarded by scientists. Given that scientific anthropologists have set the goal of knowing the world, a theory that does not fit the world better than other theories has a mark against it. The issue of data, while seemingly so basic, is one of the tougher issues faced by practicing scientists.

Other methodological principles central to scientific anthropology include operational definitions, representativeness, reliability, and validity. Scientific anthropologists use these concepts to guide their research and to decide what to observe, how to observe it, and how to interpret what they observe. Are cut marks on a human skeleton evidence for cannibalism, or for ritual defleshing before death? Are Neandertal toes divergent, or convergent? Was the Mexican village of Tepoztlan a peaceful, harmonious society, or a violent, competitive one? Assuming that a common reality is generating these varied perceptions, the job of a scientist is to ensure that idiosyncratic factors are eliminated as much as possible when making observations and recording them as data.

Operational definitions were discussed by Percy Bridgeman (1961[1927]) as he was grappling with the ontological status of physical phenomena that require tremendous inputs of theory and technology to measure. Under such circumstances, how do scientists know what they are even measuring? His answer was that scientists make definitions of phenomena based upon the operations that they must employ in order to measure the phenomena. For instance, it is difficult to discuss length without also discussing a yardstick. Scientific anthropologists have also adopted the notion of operational definitions. While noting the dangers of taking operationalism too far, Harris asserts,

> A strong dose of operationalism is desperately needed to unburden the social and behavioral sciences of their overload of ill-defined concepts, such as status, role...group, institution, class, caste, tribe, state...and many

others that are part of every social scientists's working vocabulary. The continuing failure to agree on the meaning of these concepts is a reflection of their unoperational status and constitutes a great barrier to the development of scientific theories of social and cultural life. (1979:15)

Likewise, H. Russell Bernard (1994a:28–31) notes that, despite the arbitrariness of operational definitions, they make anthropologists' data comparable. This means that data so generated can be used to test theories, and anthropologists can always construct better measures of phenomena.

Once a researcher has developed an operational definition of a concept and employed it in research, how does he or she know whether or not the data thus generated fairly represent phenomena? One issue is representativeness. If one is measuring household income, and one calls up ten households at random and gets honest answers on household income, will these data represent the distribution of income in society as a whole? Scientifc anthropologists, when in a position to gather data on many observations, strive, as in other disciplines, to gather the data in a way that ensures that the resulting data set represents the phenomenon fairly, and therefore can be used to make valid generalizations (Redman 1974).

Another data issue is reliability. A reliable measure is one that, if administered in the same situation, will provide the same result. Since anthropologists do not typically administer personality tests and sociological surveys to thousands of people, reliability is difficult for anthropologists to monitor. However, scientific anthropologists are aware of the need for reliability and the difficulties in achieving it. Because most ethnographers work alone, there is the possibility for many factors—including idiosyncracies of personality, gender, age, one's social position, and one's network of field friendships—to bias an ethnographer's observations and provide unreliable data (Pelto and Pelto 1978; Werner and Schoepfle 1987). One way of limiting the effects of such idiosyncratic factors is to have multiple ethnographers work in the same field situation (Roscoe 1995:498; Whiting and Whiting 1970:290). Another means of limiting bias and increasing inter-observer reliability is to train a team of researchers whose reliability can then be checked with standard methods (Pelto and Pelto 1978:72; Whiting and Whiting 1970:290). Cross-cultural researchers also monitor reliability, ensuring that they maintain a high degree of agreement when coding informa-tion from ethnographies (Lebar 1970:715), and providing statistical means of maximizing reliability from cross-national surveys (Rummel 1970). While reliability is difficult to achieve, anthropologists have taken steps to ensure that their observations are more, not less, reliable.

Validity also concerns scientific anthropologists. A valid measure actu-ally measures the phenomenon that a researcher says he or she is measur-ing. Measures can be reliable, but not valid. For instance, many psycholo-gists and sociologists recognize that IQ measures are very reliable, but they doubt that standard IQ tests really measure intelligence (Segall 1979; Blum 1978; Gould 1981). Anthropologists, and especially ethnographers, may be uniquely capable of addressing validity. A sociologist who administers a survey concocted in an ivory-tower office in reference to a bunch of ivory-tower theory texts can gather a lot of reliable data, but he or she may have little basis upon which to judge whether the data represent anything rel-evant to actual peoples' lives. Because of our anthropological tradition of living with the very phenomena we study, we are uniquely capable of ensur-ing that our data are valid. Roger Sanjek (1990:395) stresses that the valid-ity of an ethnographic account can be evaluated based on the theoretical candor of its author, the explicitness with which the author describes his or her fieldwork, evidence of how observations and notes are transformed into data, and evidence of actual fieldnotes. An ethnography that is a collection of observations that could be used for scientific research and which con-tains explicit statements about the theoretical position influencing the re-search, explicit descriptions of how the fieldwork was conducted, and ex-plicit descriptions about how experiences many people could have were transformed into data in fieldnotes is better than an ethnography in which these issues are vague. Why? Because explicitness serves as a check against hidden bias and provides other researchers with a means by which to judge the scientific quality and relevance of one's data.

Scientific anthropologists generate testable theories that they will evalu-ate with hopefully representative, reliable, and valid data. However, once one has proposed a testable theory, how will one go about actually evaluat-ing it with these data? There are two basic approaches to evaluation—con-firmation and falsification. In the past century, philosophers have debated which criterion works best for generating scientific knowledge, and their arguments are complex and as yet unresolved (see arguments in Ayer, ed. 1959; Bell 1994; Popper 1959 [1934]; M. Salmon 1982a,b; W. Salmon 1982; R. Watson 1992). Nonetheless, scientific anthropologists are aware of the strengths and weaknesses of each approach, and a discussion of the basic issue is warranted here.

Confirmation of theories is a principle most associated with the logical positivist philosophers and their traditional emphasis on criteria of verification (Ayer 1959; Russell 1959 [1931]:57; Schlick 1959:87–89). The basic question is how much data, and what kind of data, are necessary to confirm a theoretical statement; or when can a scientist accept a proposition as being provisionally (not absolutely) true? Some anthropologists seem to favor a criterion of confirmation.

> The degree of confirmation of the hypothesis is regarded as increasing with the number of favorable test findings and is especially strengthened by favorable results from a wide variety of tests. Diversity of evidence...new evidence...simplicity in logical form...consistency with other scientific knowledge.... (Watson et al. 1971:11)

On the other hand, some scientific anthropologists prefer the criterion of falsification. The basic sense of falsification is that because scientists cannot ever truly, conclusively, and absolutely prove a statement true, the best they can do is note when theories lead to empirically incorrect predictions. The philosopher Karl Popper was the champion of the falsification criteria, and he set forth the basic problem with the following hypothetical example (1959 [1934]:68–69). Consider the following statement, "All ravens are black." This statement could never truly be verified unless a researcher had the ability to witness every single raven that exists, that has existed, or that may in the future exist. "For the verification of a natural law could only be carried out by empirically ascertaining every single event to which the law might apply, and by finding that every such event actually conforms to the law" (Popper 1959 [1934]:63). Qualifying it by saying ninety percent of ravens are black does not help because in order to get the appropriate proportion, one would likewise need to sample the entire universe of ravens.

However, the discovery of one white raven clearly refutes the statement that all ravens are black. Popper argued, therefore, that there is a basic asymmetry between verifying theories and refuting them; it is basically easier to know when one is wrong. Popper's arguments have had an important impact on scientific anthropologists, and one encounters much falsification rhetoric in the field.

> The aim of scientific research is to formulate explanatory theories which are...testable (or falsifiable).... (Harris 1995a:64)

> Scientific knowledge is generated when both the object of inquiry and the procedures through which the inquiry is conducted are so clearly described that it is possible for anyone to investigate, and possibly replicate, falsify, or expand the results. (Carroni-Long 1996:52)

> This subjective element undoubtedly slows progress in both the physical and social sciences, but overcoming the difficulty requires not the rejection of refutation or of empirical science itself...but the adoption of refutation as a method for controlling and gradually eliminating human bias and error. (O'Meara 1989:358)

> The falsificationist criterion for evaluating our understanding sits poorly with those who want truth and who believe that we should accept as authorities only those who have never been wrong! (Lewis Binford in published e-mail discussion of *Anthropology Newsletter* 37:52)

Other anthropologists, willing to leave the debates to the philosophers, simply note that sometimes we gather data that seems to make a proposition more likely, and other times we gather data that refute our ideas. George Cowgill, in the published e-mail discussion notes that science is based on an "emphasis on some shared criteria of confirmation or falsifiability" (*Anthropology Newsletter* 37:52).

Philosophers continue to debate the merits of falsifiability versus confirmation. Confirmation is based on a more inductive approach to knowledge generation in which researchers derive generalizations from their observations and knowledge is confirmed as positive instances accumulate (Bell 1994:184–186). Falsification, in contrast, involves scrutinizing theories to ensure that they are not empirically false (Bell 1994:228–230). Applied philosophers have advocated both approaches in anthropology. Richard Watson (1976, 1992), Merrilee Salmon (1982a,b, 1992), and Wesley Salmon (1982, 1992) are among the more forceful proponents of confirmation criteria in anthropology, while James Bell (1982, 1987, 1994) stands as a champion of falsification criteria.

Bell argues that a refutationist approach has been the most important in scientific archaeology. "The refutationist view is by far the most important, especially because of its conception of the goal of science—to make progress—and its central tool for moving toward that goal—testability" (Bell 1994:7). A testable theory is one that has many empirical points at which it can fail; the more concrete empirical implications a theory has, the more testable it becomes (Bell (1994:52). Bell's point is that the more testable a theory, the more scientific it is, since one has a greater chance to scrutinize it empirically. Progress is manifest as scientists discover the false points of theories, propose newer theories that, for the time being, are less false, and continue to scrutinize these new ideas for their weak points, hopefully going on to propose even better explanations.

The philosophical issues underlying confirmation and falsification have presented philosophers of science with difficult problems that they have not as yet resolved. I suggest that practicing scientific anthropologists not try to do the job of the philosopher, but heed philosophers' arguments, look for potential pitfalls in scientific practice in these arguments, and then adjust methods accordingly so that they can better achieve their scientific goals. With that in mind, I want to comment on what value I, as a scientific anthropologist, think these principles have.

Confirmation, as an heuristic, is an attractive approach to scientific anthropology to the extent that we are trying to find out about the world, generate positive knowledge about the world, and generally attempt to get things right. It makes sense that a phenomenon with overwhelming empirical support would be somehow considered correct, or confirmed. I would argue that confirmation would be most important as a principle in exploratory research, where anthropologists gather data in order to recognize patterns that might serve as the basis for theoretical generalizations. However, confirmation alone cannot be the guiding principle of a scientific anthropology.

Even those philosophers who advocate confirmation speak constantly of testing and scrutinizing theories. "Thus from its beginnings, modern science has employed a skeptical methodology that has been judged to be successful on the basis of its practical results" (R. Watson 1991:275). R. Watson (1991:277) also notes that scientific archaeologists have adopted notions of falsifiability in their testing of hypotheses. Likewise, there is much talk of refutation by practicing scientific anthropologists who advocate confirmatory methods.

> The crux of scientific procedure is that hypotheses are formulated tentatively and then tested empirically by deductive procedure....Because the test implication is found to be true of the world does not means that the hypothesis must be. It simply means that the hypothesis may be empirically true because it has not been shown to be false (disconfirmed). (P. J. Watson et al. 1971:8)

So, refutation certainly plays a role in anthropological science. I would argue that falsification not only plays a role, but a predominant role for two additional, pragmatic reasons. First, a basic axiom of science is that all knowledge is provisional, tentative, and never absolute (Bell 1994; Bernard 1994a:12; Comte 1974 [1855]:799; Harris 1995a:67, 75; Popper 1959[1934]:37; Russell 1959[1931]: 67-68; Watson, et al. 1971:4; R. Watson 1992a:260; Wylie 1992:281). In other words, all scientific knowledge will be found to be wrong as it is replaced by better knowledge. The historical studies of science covered in the next chapter demonstrate that such revision and improvement has been a regular feature of the sciences. Improvement is not possible without refutation.

Second, simply gathering supporting data for a theory is never enough to gain a theory's acceptance; scientific anthropologists require that the data itself be subject to tests of representativeness, reliability, and validity. These requirements imply that data be gathered in such a way that the theory for which they are intended to support will have undergone maximal scrutiny, or chance of falsification. A good example is the recent debate over the controversial work on IQ and race published by Herrnstein and Murray in *The Bell Curve* (1994) and by J. Phillipe Rushton in *Race and Culture* (1995). These authors provide much data to support their claims of genetically based, racial differences in IQ. Nevertheless, scientists have criticized their data since much of it came from a particular journal, *Mankind Quarterly*. Devoted to exploring differences between races, this is a journal in which results that contradict racial difference are not likely to be published (Lane 1994). The fact that these proponents of a biological correlation between race and IQ did not gather their data in a way that could potentially have refuted their claims delegitimizes their findings in many scientists' eyes. I argue that this, once again, is an example of the primacy of the falsification principle in scientific anthropology—only those hypotheses that have survived repeated attempts at falsification can be accepted as in any way confirmed, and we expect that, ultimately, even the most confirmed hypotheses will be refuted.

Application of the methodological principles so far reviewed results in more objective research. The objectivity claimed by scientific anthropologists is neither the absolute truth or the Archimedean perspective that critics charge scientists with claiming. Instead, it is best considered a methodological objectivity that is ensured by methodological procedures and that results in more, not less objective theories and data. Lewis Binford (1982:127) points out that the objectivity desired by anthropologists is not an Archimedean, completely neutral, completely true objectivity. It would be nice to do that, but scientific anthropologists are fully aware that, given human perceptual and intellectual limitations, this will never happen. However, that does not warrant abandoning objectivity altogether; some things are more objective (less biased, less false) than others. The key issue for scientific anthropologists is how to determine what is more or less objective. The methodological principles reviewed above result in such methodological objectivity.

Science has adopted a definition of objectivity which refers to the views not of the individual researcher but of the scientific *community*, where theories are continually being tested. Nor are we put in the untenable position of affirming the consequent because of the interrelation between theory

and data. The attempt to evaluate theories frequently has surprising results. (Earle and Preucel 1987:509)

The difference between objective and subjective lies in the methods used
in the descriptions—methods that in the one case are public, replicable,
testable, etc., and in the other case private, idiosyncratic, and intestable.
(Harris 1995b:423)

These principles of methodological objectivity are standard among philosophers of science, and form the basis for scientific objectivity in general.

Science in the most general sense is an attempt to learn as much as possible about the world in as many ways as possible with the sole restriction
that what is claimed as knowledge be both testable and attainable by
everyone....Knowledge that is in the public domain is objective; private or
esoteric or privileged knowledge is subjective. (R. Watson 1991:276)

Karl Popper noted that because all human observers are subjective, only by
comparing their varied subjective stances can scientists determine what, in
those viewpoints, counts as real or shared phenomena.

A justification is "objective" if in principle it can be tested and understood
by anybody....I shall therefore say that the *objectivity* of scientific statements lies in the fact that they can be *inter-subjectively tested*. (Popper
1959[1934]:44)

By insisting on the theoretical, intersubjective, and therefore tentative
nature of scientific knowledge, by insisting on constant scrutiny of that
knowledge through testing; by requiring that theories fit empirical data (which
are never under the determinative control of scientists); and by requiring
that tests be conducted in a public, open forum, scientific ideas are exposed
to maximal scrutiny. Such knowledge is more, not less, objective. On a
more pragmatic level, scientists tend to employ these methodological principles in a cyclical fashion, and turning to that cycle will enable me to illustrate some further methodological concerns.

CYCLE OF SCIENCE

In reality, scientists are never purely deductive or inductive, confirmatory or refutational, and the practice of science involves cycling through these processes.

> Working scientists, of course, often build hypotheses inductively on the basis of inference from observations, and then test these hypotheses by checking implications deduced from them....The logic of empirical science in its completeness is a combination of inductive and deductive forms and procedures. What has just been said about science is true of archaeology conceived as a science. (P. J. Watson, et al. 1971:12)

I will propose a model of this cycle here in order to illustrate even further how scientific anthropologists conceive and practice their science. One can begin anywhere in the cycle, but before knowledge can be considered scientific, it should pass through, or be promised to pass through, all stages of the cycle (see Figure 1–1). I will begin discussion of this cycle by considering the inductive origin of some scientific ideas.

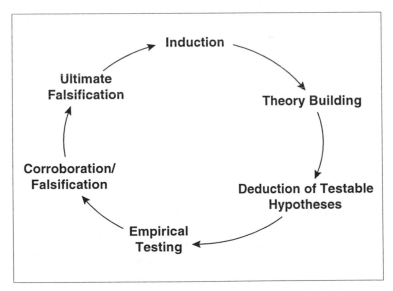

Figure 1–1: The Cycle of Science.

Induction

One obvious source of scientific theory is the experience of the scientist as he or she makes observations and gathers data. Often scientific anthropologists call this pattern-recognition or exploratory research. For instance, most archaeological projects today do not begin with a full-blown excavation of a major site, but rather with exploratory surveys designed to inform archaeologists of the range and variation of archaeological remains in a region.

Theory Building

Once anthropologists propose a scientifically appropriate problem, then they must develop an explanatory theory as discussed above. A theory that proposes a simple correlation between variables (an empirical generalization) is scientifically uninteresting; it contains a description, but not an explanation of the world. A theory must be logical, empirical, and causal.

The source of scientific ideas and theories can be other theories as well. Many philosophers since the 1830s would agree with the statement that observations are theory-laden, and therefore even observations constitute theories. Therefore, theories can originate either through deduction from pre-existing theories, or through induction from observations. Either way, it does not matter from where a theory originates, only that it is warranted (is prompted by either theoretical problems or empirical patterns, fits the definition of a scientific theory, and is testable and logical). Lewis Binford offered the following criteria for warranting a theory worthy of scientific consideration: "(a) It accommodates experience in terms of [a] broader, more comprehensive view of nature; and (b) it appears plausible" (1982:127). Once scientists formulate theories, they then need to test them.

Deduction

No matter what methodological principles a scientific anthropologist favors, at some point specific empirical propositions must be deduced from a more general theory. Anthropologists deduce logically correct statements from a general theory until these statements yield predictable consequences for the empirical world.

Testing

Testing forces scientists back into the messy world of empirical observation. At this point, scientists must operationalize the variables under investigation. Scientists use theoretical models to identify relevant variables, and the available methods for conducting research will influence how they measure these variables. For instance, if one is interested in studying risk aversion in peasant society, one must both define and operationalize the notions of peasant society and risk aversion. One may appeal to standard definitions that have been accepted and found to be reliable by other researchers, or one may propose alternative definitions and measures that one thinks have superior validity.

Evaluation

Once scientists gather new data with which to test a theory, then they must evaluate the significance of the findings. If the findings agree with predictions, then some may prefer to claim a degree of confirmation of corroboration for the theory. I point out that ultimately, all theories probably will be falsified since all theories are ultimately flawed. Therefore, if a scientist fails to find contradictory data at first, it is almost certain that someone in the future will discover such data and challenge the theory. Scientists should be cautious about falsifying a statement, and especially cautious about falsifying a theory. This is because, other than the falseness of the hypothesis in question, several things can lead to a failed prediction. These include measurement error, flawed methods, or atypical data (Duhem 1976 [1906]; Lakatos 1970, 1978; Quine 1976 [1953]). Karl Popper points out that a falsification is, in and of itself, an hypothesis that the theory is incorrect (1959[1934]:86). This is why tests must be repeated; scientists need to test the hypothesis of falsehood. This is done through replicating the research. Replicability is a fundamental principle of science. If a measurement is reliable, that means that, measured over and over again under the same circumstances, scientists would observe the same measurement. In non-experimental research meta-analysis, or the analysis of a collection of studies, is a means of achieving quasi-replication.

Repeat the Cycle

Once scientists acquire confirmatory or falsifying results, then the whole process begins again. Since scientists make no claim to ultimate truth, it is inevitable that theories ultimately will fail. If some hypotheses are refuted, a scientist may make changes to the theory so that its hypotheses are more consistent with reality. However, should a theory's hypotheses routinely be refuted, or should someone come up with a potentially better theory, the old theory will be called into question, and it may be replaced with the new one. This concern with empirical data and new theories brings us back to induction for generating new theories, deducing testable hypotheses, testing, and falsification/corroboration. The cycle becomes complete.

End Result

So, do we really gain anything through this repetitive, self-critical and endless process? Yes. First, we get a demarcation between science (human knowledge) and religion (metaphysical knowledge). This separation is increasingly lamented by artists, social critics, moralists, ethicists, and politically motivated social scientists, but it is nonetheless necessary. There are no tests of metaphysical notions, whether these deal with the existence of God, our own existence, reality, ethics, or politics. These issues will be debated as long as there are mortals around to debate them. Claiming the ability to pass final judgement on these is a claim to supernatural abilities and nothing less. Any judgement upon these matters will be based on fundamental assumptions that cannot be tested scientifically.

Personally, I think that slavery is abhorrent. I do not need a scientist to corroborate a theory that says that slavery is abhorrent. I believe it, I do not like it, and you will not change my mind on it. This is faith. I will be the first to claim that it is not science. The inappropriateness of scientific methods for evaluating ethics is a human and moral limitation of the science, and one that is unavoidable. However, once we make the demarcation between science and metaphysics, then we open a vast world of human experience that we can subject to rigorous scientific tests and upon which we can make objective evaluations. This is the strength of science.

Another strength of science is its systematically self-correcting nature. Self-correction is built into the scientific process; it is the character of the process. No other form of knowledge has this. The challenges to science reviewed in part 2 all share an essentially dogmatic set of core beliefs that are unassailable. This is true of either the literalism of creationists, the Social Darwinism of the racialists, or the socialism of many postmodernists. Religions and dogmas can change only with further revelations that are up to the caprice of supernaturals; humans have no control over the process. When humans disagree about these matters, they have no recourse to resolve the difference but to ignore one another or to silence their opponents; there is no other way.

My goal in this chapter was to present, in scientific anthropologists' own words, the science they have developed, the goals they have set out to accomplish, and some of the justifications they offer for their methods. Philosophical issues remain, and scientific anthropologists do not agree on all the details of how they should conduct their science. Nonetheless, scientific anthropologists agree on their basic assumptions, goals, and methods. Further insights into anthropological science can be gained by examining some controversial analyses of the sociological dimensions of science, which I will take up in the next chapter. Then, in chapter 3, I will provide two case examples of anthropological science that will illustrate much of what scientific anthropologists discuss abstractly.

Chapter 2

Science—
Problems with Progress

Art is I: Science is We.

Anonymous Poet
Quoted by Claude Bernard

Science, like life, feeds on its own decay. New facts burst old rules; then newly divined conceptions bind old and new together into a reconciling law.

William James
The Will to Believe

Anthropologists have developed a scientific approach that more or less accords with what philosophers of science prescribe, and scientific anthropologists have justified their practice in light of their own anthropological goals. However, having rules guarantees neither that they will be used, nor that they will work. One must address the social practice of science if one wishes to make claims that science works. In this chapter, I review three analyses of how scientists operate: Thomas Kuhn's analysis of scientific paradigms, Imre Lakatos's argument for a progressive science, and the Duhem-Quine thesis. A central question asked by these analysts is whether or not science progresses; is it a step-by-step addition of bricks upon an edifice, or as James suggests, a dynamic process ironically feeding upon its own decay? I will review these arguments briefly and evaluate them from

51

the perspective of anthropological science. Kuhn's work and the Duhem-Quine thesis are often used by critics of science to argue that scientists fail their goal of generating knowledge rationally and progressively, whereas Lakatos argues that scientists indeed engage in practices that result in progress. I will examine each of these positions in turn.

THOMAS KUHN: PARADIGMS AND SCIENTIFIC REVOLUTIONS

While many critics of science embrace Kuhn's *Structure of Scientific Revolutions* as a demonstration of the failings of science (Feyerabend 1978; Harding 1991), a thorough analysis of this work indicates that such an opinion is overly hasty. Kuhn is vague about central concepts of his analysis (like paradigm); and, as James Bell notes, "Critics and supporters of Kuhn's views on science take very different sides on many issues, but on one point nearly everyone agrees: *The Structure of Scientific Revolutions* is ambiguous" (1994:205). The central issue that Kuhn addressed is whether or not science is an accumulation of individual discoveries and therefore represents an additive process of increasing knowledge and getting closer to reality (Kuhn 1970:2). He directs his analysis at the history of the physical sciences and analyzes the major breakthroughs with which most scientists are familiar, such as Newtonian dynamics, relativity, and others. Kuhn notes that scientists hardly work in isolation; they work in groups that share common theories, outlooks, problems, and technologies. "Science is We." While his analysis is descriptive, Kuhn feels that his description has normative implications that will influence how scientists should do science (Kuhn 1970:209).

Kuhn notes that scientists within groups share paradigms. He defines a paradigm as "a set of recurrent and quasi-standard illustrations of various theories in their conceptual, observational, and instrumental applications" (1970:43). These sometimes become known as scientific traditions—Einstein's relativity and Darwinian evolution are examples. Kuhn also views paradigms as a worldview shared by a group of scientists (1970:111). The paradigm influences what scientists think of as reasonable problems and how they go about studying them (1970:37).

When a scientific discipline has one prevailing paradigm that guides the actions of scientists, there exists a period of normal science. Kuhn notes normal science means that research firmly based upon one or more past scientific achievement supplies the foundation for scientific practice (1970:10). Single paradigms are essential to the existence of normal science since scientists need to agree as to what constitutes a past achievement that can guide future research; this requires the sharing of scientific standards of practice (Kuhn 1970:11). Kuhn notes that "the results gained in normal research are significant because they add to the scope and precision with which the paradigm can be applied" (1970:36). Normal research is important for another reason: it eventually leads to anomalies and scientific crises.

Anomalies are observations and results that stand in contradiction to a paradigm. There are always anomalies in research. Scientists long ago gave up the requirement that their theories explain all possibilities, and this has become encoded in the popular (among scientists anyway) saying that a theory that explains everything explains nothing. Kuhn points out that anomalies in and of themselves are usually uneventful. However, if they accumulate and demonstrate a systematic way in which they contradict a paradigm, a scientific crisis will ensue in which some scientists will question the paradigm under which they operate (Kuhn 1970:68).

Scientific revolutions are "those non-cumulative developmental episodes in which an older paradigm is replaced in whole or in part by an incompatible new one" (Kuhn 1970:92). The issue of whether or not scientific revolutions take place in a rational manner and whether or not they result in progress are the key controversial issues broached by Kuhn. He points out that it is not a simple, rational process of falsifying the old paradigm (1970:77), although logic and reasoning do play a role. "Probably the single most prevalent claim advanced by the proponents of a new paradigm is that they can solve the problems that have led the old one to crisis" (Kuhn 1970:153). One way of demonstrating this is an ability for researchers working with the new paradigm to make more accurate measurements and predictions (Kuhn 1970:154). However, these criteria alone are not sufficient, and more subjective criteria are also involved. The new paradigm must also "appeal to the individual's sense of the appropriate or the aesthetic—the new theory is said to be 'neater,' 'more suitable,' or 'simpler' than the old" (Kuhn 1970:155). Scientists eventually accept the new paradigm based on a hope that the theory has future promise (Kuhn 1970:158). Once a new paradigm replaces the old, a new period of normal science begins.

Kuhn's identification of this messy, social, and partially subjective means by which scientists actually accept and reject paradigms is by no means a hyper-relativistic stance that the sciences capriciously jump from paradigm to paradigm based on social trends, fads, or whims. Both opponents and supporters of Kuhn's view have misunderstood this, and I clarify the point here. There is nothing frivolous or whimsical about a scientific revolution; new paradigms do not "triumph ultimately through some mystical aesthetic" (Kuhn 1970:158).

Kuhn notes that paradigm shifts are not simply Orwellian rewrites of history. A characterization which would "not entirely be wrong if it did not suppress the nature of the process and of the authority by which the choice between paradigms is made. If authority alone, and particularly if non-professional authority, were the arbiter of paradigm debates, the outcome of those debates might still be a revolution, but it would not be a *scientific* revolution" (Kuhn 1970:167). For Kuhn, the new paradigm must resolve problems in the old paradigm, while preserving much of the problem-solving capabilities of the old paradigm. "Novelty for its own sake is not a desideratum in the sciences" (Kuhn 1970:169). Furthermore, the shift from one paradigm to another should encounter resistance.

> By ensuring that the paradigm will not be too easily surrendered, resistance guarantees that scientists will not be lightly distracted and that the anomalies that lead to paradigm change will penetrate existing knowledge to the core. (Kuhn 1970:65)

The relationship between the old and new paradigms has become a contentious issue, and one that speaks to the heart of the issue of scientific progress. People have traditionally viewed science as a cumulative process that leads to successive approximations of reality (Kuhn 1970:96, 206; see Russell 1931:35). Kuhn takes issue with this view of a steady, cumulative advance of scientific knowledge, and he illustrates that it is simplistic by comparing the relationship of old and new paradigms. A new paradigm does more than just explain new data. Kuhn asserts that different paradigms are incompatible and incommensurable (1970:7, 92, 103, 121). This is because paradigms incorporate implicit worldviews and notions of appropriate problems, methods, and techniques. Different paradigms necessarily entail different phenomena and ways of studying them (Figure 2–1).

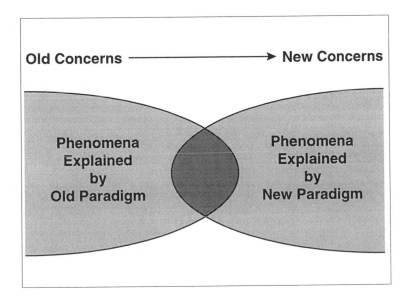

Figure 2–1. Kuhnian Scientific Revolution. Following Paul Feyerabend's discussion in *Against Method* (1978:178), this figure represents a more cynical interpretation of a Kuhnian scientific revolution.

If paradigms are incommensurable, then is there progress in science? Kuhn is very specific and congratulatory toward normal science in this regard. There *is* progress in normal science, and this is due to the fact that once scientists focus on a problem and agree as to how they will resolve it, the scientific community employs its methods very effectively (Kuhn 1970:166). The nature of scientific communities makes this type of progress possible and contributes to the limited progress of scientific revolutions. The characteristics of these communities include: concern with natural world, focus on detailed problems, need for wide acceptance by members of the community, a professionally recognized group, shared training, members are sole possessors of rules of judgement, and most importantly, freedom from being judged by heads of state or by the populace (Kuhn 1970:168). I would extend "heads of state" to mean institutional heads so that his case could generalize to institutions other than the state (e.g., the church, a university administration, a tobacco company). Kuhn points out that these criteria set the scientific community apart from all other communities of professionals, since these criteria guarantee a certain amount of expertise, focus, insulation from society, and freedom from external judgement (1970:169). He asserts that these criteria are essential if science is going to work (1970:164).

A larger issue is whether or not, through history and across paradigms, science progresses knowledge. Don't we know more about the empirical world today, after four hundred years of scientific revolutions? I would argue that we necessarily do, and Kuhn has clarified his position on this matter to suggest that there is a kind of progress that occurs through scientific revolutions. One reason for arguing that scientific revolutions result in a progressively better understanding of nature is that paradigm shifts do not result in the wholesale destruction and abandonment of old paradigms (Kuhn 1970:149).

Another reason to argue for progress can be deduced from Kuhn's statements regarding how normal science leads to revolutions. Kuhn is explicit in stating that, ironically, normal science's narrowly focussed puzzle-solving will solve the puzzles of the paradigm and find anomalous cases that do not fit the paradigm. These anomalies precipitate the crisis that leads to scientific revolution and subsequent paradigm shift (Kuhn 1970:52, 74). Scientists in normal science solve their own riddles, then push their paradigm to its limit while seeking to extend the scope of the paradigm. This is both an efficient and a thorough method by which to bring about a scientific revolution. The fact that the scientific community exhausts the old paradigm before moving on to a new one indicates that much is learned in the process. The fact that the new paradigm must explain new phenomena (the anomalies of the old paradigm) while retaining the ability to explain what the old phenomenon could (Kuhn 1970:169) indicates that a quantitative shift toward more explanation has been achieved, rather than a mere qualitative shift toward explaining only the new data.

I will use Kuhn's (1970:98–101) discussion of the scientific revolution from Newtonian dynamics to Einstein's relativity as an example of scientific progress. This may seem odd since Kuhn uses this example to demonstrate that paradigms address incommensurably different issues and therefore revolutions do not imply progress. However, I think that his example demonstrates the opposite.

> Relativistic dynamics cannot have shown Newtonian dynamics to be wrong, for Newtonian dynamics is still used with great success by most engineers and, in selected applications, by many physicists. Furthermore, the proprietary use of the older theory can be proven from the very theory that has, in other applications, replaced it. Einstein's theory can be used to show that predictions from Newton's equations will be as good as our measuring instruments in all applications that satisfy a small number of restrictive conditions. For example, if Newtonian theory is to provide a good approximate solution, the relative velocities of the bodies considered must be small compared with the velocity of light. Subject to this condition and a few others, Newtonian theory seems to be derivable from Einsteinian, of which it is a special case. (Kuhn 1970:99)

True, engineers still use Newton's laws with great success when building bridges and high-rises—it is probably fair to say that we all are thankful for that. Kuhn himself admits that Newtonian dynamics are derivable from Einstein's relativity, provided that one restrict the conditions to which Newtonian theory will apply. In other words, Newton's theories are a subset of Einstein's theories, applicable to a subset of universal conditions. This is commensurability; and furthermore, the Einsteinian revolution not only extended Newton's theories, but extended the conditions to which physical theories could apply. This certainly implies progress.

Another example will illustrate my point. Georges Cuvier (1769–1832) proposed the theory of catastrophism to reconcile the existence of extinct fossil animals with ecclesiastical interpretations of nature. His notion was that fossils were the remains of animals that were massacred in major, cata-strophic events. After Darwinian evolution took over as the prevailing para-digm in scientific biology, scientists rejected Cuvier's view. However, about a hundred years later, scientists proposed the theory of punctuated equilib-rium to account for discontinuities and seemingly rapid periods of speciation in the fossil record (Gould and Eldridge 1977), and scientists now entertain the possibility that an asteroid wiped out the dinosaurs. Does this mean that scientists have rejected Darwinian theory and have returned to Cuvier's Bib-lical view of nature? Hardly. What we have now is an improved understand-ing of how evolution occurs; this new view is an improvement over both traditional Darwinian gradualism and Cuvier's Biblical catastrophism in that it explains paleontological phenomena better and results in testable, empiri-cal predictions. Punctuated equilibrium simply happens to contain useful ex-planatory elements of both views.

IMRE LAKATOS: PROGRESS ON PROGRESS

Imre Lakatos, Popper's protege, takes up both Kuhn's challenge to progress and weaknesses in Popper's view of science. Lakatos returns to a primarily normative analysis of the evaluation of scientific theories, although he uses descriptive information on how scientists actually evaluate theories to improve upon Popper's methods (1970:117). There is a very good reason for considering what scientists actually do. Few philosophers and fewer scientists would assert that we know less about the empirical world today than before Bacon's scientific revolution. Scientists must have been doing something right, and it pays to examine what scientists actually do in order to infer the rules by which they actually operate.

Lakatos echoes Popper's most basic points. He is primarily concerned with normative analyses of how scientists should evaluate theories. Lakatos argues, as do other philosophers (Hempel 1965; Popper 1959 [1934]), that it does not matter from where scientific statements originate or for what reasons; the thing that matters is that scientists evaluate them rigorously and rationally. Falsification is central to Lakatos's method.

Lakatos proposes a sophisticated falsificationism with its attendant prin-ciples of intellectual honesty in order to improve upon Popper's original formulation. The principle of demarcation for sophisticated falsificationism maintains that "a theory is 'acceptable' or 'scientific' only if it has corroborated excess empirical content over its predecessor (or rival), that is, only if it leads to the discovery of novel facts" (Lakatos 1970:116; see Kuhn 1970:149 quoted above). A new theory must also explain what the old theory could explain (Lakatos 1970:116). The theory should not only explain empirical facts as they exist, but previously unforeseen facts as well. This places the onus of predictive power upon the theory such that in a novel situation the theory will perform better than its rivals, and in a familiar situation the theory performs as well as its rivals. Obviously, this begs the question of how we know a theory can predict something that we do not yet know. The theory needs only have the potential for predicting novel information, and scientists accept a new theory with a degree of risk that it will fail. Should it fail, then Lakatos's scheme allows for its abandonment on systematically logical grounds.

Lakatos goes further to describe and prescribe what scientists actually do and should do. He points out that scientists do not simply test theories, they test series of related theories called research programs (Lakatos 1970:118, 132). He notes that, in practice, scientists have largely been unwilling to "throw the baby out with the bathwater" whenever their theories are refuted. Just because one aspect of a theory does not work does not mean that the entire theory is false. It may need adjustment to be more correct.

His method of sophisticated falsificationism is based on what he calls a negative and a positive heuristic. Every research program has a core of concepts that scientists (initially anyway) do not question. The negative heuristic maintains that scientists are not out to test this core, but to use the core theories to generate auxiliary theories (Lakatos 1979:133). It is this collection of auxiliary hypotheses that scientists normally test and reject. The positive heuristic "consists of a partially articulated set of suggestions or hints on how to change, develop the 'refutable variants' of the research-programme, how to modify, sophisticate, the 'refutable protective belt' [around the core]" (Lakatos 1970:135). This is what typifies (and according to Lakatos should characterize) scientific research (Figure 2–2). If this were all there was to it, then science would not differ from any other body of

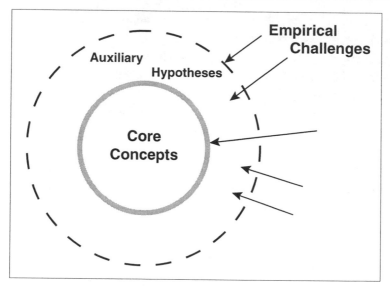

Figure 2–2. Lakatos's Negative and Positive Heuristic. Note how a set of core concepts is more or less protected from direct testing (the negative heuristic), although auxiliary hypotheses are generated, tested, and altered by empirical challenges (the positive heuristic). Note also that, in the end, even the core is permeable and ultimately can be systematically rejected through the refutation of its auxiliary hypotheses. This contrasts with a religious system of thought as seen in Figure 2–3.

knowledge based on dogmatic axioms and untestable assumptions (Figure 2–3). However, scientists are not free to change auxiliary hypotheses at will. James Bell (1994:70–83) provides an extended discussion of how scientists can make these adjustments while retaining the testability of a theory. The key is that no change should occur that renders the theory less testable.

    In addition to restrictions on changing auxiliary hypotheses, even the core is ultimately refutable, and this is extremely important. The core is refuted indirectly by the refutations of its auxiliary hypotheses. Lakatos notes that "we maintain that if and when the programme ceases to anticipate novel facts, its hard core might have to be abandoned" (1970:134). I would argue that this notion of ultimately testing the core serves as the most important principle of demarcation between science and metaphysics, especially those metaphysics based on ethical, moral, or religious faith. Therefore, nothing is ultimately unassailable in science; even the most central axioms of a sci-

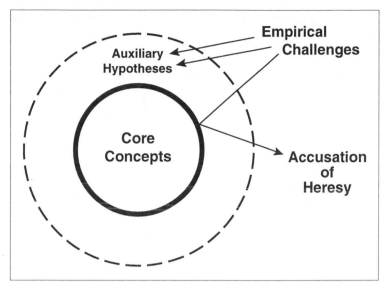

Figure 2–3. Religious Systems of Thought. Note that auxiliary hypotheses derived from core religious teachings can be altered in light of theological debate and empirical experience. However, the core is solidly and dogmatically protected. Challenges to the core are dismissed as heresy.

entific research program can be overturned using the very method that generated them. This point leads to new standards for intellectual honesty.

> The honesty of sophisticated falsificationism demanded that one should try to look at things from different points of view, to put forward new theories which anticipate novel facts, and to reject theories which have been superseded by more powerful ones. (Lakatos 1970:122)

Lakatos's system assures progress as long as any replacement (problem shift) of a theory or a program involves a replacement with a theory that explains old data, explains the present anomalies, and promises to explain unanticipated facts. Lakatos states it simply as, "a given fact is explained scientifically only if a new fact is also explained with it" (1970:119).

Lakatos's approach shares a number of characteristics with Kuhn's. A research program is pretty much the same as Kuhn's paradigm, at Lakatos's own admission (1970:132). He also notes the importance of anomalies and the fact that they can lead to scientific crises, while stressing that new thoughts that lead to better theories are also an important source of problem shifts (Lakatos 1970:121, 122). Problem shift is basically another word for scientific revolution or paradigm shift. Like Kuhn, Lakatos also argues for scientific resistance to change. He argues that only by exhausting the possibilities of a theory can scientists see what theories could better replace it.

> The dogmatic attitude of sticking to a theory as long as possible is of considerable significance. Without it we could never find out what is in a theory—we should give the theory up before we had a real opportunity for finding out its strength; and in consequence no theory would every be able to play its role of bridging order into the world, of preparing us for future events, of drawing our attention to events we should otherwise never observe. (Popper 1940 in Lakatos 1970:177)

The main differences between Lakatos and Kuhn lie in Lakatos's normative approach and his explicit view on progress. While Lakatos provides ways to salvage a progressive science, a dispute over the possibility of falsifiability has existed since the turn of the century that involves falsification as well as Lakatos's notion of research programs. This challenge to progressive science, known as the Duhem-Quine thesis, has been used by science's critics.

THE DUHEM-QUINE THESIS

Pierre Duhem began the debate in 1906 with the publication of his *Aim and Structure of Physical Theory*. He began by pointing out that all observations are theory-laden since theories lead scientists to develop certain instruments for measuring the world and interpreting measurements (1976 [1906]:3). Because of this, and the fact that hypotheses are deduced from systems of interrelated theories along with sets of background assumptions, a test of a single hypothesis really reflects upon this larger system of hypotheses and assumptions (Duhem 1976 [1906]:8). His position is known as the weak form of the Duhem-Quine thesis (Harding 1976). Not only is "no hypothesis an island," but when there is contradictory evidence, one cannot be sure that the hypothesis is incorrect, its theoretical underpinning is wrong, the observations are invalid, or the background assumptions are faulty. For instance, scientists might salvage a contradicted theory by altering the definition of what they study (Duhem 1976 [1906]:31). Indeed, this is what Lakatos suggests with the positive heuristic. For instance, if I were to harbor a theory that the state exists by virtue of taxes and I find a state that exists without taxes, instead of rejecting my hypothesis I may simply redefine *state* to include the contradictory instance.

Duhem's solution is to use "good sense" to choose among alternative theories (1976 [1906]:39). He is vague about what this means, although he also notes that experiments aid in determining what constitutes good sense. He goes on to suggest that scientists should maximize their good sense by not cluttering their minds with vanity and bias. "Now nothing contributes more to entangle good sense and to disturb its insight than passions and interests" (Duhem 1976 [1906]:39). So, in the end, Duhem argues for the testing of systems of theories based on empirical evidence and good sense, unencumbered by ideological or personal agendas. Based on the presentation of anthropological science in the last chapter, it is fair to say that scientific anthropologists would not be the least challenged by this.

Willard Van Orman Quine extended the Duhem thesis to suggest a stronger criticism of refutation/confirmation. Quine begins by denying the demarcation of science and metaphysics because we are incapable of formulating definitions or theories without making untestable assumptions (e.g., reality exists), or referring to a specific language that places constraints on our ability to conceive ideas (1976 [1953]:41). He argues that scientists can always salvage a theory contradicted by empirical data by making an adjustment somewhere in its system. "Any statement can be held true come what may, if we make drastic enough adjustments elsewhere in the system....no statement is immune to revision" (Quine 1976 [1953]:60). It is this last statement that has become known as the strong thesis, and the one that has engendered the most controversy.

Adolf Grünbaum and Imre Lakatos both have critiqued the Duhem-Quine thesis. Both authors recognize the weak Duhem-Quine thesis as stated in Duhem, and they note as well that it holds, although in a trivial way (Grünbaum 1976 [1960]:116; Lakatos 1978:98). Grünbaum argues that the strong thesis, which denies the falsifiability of hypotheses, is a non sequitur (1976 [1969]). It is a non sequitur because, in order always to save an empirically contradicted hypothesis, one must necessarily be able to generate an alternative set of auxiliary assumptions undergirding the hypothesis. There is simply no logical reason why this must be so; one can imagine that it is possible to do this, but it is not inevitable that alternative assumptions always can be derived to save the hypothesis. I would point out that Quine's statement that "no statement is immune to revision" is tantamount to saying "all ravens are black." As Popper pointed out, only one counter-example is sufficient to refute a universal statement, and Grünbaum supplies such a counter-example in physical geometry. I want to offer the following anthropological example to point out that, in anthropological practice, Quine's strong thesis is not typically practiced by anthropologists.

One of anthropology's early truisms was the unilineal progression of human society from savagery to civilization. Pioneers such as Lewis Henry Morgan (1963 [1877]:66) and E. B. Tylor (1960 [1881]:247) postulated that human societies would have passed through a matriarchical stage when the only sure line of descent was through mothers and all deferred to women's authority. Early anthropologists uncritically used concepts like patriarchy and matriarchy as explanations for the ethnographic realities they witnessed. However, as ethnographic fieldwork (and observations) accumulated, and anthropologists better understood the social workings of more societies, they began to cast doubt upon this unilinear scheme. In 1924, A. R. Radcliffe-Brown published a paper in which he noted the logical and empirical failings of the concept of matriarchy, and instead of redefining the terms or background assumptions to save these concepts, he refuted them and proposed a better alternative.

Radcliffe-Brown was disturbed by statements that the closeness of the relationship between mother's brother and sister's son in patrilineal African societies was evidence that these societies had previously gone through a matriarchal stage (1965 [1924]:15). He noted that the terms *patriarchal* and *matriarchal* were too vague to be scientifically useful, and he operationalized these terms so that he could scrutinize them empirically (1965 [1924]:22). Radcliffe-Brown provided definitions that reflected the general usage of the terms; he did not redefine the terms to save (or necessarily to destroy) them. Then, using cross-cultural, empirical accounts, Radcliffe-Brown demonstrated that no society conforms to a patriarchy or matriarchy. Instead, he argued that one's behavior toward kin is an extension of one's behavior toward one's parents (1965 [1924]:25). In a patrilineal society, where discipline and inheritance come from the male side of the family, one's father, one's father's sisters, and even one's patrilineal ancestors are treated with deference and respect. In contrast, the matrilineal kin are treated as an extension of the close relationship to one's mother. Radcliffe-Brown did not simply redefine matriarchy and patriarchy in order to account for ethnographic phenomena. Instead, he operationally defined them according to common usage, found them to be inadequate, and dealt a major blow to the nineteenth-century concepts of matriarchy/patriarchy and unilineal evolution. This type of behavior is much more typical of anthropological research than the redefinition of terms to save theories at all cost suggested by Quine.

Lakatos's main critique of the strong thesis centers on the characteristics of sophisticated falsificationism. Because the sophisticated falsificationist "allows *any* part of the body of science to be replaced *but* only on the condition that it is replaced in a 'progressive' way, so that the replacement successfully anticipates novel facts," and because of the "strong empiricist requirement" for falsification, some theories can be judged superior to others (Lakatos 1978:99, 100). In plain terms, some things will just not accord with observations no matter what scientists do to them. Only by continually checking definitions, assumptions, and theories against the empirical record, can scientists expect to generate theories that will increasingly accord with that record. And so, this diversion into the Duhem-Quine controversy leads back to the basic principles of science as stated by anthropologists.

All of these arguments, whether they be statements by scientific anthropologists about what they do or arguments by philosophers about what scientists should do, are purely academic unless they correspond to actual scientific practice. The next chapter contains two extended examples of scientific anthropology that demonstrate the correspondence between methods of evaluation reviewed in the last chapter and the sociological dimensions reviewed here, and anthropological practice.

Chapter 3

Two Examples of
Anthropological Science

Few things are harder to put up with than the annoyance of a good example.

Mark Twain
Pudd'nhead Wilson's Calendar

In this chapter, I will demonstrate that anthropologists following a scientific approach generally do what they say, although the application of scientific methods can be a messy affair. The two examples I use are the investigation of the role of hunting in forager (hunter-gatherer) societies, and archaeological research on the Hopewell phenomenon (ca. 100 B.C.–A.D. 400) in the mid-continental United States. I use these examples not only to demonstrate that anthropologists have scientific goals and employ a scientific approach, but also to illustrate the sociological dimensions of scientific practice. Values and ideological social movements play a role in these examples. As people's attitudes and desires change (e.g., pro-Native American sentiments, feminism) anthropologists re-direct their attention to new sources of data and new theories. However, in these examples, anthropologists use these shifts of focus to generate data with which to test theories, or to build new, yet testable theories. In the end, even though the anthropological quest for knowledge is suffused with human intentions and influenced by political and ideological movements, anthropologists eventually set these aside and employ scientific methods of evaluation to scrutinize all of their ideas. The result is a progressive increase in the breadth, depth, and objectivity of anthropological knowledge.

I have chosen these examples precisely because they are not clean, clear-cut examples of the triumph of textbook scientific methods. Both have a long history of research influenced by powerful social forces. Despite these real-life influences of human interest, in both cases a basic scientific commitment to generating more objective knowledge resulted in theories that better account for empirical data. By necessity, I have focussed on the most salient aspects of these examples, and my descriptions of each issue should not be considered exhaustive. I have chosen elements of each example to illustrate the issues I have so far discussed in the abstract. The result is a more realistic view of scientific anthropology. If good examples are annoying, I hope that these two glimpses into anthropological practice will be infuriating.

MAN THE HUNTER

> She went to Cú Chulaind, then, and said, "The women desire those birds from you."...Cú Chulaind sprang into the chariot, and he dealt the birds such a stunning blow....Then he returned with the birds and distributed them so that each woman had a pair....When he came to his wife, he said, "Angry you are." "I am not," she replied,... "You did right, for every one of those women loves you or gives you a share of her love, but I share my love with you alone." "Then do not be angry," said Cú Chulaind.... "you will have the most beautiful pair."
>
> The Wasting Sickness of Cú Chulaind
> Early Medieval Ireland

And so goes the stereotype of the male warrior/hunter/provider, a stereotype that, along with its equally stereotyped reactions, has influenced how people have regarded gender roles in foraging societies. The history of anthropological research on the role of hunting among foragers is a good example of how scientific methods have led to a better understanding of this phenomenon. Research on hunting also has benefitted from feminist and social-reform movements to the extent that these social/political concerns led researchers to gather data and ask questions that they had previously ignored, although excessive politicizing of forager research has also led some away from scientific research. One hundred years of scientific anthropological research on foragers has, nonetheless, generated much more accurate knowledge about foragers than what had existed before (see Ingold, et al. 1991a,b; Kelly 1995 for updates and summaries of this body of knowledge).

Foragers, or hunter-gatherers, are people whose primary economic and subsistence activities involve harvesting wild (non-domesticated) foods for consumption. Foragers have always fascinated social theorists by representing an ancient, primal past we all share. Because so little has, until recently, been known about foragers, social theorists have been at liberty to theorize these people any way they like, usually to make some political argument favoring their view of human nature. Thomas Hobbes (1962 [1651]) made his famous assertion that man in his natural state had a life that was "poor, nasty, brutish, and short," while Jean Jacques Rousseau (1954 [1762]) used his own myth of natural man to argue for an inherently rational, peaceful, and morally unencumbered human nature. Intimately bound with the Hobbesian stereotype is the idea that humans are "killer apes," fundamentally carnivorous, whose males are genetically programmed for hunting and killing. A corollary to this notion is that females, not so genetically endowed, are dependent upon males to provide the life-giving meat they are unable to procure for themselves.

The carnivorous, Hobbesian stereotype is the earliest paradigm of forager research in anthropology, and anthropologists have used it as a starting point for their theorizing. However, the anthropological practice of long-term, empirical, ethnographic fieldwork generated data that anthropologists used to challenge this stereotype and resulted in newer, more realistic theories of forager life. I will focus on the role of hunting in forager society. Cultural anthropologists have been generally skeptical of any simplistic, stereotypic view of foragers. While Marshall Sahlins notes several early anthropologists who painted a Hobbesian picture of forager life, he simultaneously notes that "the traditional dismal view of the hunters' fix is also preanthropological and extra-anthropological" (1972:3). As anthropologists gathered more data among actual foragers, these stereotypes broke down.

Important theorists like Julian Steward reflected the Hobbesian assumptions of an essentially carnivorous, male-dominated natural state of humanity. "Groups consisting of patrilineal bands [i.e. foragers] are similar...because the nature of the game and therefore their subsistence problem is the same in each case" (1955:38). Based on cursory information and the few ethnographies of people (like the Paiute and Sirionó) who seem to live in truly marginal habitats, these generalizations were not entirely unreasonable. However, anthropologists did not monolithically accept this prevailing view of carnivorous, male-oriented foragers. Elman Service noted that while in some groups males provide the bulk of the diet through hunting, this is not true of all groups; and he cites shell gathering by Yaghan women as a counterexample (1971 [1962]:33). The carnivorous generalization would not stand for long. By the mid-1960s, anthropologists had studied a number of foraging groups in an increasingly detailed and quantitative manner, and the patterns of data they presented challenged standard views.

The watershed event in forager studies was the Man the Hunter conference, held in 1966, and its proceedings, published in 1968. Richard Lee and Irven Devore (1968) summarize the results of the conference, in which anthropologists compared notes on dozens of forager groups from around the world. The new patterns constituted a new paradigm in forager research that included: foragers satisfy their basic needs and wants with little effort and are well-nourished; plant foods tend to dominate the diet (excepting high-latitude foragers); political organization is focussed on very fluid, non-territorial bands; foragers are not nearly as patrilocal as previously thought, kinship systems tend toward bilateral descent; foragers are generally well nourished and have little disease; bands are small; and mobility is a pervasive feature of foraging society. Lee (1968) went on to elaborate the typical subsistence pattern of foragers. Comparing fifty-eight forager societies, he found that only eleven emphasized hunting, although in fifty-seven cases, hunting contributed at least twenty percent of the diet (Lee 1968:42). Gathering tended to be women's work in forager societies, so this de-emphasis on hunting redirected anthropologists' attention to women's contributions to the diet; since men were no longer bringing home the bacon, women were apparently the real breadwinners.

Several influential publications coincided with or followed the Man the Hunter conference. Elman Service published *The Hunters*, a book he admitted was not well named since he noted that neither hunting nor male provisioning was the necessity anthropologists once thought it was (1966:11). Marshall Sahlins published his influential thoughts on original affluence to emphasize further the reality that many foragers do not work very hard to satisfy their needs and desires (1972). He compared data on Australian Aborigines with Lee's !Kung data and Washburn's Hadza data in Africa and noted that among these groups, people work the equivalent of only a couple days a week. M. G. Bicchieri (1972) edited a follow-up volume to the *Man the Hunter* proceedings in which he stressed the scientific need for detailed, representative ethnographies in order to challenge theory productively, and to correct for wider societal biases about foragers.

In 1981, Frances Dahlberg edited a volume entitled *Woman the Gatherer*. Realizing both the new opportunities for incorporating women in meaningful ways in anthropological theories and the older androcentric biases exhibited by some physical anthropologists (e.g., Washburn and Lancaster 1968), Dahlberg brought together ethnographers' accounts of female forager lives, adding "woman the mate chooser, woman the mother, woman the aunt, woman the communicator, woman the power, woman the ritual actor, and woman the hunter" to woman the gatherer (1981a:xi). Dahlberg notes that the women's movement of the 1960s and 1970s also increased anthropologists' willingness to scrutinize standard wisdom, although Dahlberg's approach remains resolutely scientific and evaluative. Citing cross-cultural studies that both support and challenge the Man the Hunter view, Dahlberg notes that males are largely responsible for hunting large animals, their tasks tend to be more dangerous, and they are more competent in women's tasks than women are at men's. Likewise, women are largely responsible for gathering, cooking, and childcare, and women's contribution to subsistence is not always the primary one (Dahlberg 1981b:13–15).

While Dahlberg promotes a more accurate, more truthful, more representative view of women foragers against the androcentric biases of the past, she is equally troubled by feminist mythologizing of foraging societies as a "golden androgynous past." She (1981:19–27) challenges feminist notions that foragers represent sexual egalitarianism, feminist devaluation of motherhood, and the notion that nature is a debased category among foragers as projections of feminist values onto accounts of foraging peoples.

> Research that starts with the majority—women and children—does not support a legend of man the hunter or woman the gatherer but leads to a more complicated story. (Dahlberg 1981b:27)

It is worth noting that the scientific orientation of the *Woman the Gatherer* volume is symptomatic of a divergence in forager studies, a division nicely documented by Bender and Morris (1991) between traditional, scientific ethnographers and those who have taken up more advocacy-based and literary orientations. While some ethnographers of foraging societies have taken this literary turn, a constant thread of scientific research has been directed at resolving one of the foundational problems of foraging theory—the role of hunting.

The de-emphasis on male hunting and the emphasis on female gathering that emanated from the *Man the Hunter* volume, combined with increasing cross-cultural realization that men hunt and that hunting remains an important activity for men (both economically and ideologically), led anthropologists to ask the question, "Why do men bother hunting?" The varied and high-quality vegetal diets enjoyed by many foragers, combined with the sporadic success of hunters, cast doubt upon the necessity of meat as a source of protein or calories. Yellen and Lee (1976: 40) provide a nutrient analysis of the !Kung's most commonly eaten plant foods to demonstrate that these foods are high in nutrition, and that Mongongo nuts, tsin beans, and peanuts are particularly high in protein. Truswell and Hanson found that medically, the !Kung show "no signs of protein deficiency" (1976:192). Forager men do not seem to be that good at hunting anyway. Lee (1979:267) provides data in which seven men made eighteen kills over seventy-eight man-days. This averages to 4.3 man-days of labor to make a kill. Considering that !Kung men only work about two days a week, this would mean that the average man might bring back a kill about once every two weeks. How could men be providers with such dismal success?

The first hypothesis proposed to answer how men could provision with hunting involved the concept of risk pooling. Perhaps the one social institution most regularly reported by anthropologists working with foragers is meat sharing. Hunters rarely eat a large kill by themselves, or with just their own families. Meat is almost universally brought back to camp, where it is doled out to relatives and friends who, in turn, give portions to others, until the meat is distributed throughout the camp (Burch 1991:102; Clastres 1972:169; Endicott 1991; Gibson 1991; Gould 1982; Kaplan, et al. 1990; Hawkes 1993a; Lee 1972:348; Radcliffe-Brown 1964 [1932]:43; Rogers 1972:120; Sharp 1981:240; Stearman 1989:65; Woodburn 1968:53). Lee (1979: 247, 1972:349) and Marshall (1976:357) also stressed that meat is not hoarded because it is impractical in the hot Kalahari environment, and because of an overwhelming egalitarian ethic among the !Kung.

The uncertainties involved in the hunt led many anthropologists to postulate that meat sharing was a form of risk minimization. Pierre Clastres noted for the Guayaki of Paraguay that "each hunter gives his game to others, but, in return, the others offer their own game to him" (1972:169). Richard Gould postulated that "affluence for hunter-gatherers *means* minimal risk," and noted that where resources are more uncertain and limited, foragers will extend their social networks in order to have others to rely on, thereby limiting risk (1982:76, 86). The idea that forager sharing is a form of risk-pooling was operationalized and tested among San foragers by Polly Wiessner and Elizabeth Cashdan. Wiessner concentrated on the !Kung Hxaro trade network, a generalized reciprocal network of sharing in which !Kung exchange non-food items. She points out the abundant sources of risk and uncertainty in !Kung life, and demonstrates ethnographically that !Kung manipulate the Hxaro network so as to place trading partners in various geographic areas (1982:74). The risk-minimizing value of this strategy is that in times of stress, movement to another region is a common and effective strategy. Cashdan studied Basarwa forager/cattle herders, employing insurance theory and carefully recording food exchanges between families. She then presented data on grain sharing among households, and found that the generalized reciprocity of the Basarwa indeed reduced the variance in income of Basarwa families (1985:469) .

Bruce Winterhalder and Eric Allen Smith developed theoretical models of sharing networks intended to apply to forager behavior, and I will concentrate on Smith's formulation. Smith's aim is to develop a theory applicable to forager decision making that will yield deductive predictions "in a manner that is subject to quantitative (and hence more exacting and powerful) empirical test" (1991:236). Smith questions the *Man the Hunter* view on the ubiquity of altruistic sharing that he argues has become an uncritically received view (1991:238). First, he notes that the ethnographic record on sharing is much more variable than many ethnographers now admit. Second, he exposes a logical flaw in the theory of altruistic sharing—just because the greater good can be had for all does not mean that individuals will necessarily behave that way (Smith 1991:239). He then goes on to demonstrate theoretically that sharing is a rational choice provided that there is an assurance that the sharing parties will meet again, and that there exists an effective sanction against those who will not share. Smith suggests that an effective sanction would be not reciprocating in a sharing network (1991:240).

These risk-pooling theories provided increasingly explicit and testable hypotheses about forager food sharing. Indeed, Weissner's and Cashdan's formulations attained a degree of confirmation in the ethnographic record. However, neither Weissner's nor Cashdan's research explicitly focussed on meat sharing, and the sharing of other items may be qualitatively different. Emically, many foragers probably would point this out as they have different terms for hunger, often separating meat hunger from generalized hunger. For instance, the Yuquí differentiate between "*toria i*, to be hungry, and *eyibasi*, to be meat hungry" (Stearman 1989:67). Furthermore, looking at the sharing that men and women do conflates gendered aspects of sharing. Who produces and who shares may have an important influence on the nature of sharing. Another weakness was not apparent until some anthropologists realized an uncomfortable fact—not all men are equal.

Optimal foraging theory is an application of microeconomic theory to ecological contexts. The benefits of this approach are that it is explicitly deductive and logical, and that it provides specific, empirically testable hypotheses (Winterhalder 1981:18–19). If theories anthropologists derive from optimal foraging theory are wrong, it will be obvious. A team of researchers using optimal foraging theory studied the Aché foragers of Paraguay and eventually discovered another major flaw in the risk-pooling theories. The Aché are a group of tropical foragers for whom meat is a major resource. Ninety-five percent of men's subsistence effort is devoted to hunting (Hill and Hawkes 1983:159), and men provide nearly ninety percent of the food the Aché consume while trekking in the forest. Research on Aché women's subsistence activities indicated that a major factor in their activities was compatibility with childcare (Hurtado, et al. 1985), corroborating an empirical pattern long postulated by anthropologists and found by cross-cultural researchers (Brown 1970; Ember 1978; Murdock and Provost 1973). Women generally have to conduct activities in the presence of infants, precluding the stalking of large game, and women need to feed children with regularity. Gathering activities provide both the dietary certainty and the logistical compatibility women require. For instance, in an ethnography of the Venezuelan Pumé, Gragson recorded that men had 7.5 successes for each failure in hunting events, compared to women's 16.4 successes for each failure in gathering events (1989:234). Now there existed a better empirical basis for why women gather, but why do men hunt?

Early data on the Aché demonstrated that not only was average male hunting success low (Kaplan, et al. 1990:113), but that there was marked variation among the hunters themselves (Hill and Hawkes 1983:171). During their study period, Hill and Hawkes (1983:171) estimated that 32% of the men brought back 50% of the game, and 57% brought back 80% of the game. Simply put, some men are good hunters, others stink. The Aché data were not new among forager studies. Lee early on reported that 65% of the meat in the camp he studied was provided by one of the eleven adult males in that camp (1979: 266). The implications of unequal male success rates were important. The fact that a few males are carrying the rest in the meat-sharing network contradicts the notion that all males engage in the network in order to provide a steady supply of meat for their families (Hawkes 1990, 1993a,b).

Kristen Hawkes provides an analysis of men's hunting in which she compares hunting returns to gathering returns among the !Kung, Hadza, and Aché. She points out that the potential Calories collected per hour by men in hunting falls far below those men could gain in gathering (1993a:343–

344). Furthermore, much of a man's catch does not go to himself or his family, but is widely distributed in meat-sharing networks. Considering the higher foraging efficiency of gathering, and the loss of meat in meat sharing, men could do three to eleven times better by gathering to provision their families (from data in Hawkes 1993a:343–344). The unequal return rates among men and the low income generated by hunting for a man's family refutes the risk-pooling hypotheses.

The upshot of Hawkes's argument is this: the success (or conversely failure) rates of men are too uneven for risk-pooling to be effective, and men's hunting feeds others much more than it feeds their families. Why, then, do men, and especially good hunters, participate in hunting and meat sharing at all? Hawkes suggests that men are not hunting to provide their families, but in order to gain attention and prestige from their camp-mates (1990, 1993a,b), and she provides an analytical demonstration that if men really are pursuing attention, pursuing collective goods (like large game that is shared) provides much more attention than does pursuing private goods (small game and plants) (Hawkes 1993a:349). But a man and his family cannot eat attention, so what is going on?

The answer to this crucial question came from forager women themselves. In what is arguably a gross example of androcentric bias in anthropology, all the while that anthropologists were vexing over hunting in forager society, most failed to ask women foragers what they had to say. Kaplan and Hill interviewed women on their reproductive histories and found that Aché women report an average of 2.1 fathers for a particular child, and women mentioned better hunters most often as their lovers (1985:132). This translated into the fact that good hunters had more illegitimate children than poor hunters—the attention men apparently get from hunting big game is from women, and it is sexual and therefore potentially reproductive (Hawkes 1993a:351).

The meat-for-sex economy tentatively identified by Hawkes and Kaplan and Hill should have been no surprise to anthropologists who have gathered empirical data on foragers and horticulturalists. Allan R. Holmberg provided an early and explicit description of how men used meat to garner sexual favors from women, and cited conflicts between husbands and wives that ensued after a man returns from the forest with part of his catch missing (recall Cú Chulaind's dilemma) (1985 [1950]:166-167). In 1981, Marjorie Shostak compiled an autobiography of a !Kung woman named Nisa. Nisa was clear about the relationship between sex and meat.

> When you are a woman, you don't just sit still and do nothing—you have lovers....One day when she and her husband are living as usual, her husband says, "I'm going away for a few days." She stays behind, and that's when she sees her lovers. If one of her lovers lives in a village nearby and an animal is killed, he'll cut some meat and bring it to her. It will be beautiful meat, full of juice and heavy. (Shostak 1981 271–272)

Data from horticultural societies is likewise unambiguous (Werner 1990:42). Janet Siskind entitled her 1973 ethnography of the Peruvian Sharanahua *To Hunt in the Morning*, and she details the same meat-for-sex economy.

> Prestige accrues to the generous hunter....Prestige is not a vague goal at Marcos; it brings a definite reward, the possibility of gaining women as lovers and/or wives....The successful hunter is usually the winner in the competition for women. (Siskind 1973:95–96)

Not only did anthropologists have anecdotes from their own observations and from informants' statements, but quantitative data have existed for a long time detailing the reproductive success of successful hunters and leaders in foraging societies. William Laughlin found that twenty percent of the Nunamiut in Anaktuvuk Pass, Alaska, were descended from one particularly able hunter (1957, 1968:317). Research among the Xavante Indians of Brazil revealed that the chief in this foraging group (which included thirty-six other men) produced over twenty-five percent of the offspring! (Neel, et al. 1964:94, also cited in Laughlin 1968 and Dahlberg 1981). Anthropologists are now beginning to appreciate the implications of this pattern of reproductive success.

Hawkes's meat-for-sex theory is new, and is currently undergoing intense scrutiny. Hill and Kaplan object to Hawkes's easy refutation of the

reciprocal altruism and trade hypotheses, citing a lack of data for corroborating the falseness of these theories (1993). Hawkes, in reply to Hill and
Kaplan, even examines more of her data on Hadza sharing and concludes
that her assertion that hunters' families do not benefit from their hunting
was overgeneralized; "The patterns *falsify* my more general inference that
there is no differential consumption among group members" (1993b:707).
Hill and Kaplan also note that Hawkes ignores the nutritional benefits that
people derive from meat (1993:705). Even though Hill and Kaplan dispute
Hawkes's claims, the force of the data emerging from their research leads
them to converge on similar explanations—"Men provision children directly
and indirectly (through shared food from other adults) but do trade off
parenting effort with the mating benefits from more wide-scaled sharing"
(Hill and Kaplan 1993:705). Current researchers now focus on just what
makes meat so valuable to hominids (e.g., Aiello and Wheeler 1995), and
research among our close primate relatives indicates that this meat-for-sex
economy may not be the exclusive domain of humans (Stanford 1995, 1996).

Meat and men are back in forager theories, although not in the simplistic ways that early social theorists thought they might be. Gone forever are
the dutiful husbands and their helpless wives (see Washburn and Lancaster
1968). As anthropologists gathered empirical data, they could no longer
accept these old stereotypes. Foragers went from starving killer apes to affluent (Sahlins 1972), mostly vegetarian (Lee 1968), sexually emancipated
(Shostak 1981) flower children. However, continued research into forager
sharing revealed that both sharing and sex were tools employed in more
selfish strategies (Cashdan 1985; Gould 1982; Hawkes 1993a,b; Hurtado,
et al. 1985; Kaplan, et al. 1990; Wiessner 1982). These changes were brought
about by paradigm shifts in which anomalous data overwhelmed the standard wisdom of its day and encouraged alternative theorizing. However,
these theories, whether they be of altruistic affluents, or of scheming phi-
landerers and carnivorous prostitutes, were constantly tested against the
empirical, ethnographic record. Hawkes's eager falsification of her generalization and Hill and Kaplan's treatment of falsification are emblematic of
the scientific procedures these researchers follow. Hawkes had no problem
refuting her own claims upon seeing contradictory data, and Hill and Kaplan

are very Popperian in their concern that reciprocal altruism and trade have not been adequately falsified.

The result of this scientific activity has been an exclusion of incorrect theories on meat sharing, and the proposal of what seems at this time the most reasonable alternative—meat-for-sex and perhaps reciprocal altruism. Of course, this scenario is only tentative, and anthropologists do not yet know the true extent of the pattern, or the reasons why meat is so highly valued by women. Continuing research (e.g., Hawkes, et al. 1995) will hopefully answer these questions, and most likely will lead to revisions of the meat-for-sex scenario that even more powerfully, accurately, and generally explain the sexual division of labor among foragers.

HISTORY OF HOPEWELL RESEARCH

I came to a mound, to scores of companies, among which I found long-haired Labraid. I found him sitting in the mound, with thousands of weapons....There is in the síd a well with three fifties of brightly coloured mantles....

The Wasting Sickness of Cú Chulaind
Early Medieval Ireland

When a rich Thracian is buried, the custom is to lay out the body for three days...then the body is buried, with or without cremation, a mound is raised over it, and elaborate games set on foot. The most valuable prizes in the games are awarded for single combat.

Herodotus
The Histories, Fifth Century B.C.

Little known to most Americans, the rolling landscape of corn fields and groves in middle North America contains spectacular earthen mounds that have intrigued and fascinated Western peoples for three centuries. The artifacts contained in these mounds include carved mica sheets, elaborate pottery vessels and figurines, polished stone pipes and axes, ornaments of copper and silver, and large, expertly flaked obsidian blades. Inheritors of the

Western tradition have long held a fascination with mounds, whether they be the burial places of Thracian and Sythian warriors or the ancient dwelling places of Celtic fairies. The American mounds would be no different, spawning over two centuries of speculation and debate. I will restrict my discussion to those mounds found primarily between Illinois and Ohio, dating between roughly 100 B.C. and A.D. 400 and known to archaeologists today as the Hopewell phenomenon. I also have excluded the discussion of physical anthropological research on mound burials for space considerations; this branch of the research paralleled the scientific developments in research on settlement/subsistence systems and artifacts (see Buikstra 1979 for an overview).

The earliest account of the Hopewell mounds came in the 1770s as missionaries began to settle in the Ohio River country, and many people assumed that Native Americans had built them (Silverberg 1970:16). Early settlers began the first detailed mapping and excavation of them in order to satisfy their curiosity. The Reverend Manassah Cutler even conducted tree-ring dating of mounds in order to establish their antiquity, presaging a technique that has now become indispensable to modern archaeologists (Silverberg 1970:17). Fanciful speculations about the mounds began in 1787, when Benjamin Smith Barton published a book in which he alleged that the builders of the mounds were a lost race of ancient Vikings who settled in the New World, built the mounds, and then moved to Mexico, becoming the fabled Toltecs (Silverberg 1970:18). Barton began what was to become a major theme in nineteenth-century speculation—the notion that a lost race, unrelated to indigenous Native Americans, built the mounds—and this theme was the first widespread paradigm under which people conducted mound research. The empirical basis for the speculations was logical enough because the mounds and the artifacts within them bore little resemblance to the constructions and implements made by Shawnee, Delaware, Miami, and Wyandot who inhabited the Ohio country at that time. Furthermore, the relatively small and dispersed indigenous tribes of the area did not seem to possess the personnel or social organization necessary for constructing the large mounds and earthworks. Furthermore, Native Americans themselves confessed ignorance about the origin of the mounds (Silverberg 1970:3).

The Lost Race theories vary from Mormon doctrines to the musings of famous American politicians like William Henry Harrison. The first extensive exploration of the mound phenomenon was made by E. G. Squier and Dr. D. H. Davis on behalf of the American Ethnological Society between 1845 and 1847 (Silverberg 1970:53). Squier followed inductivist principles of scientific research as evidenced in his following statement quoted in Silverberg.

> At the outset all preconceived notions were abandoned, and the work of research commenced, as if no speculations had been indulged in, nor anything before been known, respecting the singular remains of antiquity scattered so profusely around us. (1970:54)

Squier and Davis excavated over two hundred mounds and investigated about one hundred earthworks, and used they their data to generate the first comprehensive classification of mound types (Silverberg 1970:55). They thought that lowland enclosures were religious centers, enclosures on hilltops were fortresses; and they recognized that some mounds were used solely for burial, whereas others were flat-topped. They also noted that mounds of the southeastern United States were noticeably different from those of the northeast, being larger and flat-topped. Despite Squier's inductivist principles, his conclusions were all too familiar. Squier concluded that indigenous Native Americans could not have made the mounds because the pottery manufactures and art objects recovered from the mounds were too advanced (Silverberg 1970:61-62). Furthermore, pressure from the barbaric Indians was the reason that the enlightened Mound Builders built the hilltop forts and eventually abandoned their northeastern haunts for Mexico (Silverberg 1970:56).

While Squier and Davis provided much support to the popular notion of a Lost Race of Mound Builders, their regional coverage and investigation of numerous mounds provided a more representative view of the phenomenon of the mounds. They were forced to recognize the empirical variability of the mounds, a variable pattern that, once widely recognized, actually served to refute the Mound Builder myths. Squier and Davis adhered to the scientific principles of their time and provided data that scientists with other theories also could find useful. Eventually these data, and continued skepticism about the simplistic Lost Race theories, would force a reconsideration of those theories, leading to the understanding anthropologists have today.

In 1881, John Wesley Powell, director of the Bureau of Ethnology, hired Cyrus Thomas to head an archaeology division of the bureau. At the time, Powell thought that Native Americans had built the mounds, in contrast to Thomas, who declared that he was "a pronounced believer in the existence of a race of Mound Builders, distinct from the American Indians" (Silverberg 1970:86). Thomas took the charge of testing the theory that indigenous Native Americans built the mounds. "The most important question to be settled is, 'Were the mounds built by the Indians?'" (Thomas 1985 [1894]:21). From 1881 to 1894, Thomas and his assistants gathered a massive amount of data from over two hundred mounds, including over forty thousand artifacts (Feder 1990:105). Thomas used these data, along with scrutiny of evidence favoring a Lost Race, and laid the Lost Race theories to rest.

Thomas blasted ideas that Indians were too lazy and stupid to build mounds, or that Indians just did not build mounds, by noting that Spanish and other early explorers witnessed Indians building mounds (Feder 1990:106). Other evidence produced by Lost Race theorists included inscribed tablets, metal artifacts, and carvings of extinct mammals. The tablets that contained Old World writing turned out to be admitted hoaxes (Feder 1990:108), and other evidence for extreme antiquity of the mounds, like mastodon-shaped pipe figurines, also turned out to be hoaxes (Silverberg 1970:90–93). Thomas easily demonstrated that the metal artifacts found in the mounds were not smelted from ore, but were naturally occurring metallic coppers and silvers (Feder 1990:110). Thomas concluded by stating, "The author believes the theory which attributes these works to the Indians...to be the correct one" (1985 [1894]:610).

Thomas's research exhibits several classic features of the anthropological science I discussed in the abstract. First, despite his initial theoretical stance, he was open-minded and willing to change his mind as contradictory data came to him. Also, Thomas's research would never been necessary had not a very public debate taken place in the previous hundred years. The notion of hypothesis testing was central to Thomas's work. Note that he did not state the central problem as one of proving that Indians did or did not build the mounds, but one of testing the idea and getting it right. I also want to note that probably the majority of people in society, and especially the majority of those who held power, would have preferred to deny a Native American connection to the mounds (Silverberg 1970:30). This was the age of Manifest Destiny, when Americans were carrying on genocidal wars against Native Americans and when the stereotype of the savage, intractable, almost sub-human Indian was decidedly useful to many. Thomas worked for the very government that was practicing this stereotyping and conquest, yet that same government funded the very research that would make Native Americans more human, more accomplished in the eyes of many—all in the name of finding out the truth (Jeske 1992). Finally, the data, gathered in as representative and explicit manner as possible for the time, were allowed to be the final arbiters of which theories were wrong and which seemed to be correct. This was science in the nascent stage of anthropology, a science based on principles still generally practiced by anthropologists who want to get it right.

Thomas's research paved the way for a new era of mound research. By leaving behind the Lost Race theories, archaeologists concentrated on a new paradigm in which indigenous Native Americans were the moundbuilders. Researchers conducted much fieldwork in the next half century, but did a surprisingly small amount of explicit theorizing, too much remained to be found out as research on the Hopewell phenomenon entered a very inductive stage. By the early 1950s, a new round of theories emerged concerning what was by then known as Hopewell Culture.

Archaeologists utilized a then-current paradigm of culture change resembling models of European rise-and-fall theories, along with diffusionary and migration theories popular at the time. For instance, James B. Griffin considered the Hopewell phenomenon a "culture climax" in which "artistic levels were reached in this period which were not excelled" (1952a:358). Archaeologists interpreted the large earthen enclosures not only as evidence of mortuary and ceremonial activity, but as evidence for a specialized priesthood (Griffin 1952a:359; Morgan 1952:88; Deuel 1952:254). The tremendous amounts of finely worked obsidian blades, polished stone celts, pearl necklaces, stone effigy pipes, and fine pottery led archaeologists to postulate full-time craftsmen as well (Griffin 1952a:357; Morgan 1952:89). One function of increased fieldwork and data collection was the realization that not all Hopewell were the same; distinct regional differences began to emerge in pottery types, quantities of exotic materials, and mound form (see Griffin, ed. 1952; Deuel, ed. 1952). Archaeologists could no longer argue that Hopewell was a unitary political/cultural phenomenon (as was the case at the turn of the century), and researchers postulated that the Hopewell of different regions (e.g., Ohio, Illinois, Tennessee) represented culturally and politically distinct tribal entities (Griffin 1952a:360; Morgan 1952:92; Deuel 1952:256). It was also clear that the Hopewell phenomenon predated the flat-topped mounds of the Mississippian period, thereby separating these two distinct prehistoric phenomena (Griffin 1952a:361).

Hopewellian tribal entities were assumed to be hierarchical polities with distinct noble or ruling lineages and a class of subordinate commoners (Morgan 1952:89; Deuel 1952:255). Trade functioned in this hierarchical system as a means of acquiring prestige, and primarily for honoring the dead, with whom exotic items were placed (Griffin 1952a:360; Morgan 1952:89). Also, archaeologists had now firmly established that Hopewellians acquired exotic materials from very distant locales, including the Rocky Mountains, southern Canada, the Eastern seaboard, and the Gulf Coast (Griffin 1952a:360; Deuel 1952).

Finally, researchers assumed that the subsistence of these ancient Hopewellians had to be based on settled, agricultural village life. The most obvious model for such a life would be the maize horticultural villages of the Native Americans who inhabited the northeastern woodlands when Europeans arrived, a view supported by the fact that small quantities of charred corn were found at two Ohio Hopewell sites (Morgan 1952:91). Deuel suggests that the agriculture of the Hopewell would even have been more intensive, including more thorough soil preparation and fertilization (1952:254).

Not much could be said in the early 1950s regarding the age of Hopewell, with Griffin reporting only ten radiocarbon dates for Hopewell (1952b:367), only some of which today would actually be regarded as associated with the Hopewell phenomenon. These preliminary data, though, indicated that the Hopewell phenomenon began around 400 B.C., and continued through to about A.D. 0 (Deuel 1952:265). The revisions of the 1950s came about in light of the failure of the Lost Race theories and the new data gathered in the half century since their fall.

These views of Hopewell continued unchallenged until the mid-1960s, when archaeologists increasingly diverged on their views of the Hopewell phenomenon. Olaf Prufer continued to interpret the Hopewell phenomenon along the lines of Griffin and others, although he introduced certain revisions in light of new data that had been gathered in the preceding decade (1964). For instance, he softened the view that Hopewellians practiced intensive agriculture, noting that "corn need not have been the only crop of the Hopewellians" (Prufer 1964:71). This is probably because up to 1964, only three Hopewellian sites produced any corn. He also demonstrates a concern with explaining both how and why Hopewellians traded for exotic materials and buried them with their dead, noting that more research is necessary to identify mechanisms and invoking kinship studies as models of hierchical society (Prufer 1964:73).

The ecological views of Stuart Streuver (1964; with Houart 1972) were influenced by paradigm shifts toward a more explicitly scientific ecological archaeology. Streuver and Houart maintain that Hopewellian phenomena were localized adaptations to differing ecological circumstances, and that elites in Hopewell society maintained a network of trade in exotic items in order to maintain their high rank (1972) . They call this network of trade the Hopewell Interaction Sphere, and so de-emphasize any political, or even cultural unity among Hopewellian peoples. Streuver and Houart note that exotic raw materials, mound form, and especially utilitarian items (projectile points, storage and cooking pots) vary from region to region, indicating that the Hopewell people were anything but united (1972:49). Streuver and Houart also provide an important revision of Hopewell chronology, noting that the major Hopewellian centers were probably contemporaneous based on growing radiocarbon evidence (1972:51). This fact is important since contemporaneous sites could have interacted in some manner.

Streuver and Houart state that seven and perhaps twelve major Hopewellian centers were scattered throughout the northern midwest and served to channel the flow of exotic goods among elites of the region during Hopewellian times (1972:52). The locations of different exotic raw-material sources and the distribution of these materials among Hopewell sites indicated that, "the Hopewell Interaction Sphere was not a single, homogenous unit....Emerging instead is a picture of a number of interaction networks, of different types and on different scales" (Streuver and Houart 1972:60). The authors then detail Hopewellian site diversity within one region, the lower Illinois Valley, where they note that cemetery/habitation site complexes are regularly spaced up and down the valley, with local transaction centers for trade interspersed (Streuver and Houart 1972:61). Their view of the social context for such local systems is that some form of "supracommunity political integration" existed, based on sedentary communities with elites using exotic goods as symbols of status (Streuver and Houart 1972:77). Their model of Hopewellian society accorded better with the emerging diversity in regional Hopewellian data and became the new model upon which archaeologists worked.

The next major syntheses of Hopewellian research emerged in 1979 with the publication of *Hopewell Archaeology* (Brose and Greber, eds. 1979), known as the Chillicothe conference. Archaeologists presented in this volume the extreme range of variation in Hopewellian culture and made major advances in archaeological knowledge of Hopewellian subsistence. Archaeologists presented a range of new testable hypotheses to explain both old and newly emerging patterns of data. These archaeologists noted that subsistence systems and political systems from Florida to southern Canada vary with different environmental settings and differing access to exotic raw materials, as Stuart and Houart (1972) suggested, corroborating the interaction sphere theory (see Brose 1979; Fitting 1979; Johnson 1979; Kay 1979; Spence, et al. 1979).

Also, a technological advance in archaeology, the use of flotation, had far-reaching implications for reconstructions of Hopewell subsistence and society (Streuver 1964:102). In the 1960s, archaeologists realized that delicate, small organic remains, usually lost or destroyed with standard excavation techniques, could be recovered by suspending soil in solution and allowing the delicate remains to float to the top. This technique opened up a whole new window on the past to archaeologists who traditionally missed soft organic remains. Archaeologists using flotation at Hopewell sites found little maize, but many other indigenous weed seeds. These data led to the realization that Hopewell society was based not on corn agriculture, but on the intensive harvesting and cultivation of indigenous weedy plants such as goosefoot (*Chenopodium bushianum*), erect knotweed (*Polygonum erectum*), and maygrass (*Phalaris caroliniana*) (Asch, et al. 1979:83; Ford 1979:234). Furthermore, additional small samples of maize were recovered from Hopewellian sites, although the maize samples were very diverse, indicating that the maize was not being selected for high productivity and therefore was not a staple of the diet (Ford 1979:237). The reliance upon indigenous weed seeds has implications for the settlement/subsistence system upon which Hopewellian society was based. These indigenous domesticates were easily propagated in naturally occurring, seasonally flooded terraces, and so their cultivation did not require intensive labor organization and social infrastructure. Therefore, Hopewellian society, while culturally complex, was not necessarily the caste-like theocracy envisaged by earlier archaeologists.

Archaeologists achieved further insights into the structure of Hopewell society by applying newly developed theories on the relationship between mortuary ritual and social organization. For instance, Brown noted that the amount of labor involved in building and maintaining the central log crypts of the Illinois Hopewell was much less than that involved in the large charnel houses of the Ohio Hopewell, and that the large, rectangular charnel houses of the Ohio Hopewell could have housed much more social activity (1979:212-213). The larger sustaining populations and the more elaborate rituals of the Ohio Hopewell implied a more complex social organization than that of the Illinois Hopewell.

Researchers in the past fifteen years have worked hard to test hypotheses set forth in the Chillicothe conference. Robert Jeske postulated that as groups become more sedentary and territorial, non-local (i.e., exotic) lithic raw materials become more expensive to obtain in terms of time and labor (1989). He hypothesized that this increased expense will lead to a more economical use of these raw materials as manifest by increased standardization, more thorough use before discard, and increased use for non-utilitarian (e.g., ceremonial) purposes. Jeske operationalized these concepts for stone tools and found that most of his predictions were corroborated (1989:41–43). Because of the explicit links between lithic use and social systems drawn by Jeske, he was able to note that the Hopewell system at Mound City was sedentary and territorial, but interestingly, that expensive raw materials were found both in ceremonial and utilitarian contexts, indicating that there was no elite control or craft specialization associated with these materials (1989:44).

Further research into the use of maize by Hopewellians has resulted in a more precise dating of maize use as well as a better understanding of the distribution of maize in Hopewellian contexts. Riley, et al. (1994:495) list thirteen sites in which archaeologists have recovered small amounts of maize in Middle Woodland contexts. They note that the maize remains are controversial, and generally not accepted as Hopewellian, because the small amounts typically found could easily have been contaminants from later contexts. However, by using accelerator mass spectrometry (AMS) methods of radiocarbon dating (which utilize minute amounts of carbon), the actual samples of maize can be dated; and Riley, et. al. (1994) note that three sites in the midwest have produced maize kernels solidly dated to Hopewellian times. Therefore, it is clear that the Hopewell used maize, although Riley et al. (1994:496) note that the manner in which the Hopewell used maize remains a mystery.

Finally, research on mortuary practice continues to provide more detailed insights on Hopewell culture. Doug Charles (1992) combines demographic research with data on Illinois Hopewell mortuary ritual to propose a reconstruction of how elite lineages controlled power in Hopewell society. During the period of Hopewell occupation in the lower Illinois Valley, population had increased substantially from earlier times, and the valley was filling with many small lineage-based polities (Charles 1992:190). This would have presented a problem for newly emergent lineages, whose access to resources would have been limited by those already inhabiting choice areas. Charles suggests that "manipulation of both of these media [trade and mortuary ritual] by the local leadership would have solidified its authority..." (1992:191). Burial in the central log crypts is considered a measure of eliteness, and members of elite lineages would have permitted subordinate lineages to bury their dead in the peripheries of the mounds as a signal of both their inferior status and their acceptance in the group (Brown 1979; Charles 1992:191). Elites would have been able to sustain such a system of social control as long as intermarriage between communities was necessary. However, the Illinois Valley becomes very populous during subsequent Late Woodland times, with the implication that mates could be secured from within the community. The accessibility of mates would have undermined the elites' ability to control marriage, and therefore to the abandonment of the Hopewellian forms of trade and mortuary ritual (Charles 1992:191). Charles's reconstruction is scientifically superior to other reconstructions because it accounts for the fact that, in the lower Illinois Valley, there was no apparent collapse of Hopewellian civilization. In fact, population levels continued to rise, and technologies continued to develop throughout the Hopewell/Late Woodland time transition. Charles's reconstructions are based on a theoretical framework developed by Binford (1971) and Saxe (1970), which is in turn based on ethnographic data concerning mortuary ritual and social organization. While Charles's interpretation of Illinois Hopewell data is heavily and richly theorized, the theoretical connections are explicit, logical, and largely based on empirical evidence. Therefore, his explanation of Illinois Hopewell society is ultimately testable.

The extended example of archaeological research into the Hopewell phenomenon is a good example of anthropological science for the following reasons. First of all, it is obvious that the paramount concern of archaeologists throughout the entire period of research was to get it right, and the number of names cited (which is but a fraction of those involved in Hopewellian research) indicates the public nature of the debates. Archaeologists assumed that people in the past built the mounds, and they set about to find out how and why this was done. At any one time, the data were interpreted in a richly theorized manner. The background theories employed to interpret the data were drawn from predominant models of human interaction popular at the time. Different mound-types were different races of people during the nineteenth century, mound burials and exotic goods were the result of full-time priests and craftsmen during the mid-twentieth century, and crypt burials and peripheral burials are different lineages in the 1990s. While these data are indeed theory-laden, they are not laden with theory capriciously. Rather, as increasing bodies of data emerge from archaeological fieldwork, some explanations are simply better at explaining the emergent data. The revisions detailed above exemplify this drive toward better scientific theory.

Better theories developed not so much out of the confirmation of hypotheses, but out of the falsification of hypotheses. Archaeologists have largely corroborated the Hopewell Interaction Sphere concept over the past thirty years, but most theoretical developments came about when archaeologists found older theories and reconstructions inadequate to explain the data. So, once Lost Races no longer seemed tenable, archaeologists focussed on a Native American origin for the mounds; as regional differences in material culture became apparent, Hopewell lost its status as a unitary phenomenon; as anthropological theory of ranked societies became more sophisticated, the Hopewell theocracies became ranked societies with lineages competing for resources, and as new archaeological technologies became widespread, the Hopewell were transformed from intensive maize agriculturalists to small-scale gardeners of local indigenous plants. Much remains to be known about the Hopewell. If the Hopewell knew about maize, then why did they not exploit this potentially super-productive resource? Where are the Ohio Hopewell habitations sites? Just what kind of a ranked society was Hopewell, did it more resemble a South Pacific chiefdom, or Northwest Coast Indian tribe, or something different? If the past history of Hopewellian research is any indication, then we can expect answers to these questions in the future.

Critiques of Anthropological Science

2

Chapter 4

Traditionalist Critiques
of Anthropological Science

We must never make experiments to confirm our ideas, but simply to control them.

Claude Bernard

Most men have bound their eyes with one or another handkerchief, and attached themselves to some one of these communities of opinion. This conformity makes them not false in a few particulars, authors of a few lies, but false in all particulars.

Ralph Waldo Emerson

I address two issues in this chapter that have dogged anthropology since its inception—creationism and racial research. While old issues, they are perennial, and substantial publications have appeared in the last fifteen years regarding them (Futuyma 1983; Kühl 1994; Herrnstein and Murray 1994; Johnson 1991; Morris 1984; Rushton 1995; Shipman 1994). Anthropologists are trained to debunk claims from these perspectives, and so examining them will provide insight into how anthropologists have traditionally used scientific arguments against these views. Proponents of these perspectives suffer from a single-minded attempt to confirm what they already believe, and to exempt their ideas from falsification. I aim to demonstrate the unscientific nature of these approaches, while recognizing that they sometimes present anthropological science with useful challenges. Ironically, creationist attacks upon evolutionary principles and scientific practice can be used to forge both stronger theories and sounder science; racialist claims should force anthropologists to look harder into the issue of race as a biological and cultural phenomenon, as well as to contemplate the extent to which biases influence anthropological research.

CREATIONISM

One of the more popular forms of creationism is scientific creationism, promoted by the Institute for Creation Research (see Morris, ed. 1974). The main problems that these creationists have with evolutionary accounts are differences in interpretation of empirical data, different views of science, and a perception that evolutionary theorists aim to replace Christianity with an evolutionary-based religion. I will concentrate on their latter two concerns.

The basic premise of scientific creationism is straightforward—God created the earth and the universe, and He did so as described in Genesis. Creation scientists insist on a literal interpretation of the Bible, as firmly stated in the following paragraph.

> The Bible must be accepted as absolutely inerrant and authoritative on all matters with which it deals at all. Otherwise, it is not really the Word of God!...Man seeks to become God if he (whether he is a theologian or scientist or anyone else) insists that *his* word must be accepted authoritatively as to what *God's* word means. (Morris 1984:47)

This insistence on a literal translation manifests the agenda of creationism— to make science reflect a particular Christian theology. In fact, Morris considers theology the "Queen of Sciences," and the particular theology to be followed is a Bible-believing, or literalist theology (Morris 1984:47).

A major difference between scientific creationists and scientists is the former's insistence that science is simply knowledge, period (Morris 1984:26, 302; Wysong 1976:27). Given this definition, they argue that they are putting forth a type of knowledge. Their question could be asked, "If science simply equals knowledge, then what is wrong with theology as science?" Creationists feel that the sciences have unfairly excluded theologically based theories of biology. Morris (1984:36) also speaks of a scientistic conspiracy to debunk the Bible and disprove Christianity. This threat is largely a straw-man argument. Thinking scientists do not engage in attempts to disprove God, which is impossible to do since God as a religious concept is meta-physical—there is no testing an entity that is the Alpha and the Omega. Anyone's supernatural is just that, it is beyond the natural world and must be believed on faith, not proven or tested.

Randy Wysong is more explicit about the scientific method in his *The Creation-Evolution Controversy*. Wysong (1976:27) suggests that creation-ist theories, as well as evolutionary ones, should be subject to objective scrutiny and falsification. Any scientist should find his offer welcome, but one also has to have doubts about how far Wysong, a believer in creation, is prepared to carry his falsifications. Is he prepared to falsify God? For his sake as a believer, I hope not. Faith is something you either have or do not have. Creationism is a paradigm, but because no predictive theories are gen-erated from it and because it is not subject to potential refutation, it is not a scientific paradigm; a scientific paradigm is one whose central tenets, while protected by Lakatos's negative heuristic, are ultimately refutable and re-placeable.

Wysong is more explicit than Morris about scientific methodology (see Figure 4–1). In his experimental phase, you "assume hypothesis is true and test it," a theory emerges "when hypothesis is supported by a lot of experi-ments," and finally, a scientific law is established "after theory has with time and test proven true" (Wysong 1976:Figure 7, p. 42). Two things are readily apparent here: truth and proof. Wysong, like so many creationists, and as I will show later, postmodern and critical theorists, is seeking abso-lute truth. That is O.K., but science is not the path to absolute truth, as I have demonstrated in part 1. Furthermore, philosophers over the past couple hun-dred years overwhelmingly have denied that we flawed humans are capable of proving absolute truths.

Probably the creationists' most difficult challenge to standard science is the role of faith in inquiry. Morris (1984:26) begins with the acknowledg-ment that religion is based in faith. He (1984:31) also points out that scien-tists make assumptions as well, and he challenges science by asking why his assumptions are any more arbitrary than theirs.

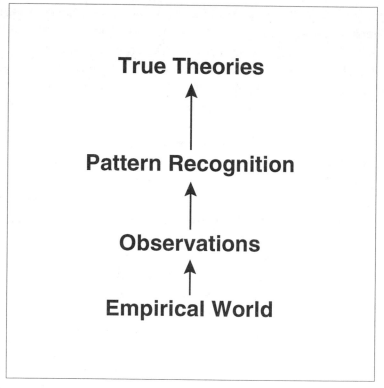

Figure 4-1. Creation Science Scientific Method.

That is, science is assumed to be, not only rational and causal and unified, but also naturalistic, banning by definition even the possibility of a super-natural First Cause....On such a basis, the possibility of true creation is excluded, not because of facts, but because of anticreationist prejudice. (Morris 1984:31)

Anti-creationist prejudice is not necessary to explain the exclusion of scientific creationism from evolutionary science. Scientific limitations on investigating the metaphysical clearly limit the phenomena that scientists can address, although they also yield a consistent means by which people can evaluate empirical statements. Scientists assume an external world, and little else. The less that one assumes correct, the more testable one's ideas are. In this regard, scientists make minimal assumptions (compared to creationists), and therefore their theories are decidedly more testable and scientific.

Phillip Johnson (1991, 1994) is a professor of Law at University of California, Berkeley, who has launched a recent attack on evolutionary theory. While he, along with Morris and Wysong, is concerned with empirical issues, his primary concern is epistemological. Johnson uses Popperian falsificationism to argue that evolutionary scientists have not lived up to their own scientific standards when evaluating Darwinian theory. Furthermore, he argues that this is because of social and ideological influences whereby evolutionary scientists struggle to maintain an ideology consistent with societal norms that also yields them direct material benefits.

Johnson begins his epistemological critique of evolutionary theory by reviewing Popper's criteria for scientific evaluation and crediting Popper with saving the scientific method (1991:147). He stresses that the basis of Popperian science is falsification, and he advocates the testing of evolutionary as well as creationist theories. Johnson (1991:148) goes on to note that Popper was not biased against metaphysics, but rather that Popper argued that metaphysical notions were legitimate sources of hypotheses, provided that they can be rendered empirically testable. He concludes by saying, "Falsification is not a defeat for science, but a liberation. It removes the dead weight of prejudice, and thereby frees us to look for the truth" (1991:154). So far, so good. I think that no anthropological scientist would have a problem with Johnson's position on these points, except maybe his use of the term *truth*.

Johnson begins to part with an explicitly scientific approach, such as the one I outlined in part 1, when he discusses Kuhn's notion of paradigm shifts. He (1991:118) accepts the notion that paradigm shifts result in new, incommensurable positions that preclude the idea of a progressive improvement in scientific knowledge. To support his argument, he accepts the idea that paradigms are incommensurable because they consist of networks of theories and untested assumptions. Johnson is adopting a line of argumentation and an interpretation of Kuhn that is curiously shared by postmodern philosophers, as I shall demonstrate in subsequent chapters. Johnson does not cite Duhem or Quine, but he goes as far as to propose the strong version of the Duhem-Quine thesis to support his notion that evolutionary theory, as scientists now cast it, is unrefutable. "The problem is that the adjusting devices are so flexible that in combination they make it difficult to conceive of a way to test the claims of Darwinism empirically" (Johnson 1991:30).

Johnson goes on to note that the most central ideas of evolutionary theory are not really tested, but rather that scientists look for confirming evidence, or make ad hoc modifications to evolutionary theory when it does not fit the facts. For instance, he notes that when paleontologists saw that, contrary to original evolutionary formulations, long periods of geologic time experienced little or no change, evolutionary scientists proposed the theory of punctuated equilibrium in order to account for data not previously accounted for by evolutionary theory. In this way, the "fact of evolution therefore remains unquestioned, even if there is a certain amount of healthy debate about the theory" (Johnson 1991:152). Johnson basically charges scientists with being unwilling to live up to their own Popperian, scientific standards of falsification.

> If Darwinists wanted to adopt Popper's standards for scientific inquiry, they would have to define the common ancestry thesis as an empirical hypothesis rather than as a logical consequence of the fact of relationship. (Johnson 1991:152)

I think that Johnson's criticism is a useful reminder for evolutionary scientists that they should not become too enamored of their theories; in the end, theories remain theories, and in some way must ultimately be tested. However, it is unfortunate that Johnson does not use Lakatos's extensions of Popperian scientific method, as this is a more accurate portrayal of anthropological science and a number of Johnson's charges can be deflected by reference to Lakatos's scheme. For instance, we would expect that the central tenets of evolutionary theory, such as descent with modification and natural selection, would not be directly tested. Being part of the core of evolutionary tenets, they are protected from direct test by the negative heuristic. Evolutionary theorists utilize core concepts like natural selection to derive more specific theories that can then be empirically tested; this is normal science.

Similarly, the invention of punctuated evolution (Gould and Eldredge 1977), as well as kin selection (Wilson 1975) and non-Darwinian evolution (King and Jukes 1969), are also expectable; they demonstrate the operation of Lakatos's positive heuristic, whereby theories scientists derive from core tenets are modified *by certain rules* when they encounter contrary data (Lakatos 1970:135). The important things to remember about Lakatos's evaluation of research programs is that the core tenets are not infinitely protected; they can themselves be falsified. This falsification is the result of either the development of better programs, or of the failure of scientists to employ the positive heuristic to modify auxiliary hypotheses. There are limits on modification because auxiliary hypotheses are modified only to the extent that they do not contradict the core tenets, and this is why the core is ultimately testable. So far, scientists have not exhausted the potential of evolutionary core ideas.

Johnson also criticizes evolutionary scientists for not falsifying Darwinian theory until they can provide an acceptable substitute (1991:154). Once again, Lakatos's philosophy of science turns Johnson's criticism into a description of expectable and appropriate science. Lakatos's criterion for a paradigm shift is not only that the new theory be able to explain what the old theory could as well as the known observations (i.e., provide an acceptable substitute), but that the new theory hold the promise of predicting novel facts (Lakatos 1970:119). Lakatos's strict criteria for a program shift guarantees that science will produce progressive knowledge, and no evolutionary scientist should be expected to abandon evolutionary theory until a better alternative is available.

The most intriguing aspect of Phillip Johnson's argument is his adoption of postmodernist positions regarding the status of reality and the demarcation (or lack thereof) between science and other ways of knowing. He adopts the social constructivist position that scientific theories merely reflect the political views of the dominant society (Johnson 1991; 1994:25).

We can only speculate about the motives that led scientists to accept the concept of common ancestry so uncritically. The triumph of Darwinism clearly contributed to a rise in the prestige of professional scientists, and the idea of automatic progress so fit the spirit of the age that the theory even attracted a surprising amount of support from religious leaders. (Johnson 1991:150)

Since Johnson reduces science to politics and ideology, he implies that creationism as another ideology has a rightful place alongside scientific explanation (Johnson 1994).

Johnson takes a strong social constructivist stance on evolutionary theory, and he cites not only material and political factors in its adoption, but also a more directed purpose behind evolutionary theory—the establishment of a natural humanist religion and the destruction of Christianity (Johnson 1991:153). I disagree that evolutionary scientists' denial of purposefulness is necessarily an attack on religion. For instance, Johnson notes that George Gaylord Simpson has written,

> Although many details remain to be worked out, it is already evident that all the objective phenomena of the history of life can be explained by purely naturalistic or, in a proper sense of the sometimes abused word, materialistic factors....*Man is the result of a purposeless and natural process that did not have him in mind* (1991:114; emphasis added.)

Johnson interprets this as a program designed to deny the existence of God's design, while acknowledging that Simpson provides this as an argument for the compatibility of religion and science. Religion and science are compatible because, in Simpson's description, scientists have nothing scientific to say about purpose or ultimate cause. These questions are beyond the purview of science, and this is why scientists must exclude the question of purpose in evolution. Simpson's statement is nothing more than a description of what evolutionary scientists are and are not capable of addressing. To the extent that humanists like Julian Huxley and eugenicists see a natural religion emanating out of evolutionary theory (see Johnson 1991:129), they are clearly overstepping the bounds of science, and creationists as well as scientists should point this out.

In light of the anthropological science I described in part 1, scientific creationism is not a science because it largely lacks the notion of refutation with empirical data. Whenever contradictory data like fossils pop up, the work of the creationist is to explain away the phenomenon, not to scrutinize the core concepts of creationism. Scientific creationists nowhere allow for the testing and refutation of hypotheses deduced from the Bible. Refutation of theories is excluded in the scientific creationist scheme since creationists consider observations a type of revelation from God in the first place. Creationists assume that believers will interpret their observations in an appropriately Biblical way. Furthermore, a scientific revolution or a problem shift is impossible since the Bible is the paradigm, and shifting out of it is beyond question. Morris excludes the possibility for anomalies by stating that empirical data can only be used to confirm Biblical scripture (1984:48), therefore excluding the possibility of a Kuhnian revolution. Likewise, the generation of a better research program following Lakatos would be by definition heresy. So, creationism's theological approach to science does prevent scientific creationism from conforming to a definition of science. Johnson's less dogmatic approach suffers the same basic weakness. While he forcefully advocates testing the central tenets of evolutionary theory, I sincerely doubt that he would be willing to apply the same stringent criteria to the central tenets of his faith. Since God's purpose is the central tenet of his paradigm, he must ask whether or not he is prepared truly to test the notion of the deity, or the purpose. If not, then his creationism cannot be science.

RACE AND IQ: SCIENTISM AND POLITICS

Another traditional challenge to scientific anthropology has been the claim that human biological races are correlated with inherited cognitive and personality traits. I will choose to call this type of research racialist, rather than racist, in order to avoid the emotional and moralistic arguments directed at the latter term. For a racialist, biological race matters as an explanatory device for behavior. Examining their claims against the mainstream scientific community will expose not only scientific shortcomings of some racialist research, but also shortcomings in mainstream scientists' own practice; bad science is bad science no matter who practices it.

Racial research has a long history in anthropology and other disciplines (Coon 1965; Herrnstein 1973; Jensen 1969 for older pro-racialist views, Boas 1940; Gould 1981 for anti-racialist views). Here I wish to address the most recent incarnation, the racialist tour de force, *The Bell Curve*, published in 1994 by Herrnstein and Murray. The argument they put forward is that the poor of America are poor because they lack the cognitive ability to compete in our highly competitive and intellectual society (Herrnstein and Murray 1994:xii). Furthermore, proportionately more people of African descent are poor than those of European or Asian descent (Herrnstein and Murray 1994:326), and they argue that this is largely because African-Americans are on average less intelligent (Herrnstein and Murray 1994:340). Their argument rests on twin pillars: race and IQ.

The authors implicitly assume that racial groups, as defined in contemporary America, reflect substantial genetic variation, and that this variation is large enough to explain differences in IQ among races (Herrnstein and Murray 1994: 299–311). Secondly, they assume that IQ scores are a valid measure of intelligence (Herrnstein and Murray 1994:105). I will examine these claims briefly, and then conclude with an examination of epistemological flaws in their research that, more than anything else, subvert their argument.

The first problematic in racialist research is the validity of race. Anthropologists since Lewontin's (1972) seminal research, have had to be skeptical about any large genetic differences among races. Lewontin tested the notion that races correspond to large genetic differences by monitoring the variation in seventeen genetic loci. He demonstrated that the amount of variance explained by common racial categories is only about six to fifteen percent. Subsequent research on human genetic variation (Cavalli-Sforza, et al. 1994) corroborates this finding. This might seem incredible, considering how obvious racial differences appear to us. I recall an outraged student's comment in my physical anthropology class who blurted out, "But it's apparent to me!" There are two responses to such a legitimate question. First, whatever physical differences that people choose to focus upon in defining races are augmented by cultural means such as dress, language, and mannerisms. Stripped naked and lined up randomly, there are fewer differences among us than one might suppose. Second, just because a few traits vary from population to population (after all, it would be ludicrous to suggest that people from central Africa are visually indistinguishable from people in northeast Asia), does not mean that the majority of our genes vary by race, or that genes underlying those traits would have any necessary connection to cognitive ability. Humans have an estimated hundred-thousand genetic loci, and only a small portion of them covary with racial groups. Due to these problems with defining races and establishing any large genetic variation among them, anthropologists maintain that race is more of a cultural phenomenon than a biological reality, despite how apparent it may be.

IQ has always been beset with difficulties. The theory behind IQ is that if testers bombard a subject with many tests that presumably measure cognition, and if these tests are correlated, then the extent to which they are correlated measures some unitary phenomenon known as intelligence (Binet and Simon 1911; Spearman 1904). This theory was rapidly transformed into a technique for measuring general intelligence that had immense practical use because it tended to reinforce the presumptions of those doing the testing, thereby justifying their decisions about how to direct people in industry (Gould 1981:174ff.). Many psychologists have debated the validity of this concept, since psychometricians never developed a rigorous theory of what constitutes intelligence and tested it. Even one of IQ's founders, Charles Spearman, was concerned that the theoretical basis for IQ was weak (Gould 1981:263). Other psychologists have proposed theories of intelligence (e.g., Gardner 1983), but they have not been as adept at operationalizing their concepts so that their theories can be tested. Some progress is being made in this area (Hunt 1995), although scientists are far from developing an adequate theory of intelligence, and therefore a valid measure of the phenomenon.

Not only are Herrnstein and Murray's two fundamental concepts far from sound, scientifically accepted facts, their argument generally suffers from a lack of theoretical underpinnings. Herrnstein and Murray have a lot of data—about twelve thousand cases in the National Longitudinal Survey of Labor Market Experience of Youth alone—and they draw correlations among variables with these data. However, empirical generalizations, if unaccompanied by explanatory theories, are ultimately uninteresting to scientists. There are a million data patterns out there; only those for which scientists can frame testable hypotheses are interesting. Furthermore, the patterns they describe are not terribly strong. Much of Herrnstein and Murray's argument turns on their theory that low intelligence as measured by IQ leads to low achievement, poverty, and an inability to live up to middle-class standards (such as controlling one's reproduction and staying out of jail). While their much-touted logistical regression equations (1994:Appendix 4) contain statistically significant results (any data set with over twelve thousand cases will), the actual variance explained in most of the real-life consequences (e.g., being in poverty, being unemployed, early marriage, criminality, having middle-class values) is quite low, from about two to ten percent, so that the empirical patterns they describe are not very strong.

Not all racialist researchers ignore the importance of theory. One racialist researcher, J. Philippe Rushton (1995), does propose an evolutionary theory to explain race differences in IQ, although this theory would, I argue, lack the rigor necessary to be properly testable. His theory is that Europeans and Asians have higher IQ scores than Africans because there has been selection favoring higher intelligence in the higher, colder latitudes of Europe and Asia. His idea is that coping with seasonal food sources requires more planning and cognition than subsistence in the warmer, tropical latitudes (Rushton 1995:262–264). Unfortunately, Rushton does not provide any detailed reasons why this should be so, nor does he detail the mechanisms by which people would have to plan and think in northerly latitudes verses tropical latitudes. His lack of detailing renders his theory untestable at this time, not to mention the fact that there are many theoretical counterarguments with which he must deal before proposing his theory as a superior alternative.

The most egregious part of *The Bell Curve* is symptomatic of the authors' political biases. They propose the term *dysgenesis*, which is a "downward shift in the ability distribution" (Herrnstein and Murray 1994:341) to describe the falling of average U.S. IQ scores. This dysgenesis is caused by a demographic shift in which too many people of low IQ are out-reproducing the smart people, or immigrating within the United States. This is, for Herrnstein and Murray, a lamentable situation, a situation of nature-gone-wrong, in which "brave, hard working, imaginative, self-starting" (1994:341) people are being out-reproduced by the undeserving dumb. Dysgenesis is an unscientific concept. The concerted work of evolutionary theorists over the past 130 years has resulted in expunging evolutionary theory of teleological, functionalist, and eugenic concepts because of their untestable and moralistic bases. First, a scientific understanding of evolution is that scientists do not suppose that evolution is necessarily going anywhere (Simpson 1949). Evolution has no necessary endpoint that we can know scientifically; there are no goals in the process. This is the reason why group selectionist arguments that genes were selected to advance the group were eventually refuted by biologists—it simply does not work that way (Dawkins 1976). Natural selection is really just a description of what happens when, in a particular environment, some individuals possess genetic characteristics that enhance their ability to reproduce (not necessarily to think). Those individuals therefore reproduce more than others, altering future gene frequencies by dumping more of their genes into the next generation than others. Should the environmental conditions that favor their reproduction persist, one would logically expect their characteristics eventually to swamp their less reproductive alternatives.

Biological fitness is central to an understanding of evolutionary theory. Fitness, in scientific and biological terms, refers simply to an organism's ability to reproduce fertile offspring. Fitness does not specify any particular characteristics such as strength, swiftness, or intelligence as being positive or negative; scientists merely use it as a measure of reproductive potential. Few people correctly understand that the only thing relevant to evolutionary theory is reproduction, for without it there is no evolution. This is why anthropologists and biologists often insist that there are no truly good or bad genes. The gene that causes sickle-cell trait, when inherited by both parents, causes death in offspring before they reach sexual maturity—this is certainly a candidate for a bad gene. However, in an environment where malaria is endemic, such a gene, when inherited with its normal counterpart, actually confers immunity to malaria, while those possessing only normal genes contract the disease at an early age. Those healthy, heterozygous individuals go on to out-reproduce others, and thereby reproduce the potentially harmful sickle-cell gene (Livingstone 1958). Clearly, there is no favoring of the group through the elimination of this potentially harmful gene, there is only differential reproduction based on how people with certain genetic compositions reproduce in a particular environment.

Another example might be strength. It may seem implicitly obvious to many people that being strong would be a desirable attribute, and therefore favored by natural selection. However, scientists know that this is not necessarily the case. The Neandertals of 40,000 B.C. were demonstrably much stronger than modern humans (Trinkaus 1978). However, where are the Neandertals now? It is very clear that evolutionary processes in the past forty-thousand years have resulted in humans who are rather wimpy compared to those that roamed the earth in the past. Once again, no particular trait or gene is necessarily always good or always bad.

Because fitness, used scientifically, describes the ability to reproduce, and because the fitness of a gene or trait depends upon environmental context, one cannot necessarily assign traits or genes to the moral categories of good and bad. This is precisely what Herrnstein and Murray do when they engage in discussions of dysgenesis. Who has valued the trait of intelligence? Nature? No. Herrnstein and Murray have. It is their (and admittedly our) human valuation of intelligence that appears in their notion of fitness—they describe fitness as intelligence, not as reproductive potential. Their definition is culturally, not scientifically based. A concept like dysgenesis, with its moralistic basis, has no place in biological science; except for applications where people impose human values upon traits, such as livestock breeding or eugenics. Their use of the term *dysgenesis*, while appropriate for situations where humans have predecided what traits they like to see in organisms, has no scientific merit as an explanatory device, only as a tool in value-laden applications.

The point here is not to deny the empirical patterns that Herrnstein and Murray or Rushton present, or to debate all the finer points of racial theories, or to argue that racialists should not ask the questions they ask. Debates concerning these issues are numerous and by now well published (Gould 1981; Hunt 1995; Jacoby and Glauberman 1995; Kühl 1994; Mackenzie 1984; Shipman 1994). My intention is merely to point out that these racialist theories do not meet scientific muster. If their authors want to be taken seriously by scientific anthropologists, they must bring their research up to scientific standards, not of proof, but of objective falsification.

So what can this flawed science do for anthropology? Beyond serving as an example of what not to do, the racialists expose the systematic biases of their detractors and force anthropologists to consider just what science is.

Is it doing research to give us the answers we want and to silence people whose views we do not like? Or is science about finding out about the world? Herrnstein and Murray point out that much research on biological race and intelligence is single-mindedly aimed at disproving such a notion to the point of never entertaining that such relationships may exist. They point out that some researchers deny any genetic influence on intelligence from the start (1994:304), and that detractors often posit their position as a hundred-percent genetic-determinacy straw-man argument (1994:311). Rushton, for his part, wonders why the concept of race is not permissible for humans when biologists use it routinely when discussing other species (1995:236), and he is puzzled as to why gene/IQ researchers are told to find the genes for IQ when biologists are rarely charged to find the genes for behavioral traits assumed to be hereditary in other species (1995:246). Finally, he is concerned with the notion that only "good" science should be done (Rushton 1995:257).

Turning to more scientifically accepted researchers who are critical of race and IQ connections, Mackenzie laments that often the reasoning used by all parties in these debates is "not merely inadequate but irrelevant to the issues involved," and that "technical arguments and criticisms often seem to be developed and put forward on an ad hoc basis, because they can be used to justify an already favored position" (1984:1214). Once again, noting that he favors environmental explanations, he nonetheless honestly reports that sociologists often resort to "special pleading...to make the description of hypothesized environmental factors more and more vague, subtle, and (as a consequence) untestable" (MacKenzie 1984:1217). Indeed, Mackenzie notes that all research into race and IQ, pro and con, is concerned more with refuting counter arguments and emphasizing correlations than with proposing any truly scientific, causal models (1984:1232). Earl Hunt, a cognitive psychologist who also doubts any race/intelligence connection, submits a more damning accusation. He suggests that the emotional turmoil this topic engenders is the result of *mokita*. *Mokita* is a word from Papua New Guinea that refers to "the truth we all know but agree not to talk about" (Hunt 1995:356); scientists are doing a disservice to knowledge as well as to those on all sides of the debate by fearing to address honestly this volatile, divisive topic in a way that actually would resolve (scientifically anyway) what is going on. I hope in the next several chapters to demonstrate that *mokita* and agenda-driven intellectual dishonesty are the expectable outcomes of the projects advanced by science's critics.

Chapter 5

The Postmodern Vanguard
Non-Traditional Critics of Science

*Go to, let us go down, and there confound
their language, that they may not understand
one another's speech.*

Genesis 11.7

The traditionalist critiques reviewed in chapter 4 have been supplemented by newer critiques of science that in the long run may prove more damaging to scientific anthropology. These critiques include philosophical treatises against the notion of objectivity, the argument that science should be used only in the advance of particular political causes, and an emphasis on the role of language in constituting reality, which leads to a pervasive relativism. The implication of this linguistic relativism, as in the biblical Babel, is that all views are confounded, rendering scientists unable to separate the less false from the more false.

Criticism of progressive science grew alongside Kuhn's discussion of paradigm shifts and Lakatos's argument for a progressive science. I will review the work of Paul Feyerabend (1978), who denies the rationality of science and holds progress as problematic. I will also discuss Sandra Harding's work. Her feminist argument (1991), while supporting evaluative science, advocates a highly moralistic agenda of feminist emancipation which, if seriously imposed upon science, would lead to a new hegemony. Finally, I discuss the development of the postmodern literary movement and the ways that critics have used it as a general critique of science. Postmodernism serves as the foundation for much of the criticism of scientific anthropology within our discipline, while the emancipatory rhetoric of Harding is reflected in the emerging critical tradition in anthropology, and all these perspectives directly or indirectly refer to the foundational work of Paul Feyerabend.

PAUL FEYERABEND: ANYTHING GOES

The iconoclastic writings of Paul Feyerabend (1978) have been a cornerstone of many left-leaning and postmodern critiques of science. Feyerabend is the most refined of the critics of science, and he has given scientists and philosophers much to ponder. However, in the end, he provides no direction for scientific conduct. I will demonstrate that not even Feyerabend himself would honestly argue for such a point, since his criticism is guided by a pervasive morality that I predict would be quickly annihilated in a system where "anything goes."

Feyerabend, like Kuhn and Lakatos, pays attention to what scientists do and compares that to the rules along which science purportedly progresses. He accepts that science has progressed (1978:23), but denies that rationality has had much to do with it. Feyerabend also makes a more fundamental argument against rationality and progress. Progress is up to different communities to decide, and he sees no necessary advantage in rationality. So, in the end, Feyerabend advocates the policy of "anything goes" in the pursuit of knowledge.

Feyerabend's argument is based upon the following points. He asserts that scientists often proceed counterinductively, violating many of the tenets of scientific methodology (1978:29ff.). Feyerabend argues that often, when a new idea is introduced, scientists retain it in the face of overwhelmingly contradictory data, inconsistency with accepted theories, and lack of demonstrable superiority (1978:35). Scientists must act so tenaciously because the very means for generating data to support a new idea usually does not exist. According to Feyerabend (1978:52), the primary reason scientific ideas survive or die is because of irrational arguments based on the political and moral appeal of the new ideas. Feyerabend's analysis of famous scientific revolutions (e.g., Galileo against the Scholastics, Einstein against Newton) are historically interesting, and they do demonstrate that scientific progress is not mechanistic. However, just because scientists in the past used illogical methods does not necessarily mean that they should continue to do so. Furthermore, James Bell points out that, in the long run, if a new theory does not conform to the world, it is not likely to prevail.

> Even granting that Galileo disregarded widely accepted scientific standards, his ad hoc arguments and propagandistic tricks would not have enabled the heliocentric theory to prevail if it had not eventually been corroborated by empirical evidence. (1994:249)

Irrational argument may have at times triumphed in scientific advance; but it has failed as well.

An infamous example of a religious, extra-rational ideology imposed upon science for the betterment of society is the Lysenko affair (Medvedev 1969). Troffim Lysenko was a Soviet agronomist who advocated the retention of an essentially nineteenth-century Lamarckian theory of inheritance, despite the clear superiority of Mendelian, particulate inheritance. His advocacy was based upon his belief in the correctness of Lamarckianism (the inheritance by offspring of traits acquired by parents in the parent's lifetime) along with its concordance with Stalinist doctrine. Stalinist dogmatists held the political position that Mendelian genetics was bourgeoise science and could not be reconciled with a Marxist, dialectical world view, a world view believed to be inherently and absolutely true (Medvedev 1969:6–9). Lysenko won favor with the Soviet dictatorship because of the political and moral appeal of his theories. He had his intellectual competitors silenced, and as a result Soviet genetics remained hopelessly backward until Lysenko lost power as a consequence of Khrushchev's 1964 resignation. This is particularly lamentable from the standpoint of the Soviets, since they employed Lysenko's flawed theories in their agricultural development applications, resulting in massive failures in the Soviet agricultural economy (Medvedev 1969:Chapter 8). Lysenko's abuses of the truth and their tragic and real consequences resulted from allowing metaphysics to intrude upon and dominate scientific inquiry. The rational scientific methods described in part 1 are a way to avoid such failures.

Feyerabend criticizes science by arguing that the consistency condition, the condition that new theories must be logically derived from accepted theories, cannot work. He correctly points out that such a condition precludes any progress, since any new idea must *a priori* agree with the old (Feyerabend 1978:36); but this argument is nothing new, as Sir Francis Bacon articulated it in the seventeenth century. Medieval scholars insisted upon such a dogmatic rule so as to protect sacralized Aristotelian theories from attack; scientists since Bacon have searched for new and different explanations in order to supersede old and increasingly failing notions. Feyerabend's definitive statement on this matter is one that few scientific anthropologists would want to counter.

> Unanimity of opinion may be fitting for a church, for the frightened or greedy victims of some (ancient, or modern) myth, or for the weak and willing followers of some tyrant. Variety of opinion is necessary for objective knowledge. (Feyerabend 1978:46)

He goes on to assert that a "scientist who is interested in maximal empirical content, and who wants to understand as many aspects of his theory as possible, will accordingly adopt a pluralistic methodology, he will compare theories with other theories rather than with 'experience,' 'data,' or 'facts,' and he will try to improve rather than discard the views that appear to lose in the competition" (Feyerabend 1978:47). This is uninteresting, since the retention and revision of theories that are weak on empirical or theoretical grounds is simply a restatement of Lakatos's positive heuristic. The important point is that, instead of dogmatically adhering to an idea, it gets revised.

Feyerabend argues in a related vein that much of science involves generating ad hoc arguments and data to support a new idea (1978:167). Once again, this is simply a statement of Lakatos's positive heuristic. Provided that scientists not dogmatically adhere to an idea to the point of rejecting the

consideration of alternatives, then there is no problem in these ad hoc explanations; they are part of utilizing a theory to its limits so that scientists might
see what other types of ideas should replace it. Furthermore, philosophers
like Bell (1994) have proposed more effective means of adjusting hypotheses so as to retain their testability.

Feyerabend also observes that no theory is consistent with all facts; and
therefore, by the principle of falsification, scientists must falsify all theory
and nihilistically dispose of all scientific knowledge (Feyerabend 1978:65).
This is preposterous since the operating principles advocated by Lakatos
and generally accepted by scientific anthropologists lead researchers to favor theories with greater empirical content, not absolute empirical content.

Feyerabend implies that all facts are so ideologically and historically
laden that they are incommensurable (Feyerabend 1978:48). It is true that
scientists must operationalize their theories and concepts, and that this
operationalization will always be constrained by observational apparatus
and historically situated ideas. However, it is a non sequitur to argue that
scientists therefore entirely make up reality and that, like the biblical de-
scendants of Noah, they merely babble past one another. Scientists may
make up ideas, but really dumb ideas about the empirical world will eventually be exposed as people attempt to employ them, either through experiment and research or through practical application (Latour 1987:29). Yes,
scientists do make up concepts, but they are not free to make up facts capriciously; principles of reality, logic, and testability constrain those facts.

Feyerabend uses his ideological basis of fact (1978:55), along with the
historical context of science and philosophy (1978:66, 146), to argue against
a demarcation between science and other forms of knowledge. He cites an
example of African mythology—and how myths are altered, but central core
concepts are not—to illustrate how science and religion are no different. He
ignores a few essential differences, because even the central concepts in
science are vulnerable, as Lakatos's (1970) and Feyerabend's own analyses
demonstrate (see Figures 2–2, 2–3). Religions are not encumbered by these
methodological constraints, and so are free to let play the full force of speculation and faith along with the dogmatic adherence to central concepts. Hin-
duism has retained the central concept of Brahma, and Judaism has retained

Yahweh, for at least three thousand years. These feats are not likely in science because of its system of systematic doubt, and so the demarcation between metaphysics and science holds historically.

Because of his equation of science with metaphysics, Feyerabend introduces politics into the issue. This is both a logical step given his argument and a calculated step given his politics. Feyerabend (1978:25) argues that appeals to reason are nothing more than political maneuvers. His primary example of this is the birth of modern science in Galileo's advocacy of Copernicanism over medieval Scholasticism (Feyerabend 1978:154, 210). He argues that Copernicanism came to represent progress to an emerging class of secular elites who regarded the church and the scholastic system as outdated, antiquated, and in their way. Galileo exploited this situation through ridicule and illogical argumentation aimed at winning support from this new class, not at convincing the monolithic Scholastics. Given this political dimension in historical scientific practice, he asserts that political arguments are therefore valid in science. "It often happens that parts of science become hardened and intolerant so that proliferation must be enforced from the outside, and by political means" (1978:196), although he goes on to note that, "Of course, success cannot be guaranteed—see the Lysenko affair" (Feyerabend 1978:51). As I will argue later in this chapter and throughout the rest of the book, the notion that science is just another form of politics is the most pervasive non sequitur promulgated by science's critics.

Feyerabend's advocacy of a politicized science stems not only from his familiarity with the history of science, but also from his own central wish— to generate a science that agrees with his own humanitarian outlook (Feyerabend 1978:52). He does not hide this agenda. In part quoting John Stuart Mill, he provides it as his second reason for writing his book.

> A scientific education...cannot be reconciled with a humanitarian attitude. It is in conflict "with the cultivation of individuality which alone produces, or can produce, well-developed human beings." (Feyerabend 1978:20)

He fears science and the monsters it may create, and argues that science should address the problems of man (1978:175). Instead of limiting themselves to narrow concerns with the empirical world, scientists should be concerned with "the development of our culture as a whole" (Feyerabend 1978:180). I want to point out that science does address the problems of humanity, and already does what Feyerabend wants; it just is not addressing those problems he favors. More fundamentally, he calls for a more subjective and anarchistic science to remedy the inhuman monster called modern science.

However, what guarantee does he offer that his anarchism will not also create monsters? I would argue that a purposefully subjective, politicized science would certainly create monsters to the extent that politics is about competing ideologies that are not necessarily commensurable. He states above that science should develop "our" culture. Does that mean Western Industrial Society? Some other culture? Who will decide what is a positive verses negative development? His system necessarily leads to a situation in which those who have the political power to define truth will see science as an ally; those on the outside will see it only as a monster. James Bell points out that a power game, as suggested by Feyerabend, "is a situation attractive to relativists. It confirms their suspicions that in intellectual matters as in everything else, politics—a euphemism for power—is all that counts. It can and does justify, at least in their own eyes, intentional use of politics and power to support their own favored theories" (1994:87). The only way of potentially circumventing this situation is to demand that scientists strive to transcend the mere politics of the day and shoot for something else—more objective knowledge of the empirical world.

SANDRA HARDING: WOMEN, SCIENCE, AND KNOWLEDGE

Feminist philosopher Sandra Harding wishes to retain science and even rationality, but wants to make it better as she argues in her 1991 *Whose Science? Whose Knowledge?* I will begin by outlining her argument, and then note those aspects that seem to support or aid the development of the scientific method and those that are empirically false or logically flawed.

Harding begins by pointing out that science does provide reliable knowledge about a real world, and that women as feminists should want this knowledge.

> Women want to know about how their bodies really work, just which so-
> cial forces are most responsible for keeping women in poverty, why men
> rape, how imperialism specifically acts on women, how women can gain
> the power to improve their condition—and we want to know these things
> now, or at least as soon as possible. (Harding 1991:173)

Harding (1991:83) is suspicious of the extreme relativism seen in postmodernist arguments such as those of the "strong programme" (e.g., Bloor 1977) against science, and their accompanying functionalism and radical relativism.

> The postmodernist critics of feminist science, like the most positivist of
> modernity's thinkers, appear to assume that if one gives up the goal of
> telling one true story about reality, one must also give up trying to tell less
> false stories.... (Harding 1991:187)

Her aim is to make a more objective science. Harding maintains that science has traditionally had a decidedly androcentric bias reflecting mens' views of nature and of women and producing knowledge and technology to serve men. Harding is particularly taken aback by the metaphors used to characterize science by its founders. "Francis Bacon appealed to rape metaphors to persuade his audience that experimental method is a good thing" (Harding 1991:43). Beyond promoting a biased use of metaphors, she argues that male bias in science (and non-science) has led to asking questions that primarily concern men, framing those questions in primarily male ways, and influencing the collection of data and the way it is interpreted (Harding 1991:40). This bias, she argues, is not just male, but predominantly European and upper class as well. Harding also critiques analysts of the scientific process who ignore the influence of culture and society on the scientific process and the politics of what scientists accept as knowledge (1991:89, 308). She even indicts the demarcation between science and religion (1991:87). These problems are pretty daunting, and Harding (1991:15) suggests that feminist studies of science can aid us not only in understanding science better, but also in re-casting science so that it may avoid some of these problems.

Harding classifies feminist scientists as either being feminist empiricists or standpoint feminists. Feminist empiricists "see themselves as primarily following more rigorously the existing rules and principles of the sciences" (Harding 1991:111) in order to eliminate male biases from science. Harding thinks that this perspective has merits, but is still too wedded to traditional notions of science. The other major feminist approach to science is feminist standpoint theory. Harding summarizes feminist standpoint theory by examining the grounds for their claims. First, women's lives have been "erroneously devalued and neglected as starting points for scientific research and as the generation of data for or against knowledge claims" (Harding 1991:121). Second, because women have not been a traditional part of science, they are better able to be open-minded and objective about what science does (Harding 1991:124). Not only are women more objective, but they are more honest, since their "oppression gives them fewer interests in ignorance" (Harding 1991:125). Harding argues that both feminist empiricism and feminist standpoint theory entail a stronger objectivity than the weak objectivity produced in traditional, Euro-male-dominated science. This is because, with the inclusion of viewpoints of women, minorities, and non-westerners, and with the realization of the influence of history and society on science, standpoint theory includes more checks on the distorted science generated by elite white males (Harding 1991:142).

Harding goes further than adopting the notion that science is best served through the inclusion of various oppressed others, and she asserts that science is just politics by other means. She gives further form to her politicized science by insisting that science should be emancipatory. "The science question asks, How can we use for emancipatory ends those sciences that are apparently too intimately involved in Western, bourgeois, and masculine projects?" (Harding 1991:49–40).

> Feminist politics is not just a tolerable companion of feminist research, but a necessary condition for generating less partial and perverse descriptions and explanations. In a socially stratified society the objectivity of the results of research is increased by political activism by and on behalf of oppressed, exploited, and dominated groups. (Harding 1991:127)

Harding argues that emancipation should extend to all women, minorities, Third World peoples, working-class peoples, and animals (1991:54, 159). The implication of all of this is that science should be guided by a certain political agenda (Harding 1991:185). Clearly, part of this agenda involves emancipating the oppressed, although Harding does not specify what emancipation entails. The frequent calls on behalf of the oppressed and her aim of stemming the flow of resources "away from the underprivileged and toward the already overprivileged" (Harding 1991:102) indicate some socialist undertones of her work. Harding (1991:49, 99, 124) also calls for a democratization of science and for a science that serves democratic ideals.

Any scientist should welcome Harding's attempt to salvage science in these turbulent postmodern times; strong objectivity makes a lot of empirical sense, and is itself a testable hypothesis. Anthropologists' work in varied cultures exposes the diversity in viewpoints held by people concerning similar phenomena, whether it be the movement of heavenly bodies or the origin of illness. Given that people may hold different ideas based on their diverse cultural backgrounds and life experiences, it makes sense that by including their viewpoints into the sciences, more potentially testable theories would result.

The other part of Harding's strong objectivity argument is that scientists should be aware of historical and social influences on theory building. If a modern scientist argues that society has no influence on what scientists study, that person is either very naive or is selling something. Anyone who doubts this need only regard the influence Star Wars technology had on science funding in the 1980s (Nusbaumer, et al. 1994), or that AIDS had in the 1990s (Gross and Levitt 1994), to see that social forces exert an influence on science. Harding makes a call for a social science of the sciences in an effort to study the influence of history, culture, and society on science (Harding 1991:15). As a scientific anthropologist, I would appreciate rigorous scientific evaluation of what we do. These elements of Harding's argument I think are consistent with the views held by scientific anthropologists. However, other elements of Harding's view are weakened by straw-man arguments, a lack of scientific research to back up her empirical statements, and finally, her strong ethical mandates.

Harding uses numerous straw men. Perhaps the most pervasive, and most deserving of the term straw *man* is her constant referral to the European, white, male elite interest as uniquely distorted, perverse, and rapacious (Harding 1991:39–50). While she admits that there are male feminists, it is clear that if you do not share her feminist views, you are part of the Elite-Euro-Male-As-Other. She also repeatedly stereotypes positivism as a scientific approach in which value-free knowledge is discovered by scientists and becomes completely objective truth that is directly observable (Harding 1991:59, 63). Even classic positivists like Carl Hempel or Auguste Comte did not make such assertions. Harding also holds a faith in and a view of the oppressed that is to me, an anthropologist who has lived with oppressed others, extremely naive and romantic.

> Less partiality and less distortion result when thought starts from peasant life, not just aristocratic life; from slaves' lives, not just slaveowners' lives; from the lives of factory workers, not just those of their bosses and managers; from the lives of people who work for wages and have also been assigned responsibility for husband and child care, not just those of persons who are expected to have little such responsibility. (Harding 1991:157)

These statements imply that non-Elite-Euro-Males are somehow more honest and objective than the elite Euro-males. This certainly begs an operationalization of the concept honesty and a test of the hypothesis. Speaking from my own experience, everyone is capable of lying and ethnocentrism; this view is supported by other anthropologists' research (Bailey 1991; Cronk 1991; Deutscher 1973; Harris 1975).

My final criticism concerns a non sequitur in Harding's argument. I agree with Harding that history, society, and culture exert an influence upon science. There is no such thing as a value-free Archimedean perspective, no one is completely objective, and science is infused with values and politics. However, there is no logical link that requires that political agendas must therefore guide scientific research. There is another possible conclusion— scientists can continue to try to rid science of as many biases as possible. If science is just politics by another means, how can people evaluate competing claims? I would remind Harding of one of her own cautions.

One cannot afford to "just say no" to objectivity....There have to be standards for distinguishing between how I want the world to be and how, in empirical fact, it is. Otherwise, might makes right in knowledge-seeking just as it tends to do in morals and politics. (Harding 1991:160)

THE DEVELOPMENT OF THE POSTMODERN MOVEMENT

Postmodernism is grounded in Western intellectual traditions in which analysts value literary form, question reality and evaluation, and are in general critical of Western social institutions such as science (Hollinger 1994; Smart 1993). I will demonstrate that many of these claims are based on certain ontological and ethical considerations, namely the doubting of reality and an almost Oedipal disdain for Western culture. The aim of postmodernists is not the criticism of Western epistemology and its replacement with improved models of evaluation, it is the destruction of Western epistemology as an end in and of itself. This anti-canonical movement nonetheless has generated its own foundational works and canons, and I review them briefly here.

Postmodernism—What a Concept

Postmodernism as a term had its inception with architecture, the term first being used in 1949 (Graham, et al. 1992:3). Architectural postmodernists embraced multiply juxtaposed motifs, a rejection of modernist and industrialist designs, and a proposed populism. These elements are expanded in postmodernism's literary and social incarnations. Postmodernism is a social movement. The central tenets of postmodernism include an elevation of text and language as the fundamental phenomena of existence, the application of literary analysis to all phenomena, the questioning of reality and representation because of the inherent flaws in language, an argument against method and evaluation, a critique of metanarratives, an advocacy of polyvocality, a focus upon power relations and hegemony, and a general critique of Western institutions and knowledge. Each of these elements will be discussed in more detail below. I am labeling as postmodern anyone whose thinking includes most or all of these elements. Postmodernists certainly vary among themselves from introspective analysts of the construction of knowledge to radical moral relativists and nihilists, from left-leaning liberals to right-wing neo-fascists (see Graham, et al. 1992; Hollinger 1993; Rosenau 1992; Smart 1993 for reviews). Nevertheless, they all share these elements.

A Brief History of Postmodernism

Postmodern thinking arguably began in the nineteenth century with Nietzsche's assertions about truth, language, and society (Foucault 1980:133). Nietzsche's criticism of truth opened the door for all later postmodern and late-modern critiques of the foundations of knowledge. He asserted that truth was no more than,

> A mobile army of metaphors, metonyms, and anthropomorphisms—in short, a sum of human relations, which have been enhanced, transposed, and embellished poetically and rhetorically, and which after long use seem firm, canonical, and obligatory to a people: truths are illusions about which one has forgotten that this is what they are.... (Nietzsche 1954[1873]:46–47)

Postmodernists point out that this skepticism about truth, and the relativism it engenders, was carried on from Nietzsche to Max Weber and Sigmund Freud, and onto contemporary postmodernists such as Jacques Derrida, Michel Foucault, and others (Hollinger 1994:15).

Postmodernists also invoke the philosophy of Ludwig Wittgenstein as a complement to the cynical tradition begun by Nietzsche (Baudrillard 1987; Lyotard 1984). Wittgenstein grappled with the issue of language as the basis of knowing, formulating his initial concepts in his *Tractatus Logico-philosophicus* in 1921, and developing his more relativistic notions in his posthumous *Philosophical Investigations* (1953). Postmodernists have extracted Wittgenstein's notion that language is an entirely internal representation (see 1972[1921]:2.174, 4.014, 4.12, 5.2), and therefore cannot be evaluated without reference to itself (Wittgenstein 1953:210ff). Lyotard argues that Wittgenstein "emphasized the *activity* of speaking a language and participating in what he called a 'language game.' Language in this sense does not represent but rather *gives* us our world" (1984:10). Wittgenstein originally spoke of a language game as a "whole, consisting of language and the actions into which it is woven" (1953:5, section 7). These aspects of Wittgenstein's philosophy have become dogma in postmodern analysis, in which language is privileged as the creator of relative truths; "*The limits of my language* mean the limits of my world" (Wittgenstein (1972 [1921]:5.6).

I am calling this foundational tenet, as it is manifest in postmodern writing, linguistic determinism (Rosenau 1992 calls it linguistic relativism), since postmodernists argue that language determines experience. The logic of this linguistic determinism implies that phenomena for which we have no language do not exist for us, and by extension, cannot impact our lives (which are obviously a construction based upon the language games that constitute our existence). This is tantamount to the rebellious Chinese Boxers' belief that European bullets could not harm their bodies—remember, the Boxers did lose the rebellion. I would add that it is trivially obvious that discourses, including those of science, must be limited to language and that language is an imperfect tool. The fact that language is so imperfect actually can be used as a further argument in favor of science; since linguistic tools of representation are so imperfect, it is all the more imperative that scientists check representations against something other than language—I suggest that something is the world of experience.

Postmodernism also is powerfully influenced by hermeneutics. Hermeneutics is a method of analysis that is open ended, and hermeneuticians emphasize both the investigator's prior biases and the transformation of those biases as the investigator encounters his or her subject. As an investigator's original views of the phenomenon change with exposure to the phenomenon, new interpretations emerge. This process can be seen as cyclical and never ending, and no final truth is to be had about any phenomenon since one's interpretations constantly change with further exposure to whatever one studies (Hollinger 1994:98–103). Postmodernists assume that such open-ended encounters refute the usefulness of scientific endeavors, and therefore of scientists' authority.

Critical theory is related to postmodernism, and the two views share a skepticism about science and Western institutions. The critical theorist Jurgen Habermas (1968) emphasizes the role of society, human interests, and biases in the development of knowledge. He develops the notion of knowledge-constitutive interests, meaning,

> the basic orientations rooted in specific fundamental conditions of the
> possible reproduction and self-constitution of the human species, namely

work and interaction....Knowledge-constitutive interests can be defined exclusively as a function of the objectively constituted problems of the preservation of life that have been solved by the cultural forms of existence as such. (1968:196)

These interests, then, establish the motivation for the search for knowledge—what is worth knowing—as well the conditions of knowledge and what people can know (Habermas 1968:212). Habermas argues that because of this, the notion that knowledge exists, purely and simply detached from human perspective, is an illusion. However, since knowledge is attached to real human needs of solving real human problems of existence, knowledge is not an ethereal phenomenon detached from reality and is therefore free to take any form possible (Habermas 1968:197). This element of realism in Habermas's work led to a split between critical theorists and literary postmodernists. In fact, Habermas has emerged as one of postmodernism's harshest critics (Hollinger 1994:154, 156; Rosenau 1992:12). The reasons for this are that critical theorists and hermeneutic philosophers have not taken a radical view of linguistic determinism, they generally assume that there is a reality to interpret, and they do not exclude the possibility of evaluation (Lyotard 1984:35; Smart 1993:92). So, critical theorists and postmodernists have always been linked in their general skepticism about science, on their advocacy of hermeneutics, and on their emphasis on the social construction of knowledge. Furthermore, most postmodernists, like the Marxist critical theorists, adhere to left-leaning political movements (Rosenau 1992). However, differences emerge in that some postmodernists actually hail from far-right political views (Hollinger 1994; Rosenau 1992), and in general postmodernists are far more critical of the Enlightenment, logic, and evaluation. One of the more foundational postmodernists is Jacques Derrida.

Derrida derived much of his perspective on language, reality, and truth from Nietzsche's emphasis on truth as metaphor and his skepticism of the possibility of truth (1976:19). Derrida emphasized that all representations of reality, since they are expressed and known in language, are texts (see also Foucault 1972). This is obviously a continuation and expansion of the linguistic determinism I noted before. For Derrida, writing designates,

not only the physical gestures of literal pictographic or ideographic inscription, but also the totality of what makes it possible; and also, beyond
the signifying face, the signified face itself. And thus we say "writing" for
all that gives rise to an inscription in general, whether it is literal or not
and even if what it distributes in space is alien to the order of the voice:
cinematography, choreography, of course, but also pictorial, musical, sculp-
tural "writing." One might also speak of athletic writing, and with even
greater certainty of military or political writing.... (Derrida 1976:9)

So, the totality of experience is language—all is text. This elevates the status of text (and therefore language) as the only metaphor of experience
(Hollinger 1994:98). Since all experience is a text or a discourse, then the
only appropriate form of analysis of anything is literary analysis (Derrida
1976:92). Derrida suggests a deconstruction, or teasing apart of meanings
and intents within a text, which is a never-ending process since an analyst's
own deconstruction is merely yet another textual construction interfused
with social interests and cultural biases.

For Derrida, the meaning in a text is not inherent, nor is it obvious to the
writer. This is because the writer is using metaphors (called tropes by
postmodern authors) ingrained in the writer's culture. The only unit of analysis appropriate in deconstructing texts is the culture itself. Every statement,
every metaphor, is thought to reveal the true agenda of either the author, or
more appropriately, the author's culture. There is an implicit assumption here
that no phrase is innocent, but rather is the outcome of some superorganic
project in which the writer's society is engaged. As an example, Derrida critiques the emphasis with logic and reason in the Western tradition dating from
classical Greek times to the age of capitalism. He calls this focus of Western
philosophy logocentrism (Derrida 1976:3) and describes its central attributes
as the concept of writing, metaphysics, and a concern with (and belief in) truth
and the concept of science. Of course, logocentrism has its ultimate development during the rise of capitalism and capitalists' attendant need for explanation, evaluation, prediction, and control. Derrida (1976:74) states that the
deconstruction of this Western logocentrism is the aim of his research. Derrida,
building upon the foundation of Nietzsche, gave postmodernists a method of
textual analysis, a justification for its use, and a target, Western logocentrism.

However, more details needed to be worked out, namely the focus on language as discourse and the recognition of power. Derrida's colleague, Michel Foucault, would supply these elements.

Michel Foucault is perhaps the most referenced postmodern author, and he provides some of its most basic concepts and positions. Foucault (1972, 1977) emphasizes the social construction of knowledge, especially that of the human sciences, and emphasizes that all knowledge is pervaded by power. Foucault (1972:5, 10) adheres to the postmodern dictum that reality is only expressed through language. He buys into the notion that different approaches to knowledge are merely language games, and therefore reality is a socially constructed, tenuous thing. He (1972:22) down plays the difference in knowledge (and in the quest for knowledge) among different language games such as philosophy, religion, and science. Therefore,

> Truth is a thing of this world: it is produced only by virtue of multiple forms of constraint. And it induces regular effects of power. Each society has its regime of truth, its "general politics" of truth. (Foucault 1984:72)

Perhaps Foucault's major contribution to postmodern thought is his notion of power relations, which is very complex and is often misunderstood by his disciples, as the notion that knowledge is constructed out of unequal, or hegemonic, relations of power among people (e.g., Clifford 1986a:10). Foucault himself points out that, "this [notion of repression] is a wholly negative, narrow, skeletal conception of power, one which has been curiously widespread" (1984[1977]:61). His abstract conception of power relations refers to the language games that are played in the production of knowledge, the linguistic and social conventions used in establishing and evaluating knowledge, and how these varied sources and forms of power interact to produce knowledge. The powers enacted in the production of knowledge and its defense (and defeat) are many, and vary from the local and immediate (resistance of subjects to be studied, a professor's need to publish to get tenure) to global (metanarratives such as the Marxist emancipation of proletariat). "'Truth' is linked in a circular relation with systems of power which produce and sustain it, and to effects of power which it induces and which extends it." (Foucault 1984 [1977]:74). Power is not,

a group of institutions and mechanisms that ensure the subservience of the
citizens to a given state...."or a mode of subjugation...," or a general system of domination exerted by one group over another...these are only the
terminal forms power takes....Power is the multiplicity of force relations
immanent in the sphere in which they operate and which constitute their
own organization. (Foucault 1978:92)

Any reduction of power to simple hegemony or repression is, in a true
Foucaultian perspective, vulgar and simplistic (Hollinger 1994:128).

Despite his criticisms of the human sciences, Foucault does not necessarily reject either reality or science. As Paul Rabinow notes, "Foucault has
described his project not as deciding the truth or falsity of claims in history
'but in seeing historically how effects of truth are produced within discourses
which in themselves are neither true nor false'" (1986:240). Foucault's focus is on ideas through history and how they have interacted with social
interests to generate truth claims and institutions such as penal systems and
health care. One example he uses is the ignorance of Mendel's discoveries
in genetics because Mendel's methods and data were simply not fit for the
audience of naturalists of the mid-nineteenth-century (Foucault 1972:224).
I would like to note that Foucault is (perhaps dangerously for postmodernists)
close to providing testable analyses of scientific practice that could aid scientists in becoming more aware of how their human and social attributes
influence their science.

Another foundational postmodern writer is an anthropologist, Pierre
Bourdieu. Bourdieu, like all postmodernists, emphasizes the experience-as-
text metaphor and literary analysis: "The mind is a metaphor of the world of
objects which is itself but an endless circle of mutually reflecting metaphors" (Bourdieu 1977:91). However, he cautions us against merely treating the world as a code to be deciphered, and he advocates concentrating on
people's practice (1991: 37). He also emphasizes the structural position of
author within society and how this may influence the text he or she writes
(Bourdieu 1977:82; Rabinow 1986:252).

In fact, the use of language, the manner as much as the substance of the
discourse, depends on the social position of the speaker, which governs

the access he can have to the language of the institution, that is, to the official, orthodox, and legitimate speech. (Bourdieu 1991:109)

Both Foucault and Bourdieu are concerned with the use of language in building truth and the role of power and social position in this endeavor. However, they both are ultimately interested in people's practice, and therefore are to a certain extent realists. More radical postmodernists have taken literary analysis and the concomitant denial of reality to new heights. The postmodern notion is that texts are really complex combinations of many texts, resulting in polyphonic space, polysemy, polyvocality, or heteroglossia (Rabinow 1986:246). Given this polyvocality in any text, and the fact that postmodernists reject giving any voice authority over other voices, it is therefore impossible to evaluate any text (Derrida 1976; Lyotard 1984).

Postmodernists also concern themselves with metanarratives, or grand narratives (Lyotard 1984:xxiv); these are grand texts (text in the most abstract notion) such as the Enlightenment, Marxism, or the American Dream. Postmodernists see metanarratives as unfairly totalizing or essentializing in their gross generalizations about the state of humanity and historical process. Skepticism regarding them is generated by the failures of these grand projects to deliver the satisfaction their proponents promise, along with the growing polyvocality and diversity that undermine their unity (Smart 1993:128). Lyotard argues that the modernist approach is to legitimize knowledge by appealing to grand narratives, and that for this reason, science has traditionally been in the service of the powerful (capitalists) (1984:8, 12, 75). For Lyotard, polyvocality and the failure of metanarratives has led to the end of "enquiry" and the beginning of "conversation." In the end, science is reduced merely to a form of discourse, and reality is lacking (Lyotard 1984:3, 77).

One of the most radical postmodernists is Jaques Baudrillard, who takes the basic precepts of postmodernism to their logical (he may not like that) extremes. His aim is entirely metaphysical and moral, although the logical extension of his arguments contradicts even these goals. "My point of view is completely metaphysical. If anything, I'm a metaphysician, perhaps a moralist, but certainly not a sociologist. The only 'sociological' work I can claim is my effort to put an end to the social" (Baudrillard 1987:84). His denial of the social (Baudrillard 1983a:65–66), mirrors his general denial of everything, including reality. Reality, if it ever existed at all, has now been overcome by simulations of reality. "Simulation is no longer that of a territory, a referential being, or a substance. It is the generation by models of a real without origin or reality: a hyperreal" (Baudrillard 1983b:2).

Since the real has ceased to exist, there can be no illusions (fakes or dreams of the real)—there is nothing (Baudrillard 1983b:38). Baudrillard's exorcism of reality follows his generally nihilistic approach to any subject he treats. Baudrillard (1983a:11) denounces any hermeneutical (or other) quest for meaning. Likewise, with the abolition of reality and the reality of the social, the justification for critique logically vanishes as he announces the "end of revolutionary convictions" (Baudrillard 1983a:22). Of course, science itself, stripped of its reality, principle must cease to exist.

> The only *a priori* for science is the postulate of objectivity, that forbids itself any part in this debate....But this postulate results itself from a never innocent decision for objectification of the world and of the "real."...all scientific movement is nothing but the space of this discourse, never revealing itself as such, and the "objective" simulacrum of which hides the political, strategic world. (Baudrillard 1983b:113)

Science, for Baudrillard, is an arbitrary, politically motivated project, based on an ethereal reality that imposes upon us hyperrealities.

Baudrillard's nihilism extends to other postmodernists. He assaults Foucault for imposing his own truths regarding the social construction of reality; this is actually an apt critique. Baudrillard notes that Foucault himself is aware of such self-deception, but that the sycophants that have followed in his footsteps remain naively, and I would argue blissfully, unaware.

> Foucault's is not therefore a discourse of truth but a mythic discourse in the strong sense of the word, and I secretly believe that it has no illusions about the effect of truth it produces. That, by the way, is what is missing in those who follow in Foucault's footsteps and pass right by this mythic arrangement to end up with the truth, nothing but the truth. (Baudrillard 1987:10–11)

Finally, Baudrillard carries his ludic exercise to its own honest and logical conclusion, a denial of Baudrillard himself. Commenting upon his revulsion toward theory and what one can do with his analysis, Baudrillard notes that, "it relies after all on an extraordinary deception—in the literal sense of the term. There is *nothing* to be had from it" (1987:135; emphasis added). So, in the end, Baudrillard provides an intellectually honest appraisal of his nihilism and asserts the ultimate emptiness of postmodernism; his discourse is reduced to silence.

SUMMARY

The new critics of science reviewed above share a number of similar tenets, weaknesses, and useful observations regarding science. All of these critics emphasize the social construction of reality, albeit with differing degrees of freedom being allotted to the construction. They emphasize the role of ideology and history in the formulation of scientific facts, and because of this, uniformly assert that science is just another form of politics or religion. Another fundamental tenet is the linguistic determinism of their views in that, ultimately, all knowledge gets reduced to mere language games which, given the influence of human interest, are seen as largely or entirely arbitrary and capricious.

These criticisms all suffer from the same fervent desire to cast empirical science as merely another form of political rhetoric with no more authority than religion, other politics, or poetry. All the authors make their cases as quasi-deductive arguments that presumably follow from true axioms such as that facts are theory-laden, language is the only means of communicating scientific ideas, or all science is politics. Here lies the deception of their work, and the reason why many of them fall prey to the non sequitur that science is just politics and therefore it should be approached as a political game, not a quest for truth. Their arguments do not really begin with axioms, but rather with politics. I would charge that in the cases of Paul Feyerabend and Sandra Harding, as among many of the postmodernists, they begin with a political/ethical agenda and then attempt to cast an argument that would support such an agenda by deductively arriving at a logical conclusion that conveniently supports their politics. It should not be surprising that in each of these logical experiments, the authors never fail to arrive at the appropriate conclusion. This type of thinking is a self-fulfilling prophecy, resulting in conclusions of what people already think they know. The strength of science is that it provides an admittedly imperfect way, but a way nonetheless, of circumventing such sophistry and solipsism. These basics of postmodernism have been well established in today's anthropology, and I now turn to that phenomenon.

Chapter 6

Elevating the Other/
Looking Back Upon Ourselves
Postmodern and Critical Anthropology

Reason betrays men into the drawing of hard and fast lines, and to the defining by language—language being like the sun, which rears and then scorches.

Samuel Butler
Erewhon

The general postmodern and critical movements reviewed in the previous chapter have gained currency in mainstream anthropology, constituting the new trend in the discipline (Gellner 1992:22; Sangren 1988:405). This chapter contains a review of this new anthropology, an outline of its basic tenets, and an exposition of its relation to the science critiques reviewed in the previous chapter. Defining this new postmodern anthropology is not easy; postmodern anthropologists comprise a diverse group of interests, including literary studies, interpretivism, Marxism, feminism, anti-colonialism, and radical relativism (Chioni Moore 1994; Clifford 1983, 1986a; D'Andrade 1995a; Fox 1991a; Harris 1995a; Marcus 1994; Marcus and Cushman 1982; Marcus and Fischer 1986; Pels and Nencel 1991; Rabinow 1986; Rosenau 1992). More strictly literary-focussed anthropologists are most appropriately called postmodern, whereas anthropologists who adopt a Marxist and advocacy stance are most appropriately termed critical theorists. There is, however, much overlap in personnel, methods, and shared values between postmodern and critical theorists in anthropology.

At the risk of being totalizing, I am lumping these diverse viewpoints together because they share several essential features. The first and foremost is either a suspicion or an out-right rejection of the scientific anthropology I described in part 1. Postmodernists commonly charge that anthropology has been the product and tool of colonialism, and therefore all traditional, scientific anthropology is tainted with an original sin of complicity with European exploitation of the world. Furthermore, these critics stereotype science as an empiricist, positivist inductivism that generalizes absolute truths. Postmodernists maintain that these problems with traditional anthropology lead to a crisis of representation (Clifford 1986a; Marcus and Fischer 1986)— do ethnographies represent the lives of the Other (Third-world peasants, ethnic minorities, women)? Can they? Should they? Who has the authority to represent? Do ethnographers have any authority at all? Not all of those I call postmodern anthropologists agree that ethnographers should not represent or do not have the authority to represent the Other, although they all see this act of representation as problematic (Fox 1991a; Marcus 1994; Vincent 1991). Reality likewise is problematic for postmodern anthropologists. Some, like Tyler (1986, 1991) seem to find the notion of reality self-evident and trivial, while ethnomethodologists like Graham Watson (1991) see reality as entirely socially constructed and still others try to salvage reality for their own political purposes (Rosaldo 1991; Scheper-Hughes 1995). Taken as a whole, postmodern ontology lies in the shadows somewhere between linguistic ideals and cold reality. Politics is central to postmodernism, and postmodern anthropologists give primacy to the political dimension in ethnography. This ranges from Vincent's (1991) recognition that all research is influenced by the political forces of its time to Rosaldo's (1991) and Scheper-Hughes's (1995) assertions that the only good anthropology is one engaged in a political struggle.

These similarities—an anti-science stance, problematic reality, colonial critique, the crisis of representation and ethnographic authority, and the primacy of politics—typify the new trends in anthropology. This movement began in the 1960s and 1970s, and gained currency and dominance in the 1980s. Its own foundational works have arisen, including Asad, ed. (1973), Bourdieu (1977, 1990, 1991), Clifford (1983); Clifford and Marcus (1986), Hymes, ed. (1974), Marcus and Cushman (1982); Marcus and Fischer (1986),

Rabinow (1977), Said (1978), Tyler (1986, 1991), and many others. The literature is vast, although these works represent the general tenor of postmodern and critical movements in anthropology.

HISTORY OF POSTMODERN ANTHROPOLOGY

Many postmodern anthropologists trace their intellectual roots within the discipline to Clifford Geertz's 1973 *Interpretation of Cultures* and Dell Hymes's 1974 *Reinventing Anthropology* (first published in 1972). Hymes (1974:36–48) began the most recent trend in critical anthropology by charging the discipline with reifying the Boasian four-field approach to the detriment of anthropological knowledge, students, and those peoples anthropologists study. According to Hymes, anthropologists fail those they study because of their adherence to dispassionate observation and Western categories of measurement, and because of their lack of attention to the political and ethical issues of our times. He calls for an ethical/political anthropology that would be critical of the domination of weaker peoples by the world's powers. "By virtue of its subject matter, anthropology is unavoidably a political and ethical discipline, not merely an empirical specialty" (Hymes 1974:48). Anthropologists should be characterized by "responsiveness, critical awareness, ethical concern, human relevance, a clear connection between what is to be done and the interests of mankind" (Hymes 1974:7). Finally, Hymes (1974:49) maintains that anthropologists have been guilty of "scientific colonialism" and exploitation of those they study by mining indigenous communities for knowledge, bringing it back to our own societies as raw material, and then producing finished products by which anthropologists profit.

Talal Asad (1973) edited the influential set of papers entitled *Anthropology and the Colonial Encounter* at the same time, and this meshed well with the arguments contained in Hymes. Asad connects the discipline of anthropology with the colonialism of Western European powers, although the manner in which anthropologists have interpreted Asad's book is curious. Pels and Nencel sum up the contemporary spin in their (1991:18–19) admonition that the exploitive anthropologist had not yet been exorcised from anthropology. Critical anthropologists routinely talk of anthropology as a tool of colonial administrators and powerful capitalists who use anthropological knowledge in the management of their conquered, dependent, and exploited charges (Scheper-Hughes 1995).

Asad's own perspective (as opposed to the one attributed to him) is less strident, more balanced, more respectful of data, and less flawed. He does assert that powerful capitalists and governments with capital interests used descriptions of a savage Other to dehumanize conquered peoples and to justify their exploitation of them (Asad 1973b:109, 117). However, he is careful to note,

> I believe it is a mistake to view social anthropology in the colonial era as primarily an aid to colonial administration, or as the simple reflection of colonial ideology. (Asad 1973a:18)

An interesting parallel is seen in Edward Said's *Orientalism* where he notes that European representations of the Middle East, while systematically biased, were not "representative and expressive of some nefarious 'Western' imperialist plot to hold down the 'Oriental' world" (1978:12).

Asad's primary attack is upon the influence that colonialism had upon indigenous societies and anthropological thinking, not on evil conspiracies between anthropologists and colonialists. He points out that, in Africa, anthropology was a beneficiary of colonialism as pacification made previously inaccessible and dangerous groups safely accessible to European anthropologists (Asad 1973b:114). Asad also notes that the functionalist description of African indigenous politics as based on consensus and reciprocal obligation is due in part to a Durkheimian social paradigm as well as to a patronizing orientation toward African peoples (1973b:112, 114).

While Asad points out ways in which anthropological theory and description has been influenced by European colonialism, he does not establish clear complicity. His exposition of possible biases in anthropological work is scientifically valuable as scientists strive to correct for biases in the pursuit of ever-more-objective representations. It is good science to recognize that early British functionalist anthropologists tended to ignore the effect of colonial rule on indigenous African politics, and it is helpful to examine the biases that come from a patronizing view of the Other. None of this delegitimizes a scientific approach to anthropology; it merely points out inadequacies in older, traditional theoretical frameworks, inadequacies that can be corrected.

At the same time that Hymes (1974) was denouncing the four-field approach and Asad (1973) was decrying anthropology's debt to colonialism, Clifford Geertz (1973) was laying the foundation for the interpretivist school in anthropology, a tradition that provided for the advancement of critical and postmodern anthropology. Geertz's main objection is to the materialist tradition in scientific anthropology, which he sees as a misguided quest for knowledge about the human condition. His interpretive school is an attempt to salvage a science of humanity by focussing on what he thinks is most important in the human condition—meaning in culture. The aim of anthropology, according to Geertz (1973:6), is to provide "thick descriptions" that elucidate the levels of symbolic meaning in people's actions. This demands much of the interpretivist anthropologist who must disentangle and decode the complex meanings of actions, words, and ideas in a culture—thick description is the ethnographic result. Thick description is an examination of a cultural form in all its complexity, including what all actors think about it, how they react to and interact with it, and its meaning in the larger cultural framework (1973:17). Geertz (1973:10) introduces the metaphor of culture-as-text as a methodological tool to emphasize the constructedness of culture and of these human experiences, and he asserts that the work of the ethnographer is more akin to that of the literary critic (1973:9). He further emphasizes that anthropological writings about culture are fictions in the sense of something made up, although not necessarily made up arbitrarily.

> They [anthropological writings] are, thus, fictions; fictions, in the sense that they are "something made," "something fashioned"—the original meaning of *fictio*—not that they are false, unfactual, or merely "as if" experiments. (Geertz 1973:15; see his reassertion in 1988:140)

This notion of fiction has led many anthropological postmodernists to go beyond Geertz's original formulation and to assert the arbitrariness and unreality of ethnographies.

I have never been impressed by the argument that, as complete objectivity
is impossible in these matters (as, of course, it is), one might as well let
one's sentiments run loose....Nothing will discredit a semiotic approach to
culture more quickly than allowing it to drift into a combination of intu-
itionism and alchemy, no matter how elegantly the intuitions are expressed
or how modern the alchemy is made to look. (Geertz 1973:30)

Geertz actually assumed that reality exists, that "a good interpretation
of anything—a poem, a person, a history, a ritual, an institution, a society—
takes us into the heart of that of which it is the interpretation" (1973:18). He
cautions, in an anticipation of 1980s postmodernism, that,

If anthropological interpretation is constructing a reading of what happens, then to divorce it from what happens—from what, in this time or
that place, specific people say, what they do, what is done to them, from
the whole vast business of the world, is to divorce it from its applications
and render it vacant. (Geertz 1973:18)

Geertz advocates the evaluation of theories according to "systematic
modes of assessment" (1973:24), and calls for an interpretive science of
culture, although he asserts that the rigorous and explicit methods of science are inadequate for understanding the rich complexity of cultural life
(1973:26). His methods favor hermeneutical approaches in which an observer enmeshes his or herself in a culture, transforming his or her view and
using this insider's perspective to decode the complex meanings attached to
the cultural form.

Geertz maintains that the aim of his interpretivism is consistent with
science—to understand the function of meaning in human culture in a systematic manner based on particular ethnographic experiences (1973:20–21).
In fact, his later work, in response to the reality-doubting postmodernists,
asserts the realist aim of ethnography. "Whatever else ethnography may
be...it is above all a rendering of the actual" (Geertz 1988:143). While
Geertz's aim mirrors a scientific approach, his hermeneutical methods, emphasis on what people say and think, and emphasis on anthropological writing, provided a fertile ground for the development of a critical, text-based,
anti-scientific anthropology.

Anthropologists fused these critical, textual trends in the 1980s with the literary postmodernist theory I reviewed in the last chapter (Chioni Moore 1994). This movement became attractive to anthropologists for several reasons. The first, and perhaps the most valuable observation of postmodern anthropologists, was the realization that all we ever have as a discipline are texts, our ethnographies (Marcus and Cushman 1982). In this sense, all culture can be reduced to a text as far as the discipline of anthropology is concerned (Clifford 1983:133). If all that anthropologists deal with are texts, then postmodernists argue that the tools of literary criticism should be appropriate for the deconstruction of ethnographies (Marcus and Cushman 1982:26; Clifford 1983:137). Marcus and Cushman's early 1980s exhortations meshed well with Geertz's decade-old assertion that culture can be read as a text, an assertion that was becoming a canon in the discipline of anthropology.

As anthropologists became more enamored of postmodern literary approaches to analyzing ethnographies and cultures, the text became the sole focus of their work. Since all text is conceived and written and therefore made up by someone, reality became more and more tenuous because anything can be written. Anthropological field data became more and more irrelevant to the evaluation of anthropological claims. This fueled the increasing skepticism about science in anthropology since empirical reality was becoming more and more vague, or at least irrelevant.

Postmodernists, with their inherently critical and often Marxist perspectives, embraced the growing criticisms of anthropology's alleged role in the colonial enterprise (Pels and Nencel 1991). Science, conceived of as a capitalist tool, could now be argued irrelevant since all that exists (and tenuously at that) is text, and all that is needed to analyze it is literary method (Clifford 1986a; Marcus and Cushman 1982; Marcus and Fischer 1986). Also, the tendency of literary criticism to be directed at Western canons encouraged skeptical anthropologists to deconstruct science as a Western philosophy, and especially encouraged them to deconstruct the foundations of their own field—including the classic ethnographies of Malinowski, Boas, Kroeber, Evans-Pritchard, and Radcliffe-Brown (see Clifford 1983; Fox 1991b:97–100; Marcus and Cushman 1982; Pels and Nencel 1991:3; Vincent 1991:51–56). The result is an anthropology in which text is privileged, reality is tenuous, and Western institutions, including science and anthropology, are suspect.

I provide this historical overview to demonstrate how different trends in anthropological thought and practice converged and combined to produce a critical, anti-science, text-based, and politically motivated new anthropology—what I have termed postmodern anthropology. I will discuss in the following sections what I see as the central tenets of this now canonical and established, if not dominant, form of anthropology. These tenets are a problematic reality, an antagonism toward science, the questioning of anthropological authority, and the impetus toward political, ethical and moral action.

THE REALITY QUESTION

The problematics of reality in general postmodern theory are mirrored in anthropological postmodernism. However, some issues are more crucial to postmodern anthropologists as they grapple with whether or not they can represent the life of the Other through their own cultural filters. Marcus (1994:41) notes that various criticisms of ethnography range from a disciplinary nihilism to reformism to experimentation with new forms of ethnography. Following his scheme, I will arrange the discussion of postmodern anthropological approaches to reality from the most radical and relativist to the most conciliatory.

Stephen Tyler has emerged as perhaps the most radical skeptic among postmodern anthropologists. His work is admittedly aimed more at tweaking his critics and sniping at the discipline than at providing a foundation for a future anthropology.

> So, the game of critique is played out, what do we do now after the crossword and the second cup of coffee?...just a little subtle perturbation here and there, a pit of parody perhaps, or some oversolicitous complicity, or maybe to play the fool, the role of court jester, and entertainer. (Tyler 1991:93)

Tyler avoids providing foundations for new directions on purpose; his postmodernism is the most bold, and he, like Baudrillard (1987), takes postmodern tenets to their logically nihilistic extremes. In this way, he is the most honest of the new anthropologists and hides nothing, there is no need for deconstructing his texts.

> Post-modernism is more interested in "playing with the rules,"...work is the "work out" that *produces nothing* beyond the sweat that signifies reduction of organic excess. (Tyler 1991:81; emphasis added)

His view of reality and even the criticism of reality and text is very skeptical, yet at the same time boldly populist. "In ethnography there are no 'things' there to be the objects of a description" (Tyler 1986:130). However, he goes on to state, "It aims not to foster the growth of knowledge but to restructure experience; not to understand objective reality, for that is already established by common sense" (Tyler 1986:135). So, for Tyler, reality is a matter of common sense. However, whose common-sense view of the world is to prevail?

For Graham Watson (1991:79), reality is wholly socially constructed; it does not exist outside of consensus. "It is important to note that accounts are not interpretations superimposed on a preexisting reality; rather, they are constitutive of that reality; they make it what it is." He (1991:80) advocates the use of 1970s ethnomethodology developed in sociology, and he criticizes Geertz (as does Tyler 1991) for trying to salvage a reality-based anthropology. Reality for Watson is merely what people socially make it out to be.

> So, it could be argued, even if we were somehow to apprehend an ultimate reality (the express train, the witches), we could never be sure that we had succeeded in doing so, because the relationship between that reality and our means of grasping it is one we can conceive of only from within the reality in which we find ourselves. (Watson 1991:83)

I might add that it is problematic whether or not a witch can harm any person one picks off the globe. It is not problematic that any person hit by a speeding train will most certainly be harmed.

While Graham Watson takes an extremely skeptical approach to reality, he adds the contradictory caveat that has become standard in postmodern writings—he says that while there is no reality, that does not mean that it does not exist and that we cannot understand it.

> This stance does not entail judgmental relativism. To say that all forms of knowledge are equally efficacious for a particular purpose is nonsense. Nor does this stance absolve us from the necessity of discriminating among the competing truth claims of fellow analysts, or deprive us of the capacity to do so. Nothing I have said invalidates available mechanisms. (Watson 1991:83)

Other postmodern authors are more ambiguous on the topic of reality, although it would be fair to say that they are very skeptical about it, but not secure enough in their textuality to abandon it altogether. Paul Rabinow (1977:150) follows Geertz's (1973) lead and stresses the fictional character of facts. James Clifford (1986a:2) focuses on the fact that all ethnographies are texts, and this dimension "serves to highlight the constructed, artificial nature of cultural accounts." He (1986a:6) lauds the notion that since ethnographies are written constructions of anthropologists, they are something made—fictions. His (1986b:119) focus on the use of ethnography as allegorical tale leads him to suggest that there is no separation of the factual from the allegorical in a text. Clifford stresses the textual, fictional character of ethnographies, but he is not ready to abandon the moorings of reality, and so he adds his own reality caveat.

> To recognize the poetic dimensions of ethnography does not require that one give up facts and accurate accounting for the supposed free play of poetry. "Poetry" is not limited to romantic or modernist subjectivism: it can be historical, precise, objective. (Clifford 1986a:26)

More recently, Marcus stresses the constructedness of knowledge and the tenuousness of realism,

> Discourses of the "real" have been demonstrated to be of a piece with the rhetoric of fiction and to possess the fully literary character of language as

narrative, subject to tropes, figuration, and self-consciousness....the basic task of social science—of creating positive knowledge of the world—is much complicated.

while reaffirming the positive goal of anthropology.

> Far from a rejection of realism, I see the following as a move toward a revitalized and defensible practice of realism. (1994:40)

This is consistent with his and Cushman's pioneering statement that, "What *is* necessary is more critical discussion by and for ethnographers of each other's works, which in paying attention to rhetoric would not lose sight of the goal of constructing systematic knowledge of other cultures" (Marcus and Cushman 1982:66).

Finally, other postmodern-influenced interpretivist anthropologists are concerned about abandoning reality for both academic and political reasons (Marcus and Cushman 1982:29). Marcus and Fischer (1986:14) wish to use literary analysis of irony in ethnographic research in order to do more real ethnographies. This is related to their concern for building a critical anthropology with something to critique.

> This insistence on a fundamental descriptive realism is what makes ethnographic techniques so attractive at the present moment in a number of different fields that claim cultural critique as their function. For anthropology, the issue is how to conduct critical ethnography at home by making use of its cross-cultural perspective, but without falling prey to overly romantic or idealist representations of the exotic in order to pose a direct alternative to domestic conditions. (Marcus and Fischer 1986:119)

Renato Rosaldo (1991:95), along with Marxist theorists (Meiskins Wood 1995; Mulhern 1995), criticizes postmodernists for ignoring the brutal realities that befall real people. Mascia-Lees, et al. (1989) caution that the anti-realism of postmodern anthropology undermines the basis of social critique. Scheper-Hughes (1995:414) is unforgiving in her criticism of some postmodernists' concern with textuality and their ignorance of the real inequalities and harms she thinks anthropology should address, calling postmodernist rhetoric "an excuse for political and moral dalliance if ever there was one." She goes on to note that in the real world, "The anthropology that most Cape Town Xhosa, Venda, Zulu, Afrikaner, and Moslem students want is *not* the anthropology of deconstruction and the social imaginary but the anthropology of the *really real*, in which the stakes are high, values are certain, and ethnicity (if not essentialized) is essential" (1995:414). The Brazilian anthropologist Roberto Damatta similarly charges postmodern anthropologists. "American 'interpretive anthropology,' besides lapsing into abstract philosophical arguments, tends toward rhetorical and programmatic exaggeration, at times slipping into what can be called an irritating righteousness" (1994:119). Vincent argues that in "engaging historicism, I would suggest, critical anthropology begins to engage this world....It has real and practical consequences" (1991: 58). These postmodern and critical anthropologists share a similar concern with more traditional scientific anthropologists over the literary turn and loss of realism in anthropology (Bernard 1994a,b; Harris 1994; O'Meara 1989; Sangren 1988).

Postmodern approaches to reality run the full gamut, although they all share the same weaknesses. Whether arguing that the cultural world exists (Scheper-Hughes, Vincent, Fox), or that it is merely a socially constructed and arbitrary consensus (Tyler, Watson), no postmodern or critical approach provides a means for evaluating which versions of reality are real. They all are purely inductive approaches to reality, whether reality is simply what people say it is, as in Watson's ethnomethodology or Tyler's common sense, or is something that immediately is perceived by the ethnographer, as in Scheper-Hughes's "witnessing" of social injustice. These approaches all lack a means of dealing with the inevitable situation when two or more parties assert contradictory realities. The lack of a means of evaluation is related, however, to the problem of representation and postmodernist calls for polyvocality in ethnography (Clifford 1983:133; Marcus 1994:48).

THE CRISIS OF REPRESENTATION

All postmodern-influenced anthropologists recognize a problem with representation (Marcus and Fischer 1986:8; Vincent 1991:49), and typically reject it as an anthropological enterprise (Clifford 1986b, Tyler 1986, 1991), although some more recent anthropologists have embraced it either for the academic health of the discipline or in the interest of political agendas (see Fox, ed. 1991). Early postmodern anthropologists uniformly confessed their sins of representation, made an act of contrition, vowed never to do it again, and searched for alternatives to representation. Clifford looked toward allegory as a way out. "Allegory prompts us to say of any cultural description not 'this represents, or symbolizes that' but rather, 'this is a (morally charged) *story* about that.'" (1986b:100). Others embraced Geertz's interpretivism ever more tightly, hoping that interpretation would avoid the weaknesses of representation (Rabinow 1977:151). For instance, Tyler (1986:129) states that evocation releases anthropologists from representation since what they evoke need not represent any particular thing.

> The whole point of "evoking" rather than "representing" is that it frees ethnography from the *mimesis* and the inappropriate mode of scientific rhetoric that entails "objects," "facts," "descriptions," "inductions," "generalizations," "verification," "experiment," "truth," and like concepts that, except as empty invocations. (Tyler 1986:130)

There are some problems with this approach. As Geertz (1973) originally argued, the act of interpreting something obviously entails that something was witnessed and that the ethnographer has taken pains to represent that something. Likewise, allegories themselves are representations of events in the story as well as of morals contained within. As Rubel and Rosman state, "There is therefore no significant difference between evocation and representation" (1994:339); and Clifford suggests that all interpretations are representations since all "ethnography is interpretation" (1983:131). This has led some anthropologists to stop worrying about the crisis and return to the job of representation (Fox 1991a; Sanjek 1990; Scheper-Hughes 1995; Vincent 1991).

Scientific anthropology is based on an assumption that reality exists, that there is something to investigate. If reality is completely socially constructed, then any attempt at science would be meaningless. Representation is related to this problem since if there is nothing to represent, representation is vacuous. These problems with reality and representation lead directly to postmodern attacks on science.

THE SCIENCE QUESTION

All postmodern anthropologists are at the least, very skeptical, and at the most, outright damning of science, or what is more appropriately labeled positivism (Roscoe 1995). Criticisms of positivism and science range from arguments stemming from the problems of representation and reality to indictments of method in general to moralistic arguments based on alleged evils that have emanated out of this purportedly capitalist invention. I will examine each of these types of criticism in turn.

Clifford asserts that "no sovereign scientific method or ethical stance can guarantee the truth of such [ethnographic] images" (1983: 119). He sees "culture as composed of seriously contested codes and representations," and asserts "that science is in, not above, historical and linguistic processes" (1986a:2). Rabinow argues that "there is no privileged position, no absolute perspective, and no valid way to eliminate consciousness from our activities or those of others" (1977:151). These statements exemplify the linguistic determinism of postmodernists. If science is simply an historical and linguistic artifact, if data are one contested code and interpretation among many, and if there can be no facts, then the empirical basis of science would be on very shaky ground. However, as demonstrated in part 1, scientific anthropologists are hardly naive about the tenuousness of facts, and that is why they frame science as a collection of methods designed to be inherently self-correcting; when a code is contested and found inadequate, it may be replaced with a code that reflects anthropologists' experiences better.

Postmodern criticisms of science do not only emanate from the crisis of representation. The notion of method is another problematic for postmodernists since the postmodern ideal evidently is amethdological.

> Modernism insists that there are, or could be, or ought to be RULES that serve as CRITERIA for RATIONAL JUDGEMENT....Rules and criteria are not necessary guides to action, knowledge, and belief as much as they are a posteriori excuses and justifications for them. (Tyler 1991:80)

A popular notion, and one asserted among postmodern critics of science elsewhere, is that method and positivist epistemology are dead. Clifford asserts "that this ideology [of empirical methodology] has crumbled" (Clifford 1986a:2). He feels that his ethnopoetics "cannot be reconciled with a notion of cumulative scientific progress, and the partiality at stake is stronger than the normal scientific dictates that we study problems piecemeal, that we must not overgeneralize, that the best picture is built up by an accretion of rigorous evidence" (Clifford 1986a:18).

While the more text-oriented postmodern anthropologists have set up a fundamental problem in accepting science, other postmodern anthropologists do not see science as necessarily impossible. As an example, Rabinow advocates anarcho-rationalism. "Rorty calls his version of all this hermeneutics. Hacking calls his anarcho-rationalism. 'Anarcho-rationalism is tolerance for other people combined with the discipline of one's own standards of truth and reason.' Let us call it good science" (1986:238). Rabinow argues for a science of humanity, yet one that would be replaced by hermeneutical methods, similar to the science advocated by Geertz (1973). I will state now, following the work of Kosso (1991), Wylie (1992a), O'Meara (1989), and Roscoe (1995), that hermeneutics and anthropological science can be formally alike, despite the contentious polarizations that have arisen around the two traditions; and I will elaborate on this similarity in the next chapter. Taken at face value, then, Rabinow's anarcho-rationalism is not contradictory to the scientific methods of anthropologists, and a growing tolerance for considering different points of view and for regarding biases (Harding 1991) in research indeed would be called, by scientific anthropologists' standards, "good science."

Finally, some postmodern anthropologists reject not only reality, not only scientific method, but the whole notion of method itself. Tyler argues that postmodern "ethnography denies the illusion of a self-perfecting discourse. No corrective movements from text to object and back again in the manner of empiricism, and no supplemental, self-reflexive movements from flawed sublation to scatheless transcendent mark its course" (1986:138). He also says, "Hermeneutics is the modern perversion of the old thanatopsis" (1991:84). This rejects hermeneutical and reflexive methods such as those advocated by Rabinow and especially Geertz (G. Watson 1991:80). According to Tyler, postmodern ethnography "prefers allegories and subject rhyme....It resists the hegemony of ontology and epistemology" (1991:83).

Much of this kind of argumentation is based on a notion that science, and the whole notion of epistemology itself, are simply the historical inventions of nineteenth-century, Enlightenment-influenced, capitalist, European society.

According to Rorty (1979:4), the need to know how we know what we know (epistemology) emerged in the late nineteenth and early twentieth centuries. This, of course, coincides with the increasingly rationalized industrial societies that emerged in Europe in the nineteenth century, where cause and effect, classification, and a discovery of how thing worked were essential to the workings of this new kind of society. Rorty (1979:7) asserts that epistemology has seen its time, has lived out its usefulness, and is now a fruitless task. I would point out that epistemology has been emergent arguably over the past twenty-five hundred years in the West (Russell 1972), and that postmodernists mount an epistemological attack of their own upon science. So, this type of argument seems to turn back on itself and criticize the very foundations of its own criticism.

I should point out in all fairness that not all postmodern-influenced anthropologists want to jettison science. Some, like the critical Scheper-Hughes (1995) and Rosaldo (1991), see value in representing the world and in developing a better method for understanding it. Rosaldo (1991: 16–19), despite his criticism of positivistic science, actually provides a good example of it in his analysis of the phenomenon of rage in grief. Based upon his own tragic realization of what Ilongot headhunters meant when they felt compelled to take heads when grieving for loved ones, Rosaldo framed a cultural object, a category of data he calls rage-in-grief. He then scanned the cross-cultural literature to find other ethnographic accounts of this powerful emotion and its attendant causes and consequences. He found that the explanation that "youthful anger and old men's rage lead them to take heads is more plausible" than other explanations offered by anthropologists (1991:19). He goes on to state that "it [anthropology] must investigate how headhunters create an intense desire to decapitate their fellow humans. The human sciences must explore the cultural force of emotions with a view to delineating the passions that animate certain forms of human conduct." This is good scientific anthropology, using anthropological sensitivity and ethnographic depth of knowledge (a.k.a. validity) to realize an aspect of the human experience and then recognize that human experience among varied groups who may share certain social and cultural similarities. He presents tantalizing hypotheses that are testable, and I find it unfortunate that he would deny the knowledge-building quality of his work.

Many postmodern criticisms of science are really based on stereotypes and misrepresentations of science, not realities (see Sangren 1988 and Roscoe 1995 for a critique of these stereotypes). The most widespread straw man are the notions that scientists produce absolute truths that are unalterable, and that scientists actually think that they do this. Clifford (1986:25) announces that in "cultural studies at least, we can no longer know the whole truth, or even claim to approach it." Likewise, Rosaldo states that the "truth of objectivism—absolute, universal, and timeless—has lost its monopoly status" (1991:21). Tyler takes a similar absolutist stance when he states, "Yet its [science's] only justification was proof" (1986:123). These statements ignore philosophical work going at least back to Hume's realization of the problem of induction, not to mention even positivists' admission that scientific knowledge is not absolute (Ayer 1959:229; Comte 1974 [1855]; Hempel 1965), along with Popper's warning that "anyone who envisages a system of absolutely certain, irrevocably true statements as the end and purpose of science will certainly reject the proposals [for falsificationism] I shall make here" (1959 [1934]:37). Of course, the presentation of what scientific anthropologists actually say and do that I provide in part 1 demonstrates the falseness of postmodernist claims. If anthropological claims were unalterable, then anthropologists would still be discussing the plight of the savage forager in his fruitless attempts to locate enough meat with which to feed his starving family, and archaeologists would still be debating whether Phoenicians or Vikings built the Ohio mounds. Clearly, scientific anthropologists have been willing to change their minds.

Postmodernist anthropologists go on to note points that to scientific anthropologists, are trivial, and about which scientists are not naive. Rabinow cites Stanley Fish's notion that "all statements are interpretations and...all appeals to the text, or the facts, are themselves based on interpretations" (1986:255), which is nothing more than the positivist's claim that facts are theory-laden (Bernard 1994a,b; Harris 1994). Rosaldo (1991:169), like Harding (1991), notes that there is no Archimedean point of view. Certainly no scientific anthropologist could argue for such a view, but rather that because such a view is impossible, anthropologists must have a method that enables them to identify those views that are less Archimedean (Harris 1994:65; O'Meara 1989:358).

Another theme in the postmodern anthropologists' rejection of science is based on a moral, ethical, and political argument. The basis of this argument is a Marxist assumption of the immorality of capitalism and the alleged complicity of science with capitalist economics. Marcus and Fischer state that "ethnography, as the practical embodiment of relativism and interpretive anthropology, challenges all those views of reality in social thought which prematurely overlook or reduce cultural diversity for the sake of the capacity to generalize or to affirm universal values, usually from the still-privileged vantage point of global homogenization emanating from the West" (1986:32–33). Tyler is more strident when he denounces the "fascism of science, democracy, and bureaucracy" (1991:82). Postmodernists charge that science is hegemonic, a hand-maiden to the powerful interests of Euro-American capitalists, and therefore illegitimate. Once again, if this were true, then the dehumanizing Hobbesian views of foragers held by nineteenth-century anthropologists would never have been challenged in favor of the (more empirically correct) view that foragers lead a life that in some ways is more affluent than that of the most successful capitalist. Given the examples presented in chapter 3, I fail to see any systematic hegemony in anthropological science.

Even if the postmodernists could substantiate such claims (and indeed there are some phenomena, such as military-industrial complexes and rationalized schemes for mass production, that would be good candidates for biasing some physical and economic sciences), where is their tolerance for a polyvocal, approach to writing the human condition? If all views are equally valid, then who ever has authority to speak?

THE AUTHORITY PROBLEM

Who is speaking for whom? Who should speak for whom? These are two important questions asked by postmodernists, the former being an empirical issue, the latter an ethical issue. These questions lie at the heart of the crisis of representation and extend to ethical dilemmas regarding the authority of statements made about a people. Postmodernists have done much to jolt the discipline into being more up-front about from where data and statements in ethnographies originate (Clifford 1983, 1986a:13). This is an empirical issue of utmost importance to a scientific anthropology, since it is crucial that anthropologists differentiate between etic observations and emic statements. An ethnographer may improperly legitimize his or her own perspective by masking it as the statement of those he or she studies. This is clearly messing with the data because indigenous perspectives, part of the essential emic data that anthropologists gather, do not always coincide with those of the researcher. Indeed, the ethnographer, in writing the definitive statements on a people, can potentially exercise a representational hegemony over his or her subjects (Clifford 1983:120). However, postmodernists have gone farther than pointing out this methodological caution, and they have asserted an ethical agenda in the discussion of representation and authority.

Much of the discussion regarding authority involves the notion of power relations developed by Foucault (1977, 1980). The concern is that anthropologists have unfairly used the positions of power they assumed while studying the Other in framing what the world knows about that Other. This inequality in power originates in the colonial and capitalist past, a past that postmodernists point out was related to the birth of anthropology as a discipline (Rabinow 1986:241). Clifford claims that,

> the unreciprocal quality of ethnographic interpretation has been called into account. Henceforth, neither the experience nor the interpretive activity of the scientific researcher can be considered innocent. (1983:133)

This alleged complicity with colonialism, and the fact that anthropologists build careers on the lives of the Other, leads Pels and Nencel to remark, "we argue that the image of the exploiting anthropologist cannot (yet) be dismissed as caricature" (1991:18–19).

The solution postmodernists propose to this problem is twofold. Some advocate more polyvocal texts in which indigenous views and words appear in ethnographies alongside, and on equal footing with, those of researchers. (Clifford 1983:119). For instance, Marcus urges anthropologists to accept the "the montage of polyphony" (1994:48). Others, overcome by Euro-American-Capitalistic-Colonial guilt, advocate abandoning the anthropology of the foreign altogether and returning home to do ethnography on our own societies, if not on our own discipline. Pels and Nencel state, "We have not yet stared at our navels long enough" (1991:16).

The move toward polyvocality is based on the notion that reality is such a slippery thing, if extant at all, that it is unreasonable for one ethnographer to have an adequate view of it, as the following quotes demonstrate. Ethnography should become a "carnivalesque arena of diversity" (Clifford 1983:133). "But once *all* meaningful levels in a text, including theories and interpretations, are recognized as allegorical, it becomes difficult to view one of them as privileged, accounting for the rest" (Clifford 1986b:103). "Such terms as *objectivity, neutrality*, and *impartiality* refer to subject positions once endowed with great institutional authority, but they are arguably neither more nor less valid than those of more engaged, yet equally perceptive knowledgeable social actors" (Rosaldo 1991:21). "The notion that a point of view gains or loses currency because it 'is' true or not carries little conviction, for we live in a global village of competing truths" (G. Watson 1991:90). So, in the end, everyone necessarily gets to be right, especially since no method of evaluation is ever proposed by these postmodern anthropologists.

The inclusion of the voices of the Other, which I heartily advocate as doing good, honest scientific research, has gained many labels including polyvocality, polyphony, and heteroglossia (Clifford 1983:119, 1986a:15; Rabinow 1986:245, 246; Tyler 1986:126). Postmodernists intend this polyphonic space to be a realm of different and contrasting voices, all of which are equally valued.

I would like to point out that since the beginning ethnographies were cooperative ventures in which the voices and perspectives of those studied were indispensable, and this tradition continues. Two nineteenth-century examples are Henry Rowe Schoolcraft's early work on the Ojibwe, which depended upon his educated Ojibwe wife, Jane Johnston Schoolcraft, and her family (Weatherford 1991:257), and his later work on the Iroquois, which depended on the prominent Seneca Ely Parker (Weatherford 1991:260). It was this same Ely Parker, trained in traditional Seneca lifeways as well as educated in Greek and Latin, who befriended Lewis Henry Morgan. Jack Weatherford points out that it was Parker who patiently and diligently impressed upon Morgan the importance of kinship as an organizing principle of society, a concept that has since been a major focus (and insight) of anthropological research. The published result of their collaboration is the classic *League of the Iroquois*, which became a model for later ethnographic work. Weatherford notes that this "first book in American anthropology...came to life as the joint creation of an Indian and a white," and that what "we now think of as cultural anthropology or ethnology was largely invented by Morgan in his studies with Parker. It became the detailed study of a people and their way of life" (1991:264). I would not deny that anthropologists have at times masked their views as those of their subjects, and that Jane Johnston Schoolcraft and Ely Parker should have been more explicitly credited by Schoolcraft and Morgan. However, the debt is there, and these talented Native Americans helped to ensure that the earliest ethnographies represented indigenous societies, not simply Euro-American stereotypes.

There is evidence that anthropology's self-flagellating trend is coming to a close. Anthropologists have always valued the position of outsider in a society as a means of seeing things more objectively (Harris 1979:35; Powdermaker 1966:9), and there is a return by some to this ideal (Rubel and Rosman 1994:339). Also, some anthropologists are tiring of this self-abuse, and their desire for doing the work of anthropology has led them to return to doing ethnography and re-asserting their authority (Fox 1991a:2; Sanjek 1990).

An example of how this may be done without masking who is speaking and without devaluing indigenous views is found in Rosaldo. "The ethnographer, as a positioned subject, grasps certain human phenomena better than others....so-called natives are also positioned subjects who have a distinctive mix of insight and blindness" (1991:19). In other words, all people have strengths and weaknesses in their interpretation of culture, and professional anthropologists have strengths that should not be ignored. I would add that the empirical validity of different points of views can be potentially evaluated via the use of scientific means, following Sanjek's (1990) recommendations. There is no need to be cast in a polyphonic sea without moorings; some views will be demonstrably more false than others, and this is what scientific anthropologists are equipped to find out.

POLITICS/ETHICS/MORALS

Power relations, politics, ethics, and morality all play heavily in postmodern anthropology. As I argued in part 1, all politics, ethics, morality, and religion are essentially metaphysical, and therefore beyond the purview of science. Some postmodernists wish to retain some science, yet want their ethics as well. This is simply contradictory, as these issues are incommensurable. Those postmodernists who wish to jettison science entirely, seem not to comprehend the metaphysical nature of their arguments and fail to provide even a metaphysical justification for the values and truths they espouse. They completely assume that Marxist notions of exploitation, feminist notions of female subjugation, and politically correct notions of racial and ethnic discrimination and their attendant evils are self-evident, all-pervasive, and true.

I am not arguing that these things do not exist. The problem with the postmodern argument is that these issues become truly allegorical and the moral import of them is assumed self-evident. I think that scientific anthropologists who study and evaluate the empirical world appreciate that it is nowhere nearly as simple as postmodernists assert, and that both the empirical realities of these issues and proper ethical courses of action require more than textual analysis or activist rhetoric. Furthermore, I am in no way suggesting that scientific research cannot be used as the basis for criticism. I happen to agree with many postmodern critiques of modern industrialized society, and I would like to see more rigorous and scientific analysis of the metanarratives that influence anthropological thought as well as of the problematics (from the perspective of those experiencing problems) of modern life. However, the arguments of critical anthropologists are not critiques, but condemnations that carry the full weight of a particular moral point of view, as I take up in chapter 9.

Postmodern anthropologists utilize the metaphor of text to assert that all anthropology, all science is ethical. Clifford asserts that the issues of ethnography are "politically significant subjects" (1983:133). Tyler claims that the "rhetoric of ethnography is neither scientific or political, but is, as the prefix *ethno-* implies, ethical" (1986:122). Rosaldo says, "The social analyst's multiple identities at once underscore the potential for uniting an analytical with an ethical project" (1991:194), and he concludes his book *Culture and Truth* with, "The choice of what we want to know is primarily political and ethical" (1991: 224). Scheper-Hughes suggests that "cultural relativism, read as moral relativism, is no longer appropriate to the world in which we live and that anthropology, if it is to be worth anything at all, must be ethically grounded" (1995:410).

These arguments are non sequiters. Just because a researcher may play multiple social roles professionally while engaged in fieldwork does not necessitate that his or her work is ethical. The choice of what "we" (who is included here?) research is not always ethical; sometimes some of us just want to know. Finally, the world does appear to be in turmoil, but that does not mean that anthropology necessarily must contribute to this turmoil; why cannot anthropologists simply generate reliable data and valid theories on the human condition that then might be used to inform the ethical debates people face?

Postmodern and activist anthropologists tend to share a mixture of Marxist and classical Western Enlightenment ideals that they feel necessarily should apply to all of humanity. Rabinow notes that politically active postmodernists have a guiding ethic. "The guiding value is the constitution of a community-based political subjectivity." He goes on to criticize this. "The risk is that these enabling fictions of essential difference may become reified, thereby reduplicating the oppressive social forms they were meant to undermine" (1986:257). Scheper-Hughes wants a "more womanly-hearted anthropology" (1995:409), and Tyler essentializes "Modernism, which we could also call 'the masculine'" (1991:90).

Postmodernists, of all people, should understand the historical situatedness of these ethical, moral, and political points of view, and they should, as Rabinow suggests, be careful that they not merely reproduce the very ethics they criticize. Their perspective on what constitutes "good" is, in their own words, totalizing and based on a decidedly Western morality (D'Andrade 1995a:405; Nader 1995:427; Roscoe 1995; Sangren 1988). Tyler's masculine modernism is just a tad totalizing. Furthermore, since when has it been decided, once and for all, what constitutes being "womanly?" Has not the thrust of the anthropology of gender over the past several decades provided ample data to indicate that definitions of gendered anything are often socially and culturally contingent (Morgen 1990:4; Zimbalist Rosaldo and Lamphere 1974:6)? The attempts at promoting a certain transcendent ethic upon anthropology, and by extension the world, are more characteristic of religious proselytizing than of any investigation of the human condition.

Much of this postmodern-influenced anthropology has a downright religious tone and intent. This is manifest by appeals for the semi-sacred status of humans, for more spiritual ethnographies, to belief over rationality, and to exhortations to engage the eternal battle between good and evil.

> The specific accounts contained in ethnographies can never be limited to a project of scientific description so long as the guiding task of the work is to make the (often strange) behavior of a different way of life humanly comprehensible. To say that exotic behavior and symbols make sense either in "human" or "cultural" terms is to supply the same sorts of allegorical added meanings that appear in older narratives that saw actions as "spiritually" significant. (Clifford 1986b:101)

Postmodern ethnography is supposed to have evoked "memories of the *ethos* of the community and thereby provoked hearers to act ethically....It has the allegorical import, though not the narrative form, of a vision quest or religious parable" (Tyler 1986:126). In the end, Clifford exhorts anthropologists to "tell stories we believe to be true" (1986:121), and Tyler urges anthropologists to believe, not evaluate.

> Belief is the OPENING, the DEPARTURE, the ex-hodos, dissemination, orgasm without climax, the ESCHATON where each end is already a new beginning. (Tyler 1991:86)

Finally, anthropologists are prodded on to vanquish evil by activist-oriented anthropologists such as Scheper-Hughes, who admonishes, "Since when is *evil* exempt from human reality?" (1995:416). Her essentially religious approach manifests itself in the following statements.

> To speak of the "primacy of the ethical" is to suggest certain transcendent, transparent, and essential, if not "precultural," first principles....I cannot

escape the following observation: that we are thrown into existence at all presupposes a given, implicit moral relationship to an original (m)other and she to me....If "observation" links anthropology to the natural sciences, "witnessing" links anthropology to moral philosophy....It is the act of "witnessing" that lends our work its moral, at times almost theological, character. (Scheper-Hughes 1995:419)

As I stated in part 1, and as philosophers have labored so diligently for centuries to clarify, these matters are metaphysical—empirical scientists cannot evaluate these moral issues. If anthropologists had some means of evaluating whether or not Scheper-Hughes' earth mother exists and whether or not her transcendent morality is indeed based on the writings of Karl Marx, then perhaps they could export anthropological morals into different disciplines and different societies. However, mere mortals lack these abilities, and it seems to me that the most scientifically sound, the most ethically/morally/politically respectful stance is not one of strident moralism, but one of careful observation, self-critical testing, and hopefully more objective discovery of the human condition. The moralists and philosophers will then, at least, have a sound basis of knowledge upon which to base their decisions.

SUMMARY

I have outlined postmodern-influenced and activist anthropology in this chapter, concentrating on examining the elements of this new anthropology that its proponents share. These elements included a rejection of or at least ambiguity toward reality, a suspicion or rejection of science, a lack of explicit guidelines for evaluating statements, an empirical and ethical concern over representing people's lives and anthropological authority, and a blatant, religious moralism based on a democratic socialist ideal.

There are a number of weaknesses in these postmodern arguments. First, they have set up a scientific straw man for deconstruction to which they contrast themselves. This straw man allegedly is a science that produces global statements of absolute truth that are monolithic and unalterable. Their view of science is a very inductive one in which Western scientific experts observe the world and then hand down their dictums from on high. They allege that science is merely a ruse for a technological machine geared toward exploiting and denigrating non-Western, non-male, others so that the capitalist powers can amass more wealth. Based on the review of scientific anthropology in part 1, this view of anthropological science is patently false. Scientific anthropologists, through their cautious observation and constant testing and falsification of theory, are the ultimate revisionists.

Despite some postmodernists' relativistic denial of reality and judgement, all postmodern anthropologists seem very assured of their view of injustice in the world, and very assured of their critique of anthropology, except perhaps Tyler (1991). This is a major contradiction in their argument. While denying the representations of reality of their foes, postmodernists assert their own versions of reality as immanently true. How is this possible if there is no reality, or if reality exists as competing, multiple voices, each of which is equally valid? This contradiction exposes the essential nihilism in postmodern approaches in general. In denying reality so as to discredit their opponents, they deny themselves the very reality to which they appeal to expose social injustice. These authors dance around this issue, with only Tyler (1991) actually addressing it and concluding that, because of the tenuousness of reality (in a postmodern view), criticism is not possible. He honestly and forthrightly takes postmodernism to its logical conclusion, a conclusion that "produces nothing."

Ethical issues permeate postmodern writing, a goal to which postmodernists strive, and a claim they make of all writing. The strategy is to politicize everything, thereby hoping to gain legitimacy for their own predominantly political writings. I would never deny that all anthropological work is subject to political uses once it is disseminated (Vincent 1991). We have no control over how our audiences will take and interpret our work. This is nowhere more evident than in the ambiguous interpretations given to patterns noted in the anthropology of gender. Is the seclusion of women in menstrual huts a denigration of their femaleness intended to inflict hardship and humility? Or is it an expression of female power, voluntarily sought for its spiritual strengthening and peaceful solitude, not to mention the opportunities for liaisons with lovers (Buckley and Gottlieb 1988)? Is women's labor in horticultural societies such as Creek and Iroquois and Mundurucú an example of pre-capitalist exploitation of women's labor or an example of women exercising their monopolistic and emancipatory control of production (Friedl 1984 [1975])? If women assert the positive aspects of these behaviors, are they asserting their independence from and equality with men or have they simply not been enlightened by Western feminists? Female Native American advocates have bristled at feminist stereotypes and have spoken out against the appropriation of their identity by upper-middle-class white feminists (Jaimes and Halsey 1992:331–334). Postmodern anthropologists very much coopt the identity of their subjects by imposing a moral agenda upon their representations.

The moralistic, inductive, self-evident approach proposed by postmodernists leaves no room for revision; it is based on self-evident common sense. One either accepts their truths, or sinfully rejects them as a callous act, probably in the interest of capital accumulation. There is no justification put forward for postmodern views—one must "just get it." If one does not "get it," then postmodernists assume that one is not a member of the postmodern, politically correct elect. Scientific anthropologists insist that a researcher constantly question his or her views, and guarantee that those views will someday be superseded by even more realistic theories; empirical justification is a constant concern of scientific anthropologists. However, if one is engaged in proselytizing, justification is onerous and distracting—one wishes only to assert truth. This is evident in postmodern ethnography, but its effects can be checked as the polyphonic voices of the Other can speak out and challenge their broad generalizations. The situation with the past is more critical because postmodern archaeologists have coopted the past in the interest of their own political and ethical agendas. Unfortunately, the people of the past cannot fight back, their voices are necessarily silent. The next chapter examines how postmodern archaeologists use the past in their own grand narrative.

Chapter 7

The Mutable Past

Postmodern Archaeology

The mutability of the past is the central tenet of Ingsoc. Past events, it is argued, have no objective existence, but survive only in written records and in human memories. The past is whatever the records and the memories agree upon.

At one time it had been a sign of madness to believe that the earth goes round the sun; today, to believe that the past is inalterable.

George Orwell
1984

These words from Orwell's prophetic 1949 novel may chill Holocaust survivors and perhaps give Native Americans pause, considering the ways these peoples are often stereotyped. These words also describe what is considered by some archaeologists to be the state of the art of today's archaeology. For the past thirty-five years, archaeologists have realized that they do not possess the truth about the past, but they assumed that there was an immutable past to which they could compare their interpretations. That immutability is now gone, according to some postmodern and critical archaeologists. I am treating archaeology separately from cultural anthropology because of the special problems that arise with interpreting the past, and because of the increased abuses of knowledge that are possible with archaeology. Postmodern archaeologists construct their argument against the scientific archaeology known as processual, or new archaeology, and I will begin with a review of its tenets. Then I will look at the postmodern alternative.

PROCESSUAL ARCHAEOLOGY: AN OLD NEW THING

Processual Archaeology emerged as pioneering archaeologists such as Kleindienst and Watson (1956), Taylor (1948), and Willey and Philips (1958) began to ask whether or not they may get beyond artifacts and to the lives of people in the past. The work of Binford (1967, 1977, 1982), Binford and Sabloff (1982), Fritz and Plog (1970), Schiffer (1976), and Watson, LeBlanc, and Redman (1971, 1984) characterizes the scientific emphasis of this approach. I incorporated the views of processual archaeologists in part 1, and their approach to science is essentially equivalent to the approach advocated by cultural anthropologists. Processual archaeologists are concerned with the evaluation of claims against an empirical record and the logical constitution of anthropological theories. It is also axiomatic that this record was created by real people who existed in a real past; the past itself is immutable. Interpretations of that past may be subject to change, but there is a fundamental reality against which archaeologists must check their interpretations.

Processual archaeologists stress that archaeological knowledge of the past consists of inferences that archaeologists make about the dynamic past, based on the static residues that remain from that past (Binford 1983:416; Figure 7–1). After the new archaeology, archaeologists could never again assert that they somehow directly know the past from their observations of archaeological remains (Bell 1994; R. Watson 1991). This is a daunting realization; but because of their scientific commitment, archaeologists rose to the task and began to address how they might reasonably make these inferences (Binford 1967; Hodder 1982, 1991a:2; Schiffer 1976).

There was an additional problem for the processual archaeologist. What is the relationship between dynamic behaviors and residues in the first place? Binford borrowed (and redefined) the sociological notion of middle-range theory to address this problem of inference (Binford 1977, 1982). Middle-range theories are theories of archaeological residue formation; they relate dynamics to statics. Binford argued that until archaeologists developed a

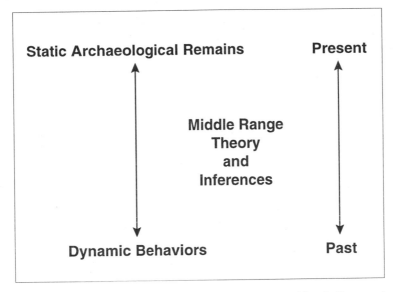

Figure 7–1. Relationship between Archaeological Present and Past in Processual Archaeology. Middle-range theory contains the theoretical guidelines for making inferences about what the dynamic past was like based on the static archaeological residues that remain in the present.

body of middle-range theory, they would not be able to make scientifically reliable inferences that in turn could be used to test anthropological theories. Archaeologists since have approached the construction of middle-range theory by butchering elephants with bone tools (Frison 1989); experimentally wearing down stone tools (Keeley 1980); living among modern-day foragers (Binford 1978; Gould 1980; Yellen 1977), herders (Chang 1984; Gifford 1978; Hodder 1982; Kuznar 1995a) and potters (Arnold 1993); and even excavating the Tucson city landfill (Rathje 1973). All of these studies have provided invaluable information upon which archaeologists can base inferences of the past. The important point is that middle-range theories are supposed to be just that, testable theories about how to interpret archaeological residues.

I have offered this brief description of scientific archaeology to demonstrate what it actually is, and as a preliminary to answering its critics who hold that scientific archaeology has been a simplistic task of merely reading the truth of the past directly off of its remains for nefarious purposes.

A RE-CONSTRUCTED ARCHAEOLOGY: THE POSTMODERN PAST

Ian Hodder's post-processual approach (1991a, first published in 1986) has been influential in opposing processual archaeology, leading to the stronger anti-science stance taken by Michael Shanks and Christopher Tilley in their *Re-Constructing Archaeology* (1987a) and *Social Theory and Archaeology* (1987b). These works have become foundations of the postmodern approach in archaeology and are therefore the texts upon which I shall focus. As Shanks and Tilley take the postmodern approach more nearly to its logical extreme, I will concentrate my analysis on their work. Postmodern archaeology shares many features with critical and postmodern ethnography, although its subject matter—the past—lends to it a special quality. Because the past is so remote from our experience and can be understood only in the most indirect way, interpretations of the past have few constraints—the dead cannot come back and tell archaeologists they are wrong. Postmodern archaeologists, in contrast to processual archaeologists, exploit this situation to the hilt.

Postmodern, post-processual archaeologists begin, as do most postmodernists, by stating that traditional archaeology has been part of the modernist/capitalist project to dehumanize, colonize, and alienate non-European others in order to appropriate their labor.

> That archaeology does not appear to have been successful in encouraging alternative perceptions and experiences of the past, may be linked to the role of archaeology and archaeologies in power strategies in Western society. (Hodder 1991a:174)

> The truth in scientific archaeology's denial of subjectivity is its reflection of the fetishized position of people in contemporary capitalism. (Shanks and Tilley 1987a:12)

This alleged alienation and reduction of humans is problematic for Shanks and Tilley, and a central tenet of their position is that humans are not reducible to scientific analysis. Consequently, reason and science are dehumanizing and deny the essentially metaphysical character of humankind. "People are not natural entities if we accept the primacy of sentience, intentionality, linguistic and symbolic communication" (Shanks and Tilley 1987a:34).

The theory-laden nature of facts is another of their targets. They point out, following Hodder (1991a:16–18), that all facts about the past are theory-laden, and that there is no such thing as a value-free science (Shanks and Tilley 1987a:110). Since they argue that there is no value-free science, objectivity is impossible, and this leads to a mutable past (1987a:46).

The literary turn obvious in postmodern ethnography also powerfully influences postmodern archaeology. Ian Hodder begins by using a text analogy, equating archaeological data with a text (1991a:153). Shanks and Tilley focus on the actual writing of archaeology. "Archaeologists observe the traces of the past then record and write about them. Archaeologists produce texts" (Shanks and Tilley 1987a:16). They argue that since archaeology exists only as text, the literary techniques of postmodern criticism are appropriately directed at archaeological texts. Finally, the cynical mark of the postmodern pioneer Nietzsche is obvious in their work, as Shanks and Tilley emphasize the interpretive nature of archaeology (see also Hodder 1991a:150–152). "The truth of the past is metaphorical....Like a metaphor the past *requires* interpretation" (Shanks and Tilley 1987a:20–21). This textual basis lead Shanks and Tilley to state that there are many texts with which to view the past.

> There are multiple and competing pasts made in accordance with ethnic, cultural and gender political orientations. (1987a:11)

Likewise, Ian Hodder states that "the past is subjectively constructed in the present, and secondly, the subjective past is involved in power strategies today" (1991a:166), and he details some of these alternative pasts in his book.

The reality of the past is crucial to these arguments since, if people promulgate alternative pasts, it might indict the notion that any one past is more real than the others. On one hand, Shanks and Tilley maintain that, because of the theory-laden nature of observations and the impossibility of

value-free science, all interpretations of the past are equally valid
(1987a:245).

> Understanding material culture is an act of translation. Meaning depends
> on context and the position of the interpreter in relation to this context,
> whether prehistoric social actor or contemporary archaeologist. There is
> no original meaning to be discovered. (Shanks and Tilley 1987b:211)

On the other hand, they are adamant about realism, and they maintain
that not all points of view on the past are equally valid. They begin their *Re-
Constructing Archaeology* with the statement that their "intention is not to
sacrifice objectivity and replace it with an extreme and disabling relativism" (Shanks and Tilley 1987a:7, see also p. 110). They contradict their
position by advocating "radical pluralism" and "multiple pasts," but then
they immediately state the caveat, "We do not mean to suggest that all pasts
are equal" (1987a:245). Hodder is less ambiguous, and never denies that
some real past existed (1991a:179, 185). The real crux of his argument considering alternative pasts is how archaeologists can use challenges to established views in order to expose biases (1991a:179, 1991b).

Shanks and Tilley do not want to let archaeologists wander about in a
non-grounded archaeology where anything goes. They, like Hodder
(1991a:150, 1991b:10) propose a hermeneutic and dialectic approach for
interpreting the past (1987a:107–108). They, however, note that hermeneutics
alone lacks a notion of structure and ignores power and ideology. They seek
to solve these problems by introducing Marxist dialectics to the interpretive
process. They recognize that archaeologists cannot perceive the past directly,
but that archaeologists perceive the past in light of their theories. Because
of this, there is a dialectic between theory and data (1987a:111). They argue
that once archaeologists realize this interdependence between theory and
data, archaeologists can transcend the notion of subject and object that un-
derlies the scientific notion of testing and verification. They also propose
that archaeology, because its facts are theory-laden and because of its inherent subjectivity, cannot escape being a political act; archaeology becomes
another form of politics. "Archaeology is historically and socially situated—

a political practice" (1987a:115). This leads them to propose archaeology as political action.

> No discourse on the past is neutral. The validity of a theory hinges on intention and interest: it is to be assessed in terms of the ends and goals of its archaeology, its politics and morality. (Shanks and Tilley 1987b:213)

Ian Hodder touches upon the same notion by stating that "a fully critical and responsible archaeology must be able to use the objectivity and reality of the experience of its data to shape and transform the experience of world" (1991a:180). His argument for an interpretive archaeology (1991b:14) is also based on the notion that archaeologists should aid subordinate peoples in interpreting the past the way they want it interpreted. However, he realizes the political dangers in advocating a purely subjective past and provides the following caution.

> With the data described as totally subjective, the archaeologist would have no recourse to the data in objecting to "misuses" of the past. The past which was so disseminated would depend entirely on power, and the ability to control theory, method and communication. In this volume, however, I have argued that the data from the past do have a contextual reality in relation to theory. (Hodder 1991a:179)

In summary, Hodder and Shanks and Tilley share a number of points in their view of a post-processual, or postmodern archaeology. They stress that facts are theory-laden, share a literary and hermeneutic approach, and note the role of subjectiveness and politics in alternative creations of the past. However, Shanks and Tilley are more strident in their denial of the reality of the past (something that Hodder rejects), their ethical mandate for doing so, and their advocacy of a politicized archaeology. Since these are common outcomes of postmodern approaches, I will focus my criticism primarily on Shanks and Tilley's work.

DECONSTRUCTING RE-CONSTRUCTED ARCHAEOLOGY

The problems with Shanks and Tilley's argument lie in their religious pros-elytizing, their coopting of scientific method, and their misrepresentation of scientific archaeology; there are also fundamental contradictions in their exposition. Ian Hodder's post-processual approach, while not as extremely anti-scientific, shares in some of these weaknesses. These shortcomings lead Shanks and Tilley to propose a number of non sequiturs that are damaging to their argument and, I would argue, damaging to archaeology.

Shanks and Tilley have a religious devotion to the notion that humans are special, above and beyond the objects of nature. Richard Watson points out yet other essentially religious and metaphysical elements of Shanks and Tilley's reasoning than those I list here (1990:678). Shanks and Tilley state that humans act with intentions, and that this is fundamentally different from animal behavior or the behavior of molecules (1987a:34,35); and Hodder thinks that it is contradictory to use scientific approaches to the natural world to study cultural phenomena (1991a:186). How do these authors know this? The assumption that humans and culture are fundamentally and qualita-tively different phenomena than other aspects of nature is hardly different from the Medieval assumption that man was semi-sacred. How do postmodern archaeologists know that animals—or even molecules for that matter—do not have some sort of consciousness as well? This is much more than an operational assumption, but a truly ethical statement regarding the distinctness of humanity. Being an ethical matter, it is clearly outside of the purview of science and best left alone unless one is looking for absolute truths. As R. Watson states, "Scientists are not metaphysicians!" (1990:683).

Shanks and Tilley will not even entertain the possibility that humans are part of the natural world and perhaps are not so special. "The concepts of function, adaptation and evolution have no explanatory role in a consider-ation of the social" (1987b:210). Another indication of their intolerant and religious approach to archaeology is their denial of demarcation between sci-ence and metaphysics (1987a:43). This said, it is clear that scientific refuta-tions are ultimately irrelevant to empirical claims under the re-constructed archaeology in the same manner that science is ultimately irrelevant to the claims of creationists.

Moving on, these critical and post-processual archaeologists introduce revelations regarding the nature of science and archaeological method that are merely restatements of the very views they criticize. They repeatedly point out that data are theory-laden (Hodder 1991a:16; Shanks and Tilley 1987a:21, 37, 104, 106, 109, 110; 1987b:209). This is nothing different than what positivists have said since Comte; this is no revelation.

Shanks and Tilley also state a number of curiously scientific ideals. They share scientists' and philosophers' admission that knowledge is always subject to change (1987a: 109). They advocate a common-sense realism and the realization that observations are theories in and of themselves (1987a:111); and they also state, "data represents a *network of resistances* to theoretical appropriation" (1987a:104). I fail to see the difference between this and theory testing. Peter Kosso, a philosopher, addresses this very issue with respect to Ian Hodder's post-processual archaeology. Kosso (1991) points out that the differences between Binford's scientific processual archaeology and Hodder's post-processual archaeology are more a matter of theoretical differences and the posturing of the writers, than of any real differences in interpretive method or philosophy. The notion that the scientific method, with its cycle of observation, theorization, testing, revision, and further observation is itself an hermeneutic has been noted by other anthropologists as well (O'Meara 1989; Roscoe 1995).

It is more accurate to regard the structural principles [Hodder's approach] as part of the theories. Recall that the operative notion of a middle-range theory places no restrictions on the content or degree of generality of the claim, only on its use for making sense of (finding information in) the evidence....Middle-range theories, recall, are just ordinary theories. They are tested and justified like any other theory, including the ones whose observational evidence they laden. Middle-range theories are tested and justified by comparison to evidence, that is, to observations. There is then a kind of circularity. (Kosso 1991:625)

The methods of natural science, and those advocated by Binford for archaeology, are more like the contextual, hermeneutic, back-and-forth model than Hodder's original opposition seems to recognize. (Kosso 1991:627)

Ian Hodder himself states,

> I have in this book accepted that as archaeologists we need to test theory against data....in fact the use of scientific means of analysis...is equally relevant with a hermeneutic approach. (1991a:185)

In fact, there is no fundamental difference between the theory testing advocated by scientific anthropologists and the hermeneutics advocated by Hodder and Shanks and Tilley. As long as scientific archaeologists repeatedly test, revise, and reject theories with data, then they practice an essentially hermeneutic approach in which they confront data with preconceptions (theories), alter those preconceptions in accordance with data, and then return to archaeological data with a new view (new theories). This is science.

Shanks and Tilley try to illuminate us on a number of points well-covered by Binford and others when they recast processual archaeology. These ideas include the notion that the past is over and cannot be relived (Shanks and Tilley 1987a:9,12). This seems little different from Binford's (1977) revelation regarding the difference between the static present and the dynamic past discussed earlier in this chapter.

Shanks and Tilley (1987a:21) and Hodder (1991b) are adamant that the past is not directly accessible, but that archaeologists must interpret it, although this is no different from processual archaeologists' concern about making inferences about the past (Binford 1977:6). All parties are agreed that the past is not directly accessible and therefore must be interpreted. Shanks and Tilley also misrepresent scientific archaeology by constructing and then deconstructing a number of straw men.

The first and most glaring is the notion that standard archaeology is a simplistic task of reading off objective, true facts of the past from artifacts (see also R. Watson 1990:680). "Equally, the apparent ease with which contemporary scientistic archaeology claims stringent objectivity, via a restricted set of methodologies, has to be rejected" (Shanks and Tilley 1987a:108). I think that the historical development of processual archaeology and the issues with which its proponents have grappled are testament enough that archaeologists have been consumed with the notion of how they generate theories, not truths, by using materials from the past.

Their view of biology and evolutionary theory is narrow and mistaken. According to Shanks and Tilley, evolutionary theory implies that "the only political action which could alter social life as it is today would be eugenic" (1987a:56). If evolutionary theory was like Herrnstein and Murray's work described in chapter 4, they might be right. However, as I took pains to demonstrate in that chapter, that type of research confuses ethics, politics, and science and is unscientific by anthropologists' standards. Moreover, biologists and bioanthropologists agree, as the outpouring of scientific correctives to the eugenicist view in popular science outlets attests (Diamond 1994; Gould 1994). Shanks and Tilley ignore the complex models of genetic and social interaction found in Chagnon and Irons (1979) and more recently in Boyd and Richerson (1985), or in Rindos (1984). Even if their view of simple additive genetic and environmental influence was the one held by evolutionary biologists, this still would not lead to eugenics. There is always the environment to manipulate if one wished.

While I think that Shanks and Tilley's restatement of processual basics is a useful exercise, and that their and Hodder's discussion of hermeneutics can aid archaeologists in realizing the tenuousness of theories, I think there is a major contradiction in their postmodern approach that weakens what they can do for archaeology. Does reality exist or not in the re-constructed archaeology? They clearly want a reality, since ultimately they would like to refute claims about the past with which they disagree. This is clear in their statement that the archaeological record may challenge theories (Shanks and Tilley 1987a:104). However, if a reality exists, and its existence is robust enough to challenge theory, how is it that there "is no original meaning to be discovered"? (Shanks and Tilley 1987b:211). If their point is that all factual statements about the past are theoretical and that archaeologists cannot see the past directly, this revelation is nothing new in archaeology and is as old as David Hume's philosophy. Further clues as to their meaning of reality and its use can be found if one looks at the last set of weaknesses in their criticism of archaeology.

There are a number of non sequiturs in their argument. The first is the notion that because facts are theory laden, and theories also influence methods, archaeologists are never capable of finding novel knowledge. "There can be no 'logic of scientific discovery' since it has already been decided what there is to discover" (Shanks and Tilley 1987a:43). Therefore, "methodology is to be criticized as determining the past in advance of its confrontation with archaeological practice" (Shanks and Tilley 1987b:209). This is a gross overstatement, and in fact a non sequitur.

Clearly, the questions archaeologists have in mind guide what methods they use, and this admittedly has an effect upon what archaeologists discover. However, once an archaeologist confronts the empirical world, any result is possible. Despite the influences from cultural and personal biases upon theories, methods, and actual work, these influences are never so all-determining that archaeologists find exactly what they theorize. Any archaeologist who has ever excavated a site can tell you that! If anything, the work of archaeology is fraught with anomalies, with archaeologists scratching their heads and wondering, "What in the hell is that?" True, theoretical perspectives give archaeologists a framework into which to fit observations, but especially in archaeological work, there is always a lot left over that one does not explain. Archaeological work produces a repository of anomalies, anomalies that eventually challenge pre-existing theories and that eventually lead to change. The accumulation of anomalies in Hopewellian mound archaeology led to revisions from Lost Race theories to Native American theories as described in chapter 3. The scientific method does not predetermine what archaeologists discover; the scientific method can be used to challenge existing knowledge; the scientific method systematically leads to change and therefore is a method of change, not a method of stasis. It is not logical that method predetermines knowledge, provided that the method is scientific.

The other major non sequitur in their approach is their conclusion that archaeology is a necessarily political act. Scientific anthropologists agree with the view that facts are theory laden and that theories can reflect biases. I therefore agree with Shanks and Tilley's statements that "values cannot be eradicated from archaeology...we should attempt to make the values we bring to research explicit," and that in the end this would result in "a more honest view of what we are doing" (1987a:67). However, going from "values impact scientific knowledge" to "science should be value-based" is a non sequitur similar to those found in the philosophical work of Paul Feyerabend and Sandra Harding, foundational postmodern texts, and postmodern ethnography. It confuses an "is" with a "should" (Watson 1990:685). Shanks and Tilley, however, insist, along with other postmodern critics of science, that because science is influenced by values, archaeologists should give up the attempt to limit this influence and make science a value-dependent enterprise.

What their approach seemingly does for them is to permit their politics to come first (see also R. Watson 1990). Throughout their philosophical discussions, they argue that a final set of conclusions logically follows from their intellectual labors. These conclusions are not only that archaeology must be value-based and critical, but that it likewise must be socialistic and emancipatory. Hodder also takes this view.

> Peoples around the world use archaeology to help maintain their pasts in the face of the universalizing and dominating processes of Westernization and Western science. The physical archaeological remains help people to maintain, reform, or even form a new identity or culture in the face of multinational encroachment, outside powers, or centralized governments. (Hodder 1991b:14; see also 1991a:167–174)

This is fine, but what if the "new identities" indigenous peoples wish to create are empirically false? Do archaeologists lie? Hodder assumes that his guarded objectivity will only help indigenous peoples (1991b:15). What if it doesn't? Finally, what are archaeologists to do when an indigenous people wishes to use the past for the subjugation of other peoples, as in Serbian claims that they are entitled to re-create a Greater Serbia, and their claim that wherever Serbs are buried is Serbia (Stiglmayer 1994)?

I doubt that Hodder and Shanks and Tilley began this enterprise and woke up at the end of it committed socialists working on behalf of subordinated peoples. I rather suspect that they began as committed socialists and great emancipators of the oppressed (women, minorities, and Third-world and indigenous peoples). The contradictions that I have exposed in their work are the result of their trying to construct a logical (and yes, methodological) framework that would undermine an established science of which they disapprove and that could incorporate their pre-existing political views. I think that it is very important to ask them whether or not their biases and hermeneutics have not pre-determined what they will find in the archaeological record and especially how they will interpret it. If anyone's approach is pre-determined, it is theirs.

If one accepts Shanks and Tilley's postmodernist dictates that politics come first in scientific enquiry and that there exist multiple valid views of the past (or anything for that matter), where does this leave us? How do we evaluate competing claims? Foucault provides the answer: Power. Shanks and Tilley maintain that power is the means by which scientists and archaeologists validate claims. "Power is central to social analysis; power (both productive and repressive) is coextensive with the social field" (Shanks and Tilley 1987b:210). The implication is that the past must be interpreted in light of these projects, and if data contradictory to these political claims about the empirical world were encountered, they should be repressed. This is a case where Shanks and Tilley's loose treatment of the past and their insistence on a literary approach to archaeology may come back to haunt them.

> The distinction between archaeology and literature breaks down in that archaeologists construct what may be termed facts and all archaeologists use heuristic fictions. (1987a:111)

If this is so, then perhaps Orwell's fiction of a society ruled by a totalitarian state that willingly alters the past in light of political concerns is not a fiction, but today's archaeological reality.

Analysis
of the
Debate

3

Chapter 8

A Comparison of Challenges to Scientific Anthropology

Politics makes strange bedfellows.
Charles Dudley Warner

What could racialists, fundamentalist Christians, literati, and left-wing radicals have in common? Much more than may be apparent. The critics of scientific anthropology hail from a diverse set of cultural and social backgrounds, world views, and religious or moral points of view. Nonetheless, they are united in their opposition to both the practices and the resultant knowledge of scientific anthropology. More importantly, they share a number of characteristics that place them on different sides of what is fundamentally the same coin—dogmatic religion. I will argue that these attributes are negative if one wishes to construct sound knowledge about the world using logic and empirical data. I also will argue that these challenges can be useful to scientific anthropology. Religious fundamentalists, right-wing politicians, poets, and left-wing socialists may have had fun raining on science's parade, but the silver lining of these clouds actually promises a stronger anthropological science.

These challenges share five attributes. First, most of these critics (racialist research excepted) elevate text as the fundamental representation and arbiter of what we regard as reality. This textuality absolves them from dealing with the messy and often contradictory empirical world. Second, they profess what is a misunderstanding of the scientific process. Often, they accuse scientists of trying to prove absolute truths, and when they advocate a science of their own, it is decidedly inductive, ad hoc, and probably more at home during the Middle Ages. Third, these critics share a basic paranoia that, somehow, the scientific establishment and its cronies are out to get them. Fourth, their arguments regarding science are weakened by numerous non sequiturs that expose political agendas that have little to do with the state of the world. The fifth and most pervasive characteristic of these challenges is that they are ethically and morally driven, and part of their proponents' own grand narratives.

A LITERARY BENT

The first similarity among most of anthropological science's critics is a decidedly literary orientation in their work. Those who dislike scientific knowledge assert that the texts, not the experiences that scientists strive to evaluate, describe, and explain, constitute reality. Creationists most obviously appeal to text in their assertions about what constitutes reality, and they appeal to the same revered text—the Bible. Most creationists contend that only a literal interpretation of the Bible is appropriate, and they look toward the Book of Genesis for their view of the creation of the cosmos, earth, and humanity (Morris 1984:47; Rimmer 1945; Wysong 1976). What they observe in nature must always be interpreted in light of the Truth contained in this text. "God's revelation in nature, therefore, must always supplement and confirm his scripture. It cannot be used to correct or interpret it" (Morris 1984:48).

This fundamentalist literalism is not unique to creationism. Ernest Gellner, discussing Islamic fundamentalism, aptly notes that "The underlying idea [of religious fundamentalism] is that a given faith is to be upheld firmly in its full and literal form....it presupposes that the core of religion is *doctrine*...which further presupposes *writing*" (1992:2).

Postmodernists are also explicit in their elevation of text, and this is clearly a defining feature of the postmodern movement (Chioni Moore 1994; Clifford 1983, 1986a:2; Gellner 1992; O'Meara 1989; Sangren 1988; Scheper-Hughes 1995:414). While postmodernists embrace Wittgenstein's philosophy of language as an internal representation, they also assert their texts as somehow true and to be believed. Since there is no reality that can judge texts, texts themselves are reality, elevating text to the level of being the only reality (or non-reality) that matters.

The privileging of text is not without its scientific critics in anthropology (Gellner 1992). For example, O'Meara notes that the truth-giving power of adopting postmodernism is that, "Unlike explanations, metaphors cannot be wrong" (1989:365), and he goes on to note that from a scientific perspective in which reality is assumed to exist, "while 'viewing' social phenomena *as if* they were texts may help researchers see new relationships, life does not thereby *become* a text of symbols." Sangren, arguing from a materialist Marxist perspective, notes that "society is not a text" (1988:419); it is something real and lived by real people.

The creationist approach is meant to be dogmatic; but in a curious irony, the postmodernists and critical anthropologists, in their push against monovocal hegemony, provide views that are no less dogmatic (Roscoe 1995:493). Sangren, along with noting postmodernists' fanatically religious fervor, accuses them of "positivistic, assertive, unargued, and highly mythologized assessments of the historical causes and intrinsic value of other social theories and the case they make for relativity, subtlety, dialog, and pluralism in ethnographic treatments of the 'other'" (1988:409).

This strategy of denying an external reality and maintaining that the only reality is in text serves postmodern and creationist agendas—it permits ignoring the empirical world. If the only reality that matters is in a text, experiences and observations that contradict that text can be dismissed as satanic illusions or capitalistic propaganda, and so can be re-interpreted in light of the essential truths contained in the text. This elevation of text is equivalent to the Scholastic method that reigned during the Middle Ages and against which Sir Francis Bacon rebelled. Because it leaves texts and their truths intact, the elevation of text serves a fundamentally moral purpose that I will review at the end of this chapter.

MISUNDERSTANDING THE SCIENTIFIC PROCESS

The misunderstandings of the scientific process held by critics of scientific anthropology center on their stereotyping science as wholly inductive and resulting in proven truths. Words like *proof* and *truth* are far too strong for what scientists (especially anthropologists) do and should be jettisoned from the scientific vocabulary. Our fundamental limitations as human animals preclude our proving anything absolutely true. These limitations involve our perceptual capabilities, which have some strengths, but also weaknesses peculiar to our species. Scientists use technology to extend these perceptual capabilities, but still, only extending those certain abilities inherent to our species. Our human mental capabilities are also likewise limited, and our memories are finite; we have to work to develop our logical and analytical abilities, and psychologists have long pointed out that we generally can deal with only a few ideas at once (Miller 1956). Our lack of omnipresence and omniscience are fundamental limitations that require consideration when doing science.

The scientific method, as developed over the past twenty-five hundred years—or four hundred years, depending on your point of departure—has been altered to deal with and correct these limitations as much as scientists can (see brief reviews in Harris 1979, or Bernard 1994a). Scientific anthropologists, benefitting from the lessons of centuries of science as well as their own discipline's history, have incorporated the basic principles of science into anthropology. A brief review of these tenets, as elaborated in part 1, will reinforce what scientific anthropologists really do. Scientific anthropologists assume that there is an external and structured reality to be understood (Bernard 1994a, 1994b:168; Hammersley 1992:51; O'Meara 1989:360; Roscoe 1995:499), and that theories must be rigorously tested with empirical data (Bernard 1994b; D'Andrade 1995a:404; Harris 1994; O'Meara 1989:358). These scientists demarcate their work from metaphysics by focussing on the empirical and admitting only those theories into their knowledge base that are empirically testable or falsifiable. Scientific anthropologists maintain objectivity, but it is a methodological objectivity (Harris 1995b:423). As I detailed in chapters 1 and 3, scientific anthropologists are self-critical, open to change, and progressive in the sense that the knowledge scientific anthropologists generate conforms increasingly to experience, with one proviso—that any theory must be empirically testable.

These few paragraphs summarize my conclusions in part 1, and represent the fundamental tenets of scientific anthropology. As I stated earlier, any fault of scientists to adhere to these principles is not a fault of the method, but of the scientists themselves. Such faults do not invalidate science, they indict scientists. These tenets are often misunderstood or totally ignored by the critics of science.

Their first misunderstanding about science is that it is, purely and simply, society's pool of knowledge. This is most obvious in the arguments of creationists who use popular definitions of science in dictionaries of common usage (Morris 1984:31). Postmodernists, who equate the project of science with that of capitalism, colonialism, and the Enlightenment, also suggest that Western knowledge as a whole is science (Clifford 1986a:2; Tyler 1986; 123, 1991:80, 91). However, not all knowledge is scientific, and science does not supersede all knowledge. Scientific knowledge is that knowledge generated by scientific methods. Ultimately, scientists consider all scientific knowledge theoretical and therefore open to scrutiny and change.

Another misunderstanding is that scientists claim to possess truth, and that science is an inductive exercise of discovering truth. Postmodernist writers and critics of science are clear in their assertion that scientists have claimed to provide truth (Harding 1991:45, 59; Tyler 1986:129). Statements by Rosaldo (1991:21) such as the "truth of objectivism," and by Tyler (1986:123) that "its [science's] only justification was proof," are examples of this incorrect stereotype. Anthropological scientists are hardly naive about the limits of induction and their inability to discover absolute truth, and this is why they ardently advocate rigorous testing of theories as demonstrated in chapter 1, and also why they ultimately do test all theories as detailed in chapter 3.

> The success of science is due primarily both to the norm of presenting generalizations in a form that makes it possible to dispute them with evidence and to the norm of carrying out extensive tests of other people's generalizations. (D'Andrade 1995a:404)

Marvin Harris (1994:64) notes that "scientific theories are held as tentative approximations, never as 'facts,'" and Bernard (1994b:172, see also 1994a:12) notes that "perfect objectivity is impossible." The value of scientific objectivity is in its ability to produce progressively objective knowledge, not totally objective knowledge.

Science's critics evidently see their own approaches as yielding these types of final, total knowledge. This ranges from the creationists' quest for God's truth through science to the critical anthropologists' assurance that they know oppression when they see it (D'Andrade 1995a). For instance, Morris (1984:48) notes that truth is found in "God's revelation in nature," and that it "must always supplement and confirm his scripture." Johnson (1994:26) boldly asserts, "We need to stop talking about the separate realms of religion and science and start talking about truth." For Herrnstein and Murray (1994:340), the differences between the races are clear, and their genetic cause is undebatable given their assertion of the weight of the data.

Reality, for Stephen Tyler, is self-evident, and therefore the methodological trapments of science appear like useless and actually misleading baggage to him, and he labels scientific concepts an "inappropriate mode of scientific rhetoric" (1986:130). Postmodern archaeologists want to assert their interpretations of the past as truth. "The truth of the past is metaphorical" (Shanks and Tilley 1987a:20–21). Critical anthropologists also hold an inductive, truth-giving view of the knowledge quest. Scheper-Hughes (1995:419) advocates that anthropologists bear "witness" to life's injustices with the intent to correct them; there is no room for testing of one's observations in such witnessing.

Racialist research, as described in Chapter 6, is entirely inductive. Herrnstein and Murray (1994:19) claim to adhere to a "classical tradition" of science, based on "accepted standards of what constitutes scientific evidence and proof." For them, science consists in developing an instrument (IQ), and then uncritically using it to look for those differences they not only suspect, but have already decided exist. Once racial differences in IQ are found, they then conclude that they have proven their theory of racial inequality in intelligence (Herrnstein and Murray 1994). This type of inductivism also leads to questionable scientific practice in Race and IQ research such as using poor and unsystematic data on penis size, or comparing crime rates across nations and cultures that define and report criminal acts in radically different ways (see Rushton 1995). Finally, this inductivism is explicitly stated in the writing of many creationists (Wysong 1976:40, 42); "Science thus involves observed facts and demonstrated laws" (Morris 1984:302). All of these authors should heed Hume's observation that "appearance can never afford us any security" (1956 [1735]:182).

These stereotypes of science constitute straw men set up by science's critics for eventual destruction or deconstruction. Of course, a straw man is not a real person, and their stereotypes are demonstrably false (see Carrithers 1990; D'Andrade 1995a; Hammersley 1992; Harris 1994; O'Meara 1989; Roscoe 1995 for refutations). Critics' use of straw men leads to other incorrect characterizations of science. Harding (1991:63, 77, 87) asserts that scientists perceive reality readily, and that science is as scientists do. The incredibly complex and expensive apparatuses scientists use and the philosophical debates on what scientists perceive that have always taken place in physics (e.g. Broad 1972 [1914]) should be enough to debunk these straw men. In anthropology, our obsession with cultural relativism, the breakdown of personal cultural biases through the fieldwork experience, and our own consideration on how to record cultural knowledge (Bernard 1994a; Naroll and Cohen 1970; Pelto and Pelto 1978; Spradley 1979, 1980; Werner and Schoepfle 1987) indicate that scientific anthropologists are hardly naive about perceiving reality.

Rosaldo (1991:169), Clifford (1986b:103), G. Watson (1991:90), and Harding (1991) assert that there is no Archimedean point of view in science, as though scientists claim such omniscience. None of the scientific anthropologists I reviewed in part 1 asserted such an Archimedean point of view. If scientists had access to an Archimedean point of view, then they would not need to evaluate their theories—truth would be self-evident.

The issue of an Archimedean point of view is the main way in which the postmodern and critical anthropologists differ from the creationists and racialists, although even postmodern and critical theorists imply a certainty that they are correct on some issues. The racialists assert that science is on their side, and that they have seen the truth of racial differences in IQ (Herrnstein 1973; Herrnstein and Murray 1994; Jensen 1969; Rushton 1995). Creationists also assert their dominance over the truth, but the source of their authority is not a set of invented and practiced human procedures, but rather the Word of God.

Another straw man is the notion that scientists are naive about facts being theory-laden. Even the original positivist Auguste Comte (1974 [1855]:474) admitted that observations are influenced by the theories that guide research, and positivists developed the notion of operationalization to make this explicit (Harris 1979:14). Ironically, the critical Marxist and postmodern analysts possess a much more naive view of the way the world works than do scientific anthropologists. D'Andrade charges that these critics suffer from a naive and "powerful tendency to believe that good things produce good results and bad things produce bad results" (1995a:406). Likewise, Hammersley (1992:152) notes that the utopian assumptions about the truthfulness of the oppressed and the evil of science are likewise based upon a naive realism that fails to appreciate the subtleties of real life. Nonetheless, postmodernists accuse scientists of such naivete (G. Watson 1991:76). This point is another one upon which creationists and racialists differ from postmodernists and critical anthropologists. For anthropology's traditionalist critics, a fact is rather brute and obvious, whether it be the alleged promiscuity of Africans (Rushton 1995) or the geological evidence for the Flood (Morris, ed. 1974).

THE CONSPIRACY THEORIES

Science's critics, especially those critical of a scientific anthropology, share a view that science is not only a flawed way of looking at things, but that it is actually malevolent. Morris is primarily concerned with science as an agent of secularization; "The philosophy of scientific determinism has been invoked to disprove Biblical miracles, for example" (1984:36). Rushton (1995:256) is not concerned with secularization, but rather a politically correct leftist conspiracy among scientists to cover up the genetic basis for racial differences in IQ. Postmodernists also assert that scientists are complicit with the postmodernist's main target—capitalism (Rabinow 1986:221; Shanks and Tilley 1987a:12).

I argue, along with other scientific anthropologists and ethnographers (D'Andrade 1995a; Hammersley 1992; Kuper 1992:69), that it is worthwhile to examine the ways in which colonialism and the rise of capitalist economies influenced the birth of anthropology and its subsequent development. However, just because anthropology originated at the same time as colonialism and capitalism does not means they were in league (Asad 1973a:18; D'Andrade 1995a; Hammersley 1992:152). Anthropologists commonly stood in opposition to colonial forces in fact (Boas 1940; Kuper 1973). The fact that archaeologists, working for the United States government, concluded that the Ohio Hopewell mounds were actually the product of indigenous Native Americans should be evidence enough that anthropologists have not automatically supported the policies and practices of their colonial, capitalistic powers (Chapter 3). Correlation does not imply causation, and the simultaneous development of these social institutions does not necessarily indicate complicity. Perhaps anthropology did not develop to enable wealthy capitalists to exploit the world; maybe it developed out of the simple curiosity of a people (Western Europeans) who had become (through their conquests and technology) familiar with a world beyond their own continental borders. Maybe anthropology has more to do with curiosity and edification than with capitalism and exploitation.

Science's critics also assert more than guilt by association, and they level the charge that science is actually the storm-trooper of Western Enlightenment colonial capitalism whose aim is to search and destroy all ideologies that may threaten to breach the walls of this Western edifice. (See Johnson 1991:150). Creationist Phillip Johnson (1994) even adopts the social constructivist assertions that science is reduced to politics and ideology, and that creationism as another ideology has a rightful place alongside scientific explanation. Indigenous peoples have levelled the charge that anthropology has been merely the handmaiden of colonial powers (Deloria 1969). Shanks and Tilley (1987a:28) equate archaeology with colonial exploitation, and Pels and Nencel mince no words when they assert that "the image of the exploiting anthropologist cannot (yet) be dismissed as caricature" (1991:19).

These accusations and the attendant guilt that has followed them has led to a rash of self-flagellating and self-debasing accounts by anthropologists, amounting to a new version of the "white man's burden." Anthropological self-loathing has led one literary observer to label the new, postmodern anthropology, "Anthro(a)pology" (Chioni Moore 1994). He notes that an interesting phenomenon has accompanied the so-called West's recent discovery of the Other. It has inspired and rejuvenated literary criticism as literary critics are actively seeking out the Other, while in anthropology it has led to a retreat from the Other out of guilt over alleged exploitation. Chioni Moore (1994:354) laments this retreat since no one does better what anthropologists do.

Bruno Latour, famed and vilified ethnographer of science, takes a critical stance against the notion that scientists are in league with Western Euro-capitalism. He (1987:62) lambastes semioticians for being paranoid conspiratorialists and points out that social analysts' criticism of science is misplaced because they take control of science out of the hands of scientists and into the realm of mysterious social forces. "Our travel through technoscience should then be full not of microbes, radioactive substances, fuel cells and drugs, but of wicked generals, devious multinationals, eager consumers, exploited women, hungry kids and distorted ideologies" (Latour 1987:175). Latour actually proposes something more plausible, that the systematic biases that enter science are the result of the social struggles of scientists to generate enough support for their views in the interest of securing their often tenuous positions and advancing their careers. This dimension, amenable to scientific study, also has been suggested by postmodern-influenced anthropologists (Rabinow 1986:243, 1991; Vincent 1991). While I argue that scientists are a bit more selfless than this, at least Latour and Rabinow's proposition is testable and brings home any fault for not doing sound science to the scientists themselves.

So, in the end, there is no demonstrable smoking gun, no network of generals, no industry moguls, no clique of greedy rapacious males, and no network of satanists; there are only scientists. Scientists operate in a social world of academia that suffers from its own idiosyncratic constraints, and that world in turn is influenced by sources of funding, economic trends, and special interest groups; the whole mess is undoubtedly exacerbated by scientists' own baboon-like egos. However, the manners in which these forces influence science is as yet poorly understood, which is all the more reason to apply rigorous scientific methods to test the various theories people propose. Furthermore, improvements in scientific knowledge, both within and without anthropology, indicate that the methods scientists employ to study the world work against these constraints.

NON SEQUITURS: AN ACHILLES HEEL

Non sequiturs are most obvious in postmodern and critical perspectives on anthropology and science. Sandra Harding's argument, while providing much that is useful, ultimately is subverted by her assertion that because politics and perspective permeate all science, science necessarily must be a moral act. Harding asserts that sciences are "created through political struggles, the only ones we ever had" (1991:10). Furthermore, "science...is politics by other means" (Harding 1991:308), although she in the same sentence notes that science "can produce reliable empirical information." If science is just political argument, then how does it produce reliable information? Is the information reliable only in a particular political context? Or can scientists transcend politicized points of view and judge competing claims about the empirical world? Much of Harding's argument indicates the latter, invalidating her claims for a moralistic, emancipatory, political science.

Similar sentiments are made by critical anthropologists, who jump from the recognition that facts are theory-laden and cultural biases impact science to the notion that anthropologists must therefore embrace a political agenda in their research. (Rosaldo 1991:194; Shanks and Tilley 1987b:213) This conclusion is illogical. As Bernard emphatically states, "Objectivity does not mean (and has never meant) value neutrality" (1994b:173). The point is whether or not scientists conduct research in an un-biased (or at least minimally biased) way.

It [science] makes no claim to being 'value free.' Rather it proposes to overcome the inevitable biases of all forms of knowledge by methodological rules that insist upon opening to public scrutiny the operations by which particular facts and theories come to be constructed. (Harris 1994:64)

Critical analysts, who correctly point out that there is no such thing as value-free research, incorrectly conclude that we must embrace this and use research to advance a particular cause. This is preposterous. Bernard, citing Geertz (1973:30), notes that "just because perfect objectivity is impossible, this does not let us off the hook. The economist Robert Sarlow is reported to have observed that, while a perfectly aseptic environment is impossible, this doesn't mean we might as well conduct surgery in a sewer" (Bernard 1994b:172). What scientists choose to study often is influenced by what they perceive as problematic in the world. Furthermore, personal backgrounds and cultural biases may very well influence what scientists choose to observe and how they interpret it. Finally, once scientists have done research, they have little control over how it is to be perceived and the consequences it will engender (Vincent 1991:58). However, scientists do not have to be happy about bias. They could, as I argue and as Harding (1991) often argues in her work, choose to expose these biases and correct for them.

In a related vein, Shanks and Tilley's (1987a,b) assertion that because theories influence methods, scientists cannot discover novel information is also flawed. Yes, theories do influence methodology (the logical positivist's operationalization). However, nature does not have to conform, and often does not conform, to theoretical presuppositions. So even when scientists have instruments developed under a certain paradigm that bias them toward seeing certain kinds of phenomena, nature may very well thumb her nose at them and provide them with no or contradictory data. Bruno Latour (1987:98) goes beyond much of the criticism of science and points out that nature is also part of the process, and indeed an indispensable part. He uses a parliamentary analogy. Nature stands in the background, like Queen Elizabeth II, waiting for the muddling scientists to get their theoretical houses in order, just as the Queen attends the blusterings of legislators. However, in the end, scientists appeal to nature. If the idea is dumb and the technology unsound, it will be refuted in the real world. Reality serves as a check on just how far scientists can go with their social construction of facts.

These logical flaws expose the fact that what lies at the root of challenges to science is not necessarily competing views of the empirical world, but explicit and implicit political, ethical, and moral agendas. The above authors jump from reasonable statements regarding the shortcomings of science, directly to the predetermined conclusions about how they would like science to operate or not operate.

ETHICS AND MORALITY: THE ENGINE OF SCIENCE'S CRITIQUES

There is more to these attacks on scientific anthropology than simply competing views of reality; these critics each have their own political, ethical, or moral agendas that constitute their own grand narratives. Furthermore, these agendas are not dark, secret conspiracies—science's critics are usually up front about their agendas.

Creationists are quite honest about their agenda, which they primarily cast as a religious and moral project. Morris, ed. (1974:14–15) argues that there is a moral need for introducing creationism into our schools. He and others (Johnson 1991, 1994; Wysong 1976) lament the moral condition of today's youth, and they perceive that secular humanist education is to blame. Christian fundamentalism is the fundamental purpose of the creationism movement, and creationists have even produced a text, appropriate for secondary school teachers, to push this agenda (Morris ed. 1974).

Racialists thinly veil their agenda by invoking the scientific import of their research (Herrnstein 1973; Herrnstein and Murray 1994; Jensen 1969). However, their agenda is also rather up front, and they use their research to address issues such as public education, Head Start, the class structure of our society, and welfare. They conform to an agenda that sociologists label organic conservatism (Williamson, et al. eds. 1985). The basic elements of organic conservatism are that individuals achieve based on their biologically determined abilities, and that justice is served as people attain those statuses that biology, or God, has ordained for them. Those who attain great wealth have done so because they were born with the talents, especially intellectual ones, requisite for achievement. Any attempt to redistribute wealth, status, or opportunity disrupts the balance of this justice and creates strife; it goes against nature. Those who have not been so endowed need to learn to become content with their lot (Herrnstein and Murray 1994:551–552).

Postmodern writing is also critical writing. Ironically, Tyler denies the possibility of criticism while being totally critical of modernism; "This is not a critique, for in our time, which is the time of the GESTELL, there is no place for critique, no neutral topos from which to launch a critique" (1991:91). Nonetheless, he betrays his essentially moral agenda in other passages. Tyler (1991:91) immediately goes on to label science "hegemonic" and elsewhere he asserts that the "rhetoric of ethnography is neither scientific or political, but is...ethical" (Tyler 1986:122). Postmodern archaeologists are also committed to ethical action first. "A critical archaeology is value-committed, a willed personal act with the aim of transforming the present in terms of its conceived connection with the past" (Shanks and Tilley 1987b:213). The agendas postmodern archaeologists embrace include socialism, feminism, and nativist movements as the politically correct moral view to advance with their work (Hodder 1991a,b; Shanks and Tilley 1987a:14, 246).

The rhetoric of some postmodern ethnography is downright religious. D'Andrade (1995a:400) notes that postmodern and critical anthropologists use religious "god" terms, and Sangren (1988) provides a similar analysis. Postmodern authors exhort scientific anthropologists to abandon skepticism and methods of evaluation, and to embrace belief (Clifford 1986:121; Tyler 1991:85, 86). As I pointed out in part 1, the basis of religious belief is faith, and faith is the cornerstone of religion. This faith comes from the postmodern regard for man and his language as semi-sacred (Clifford 1986b:101; Marcus and Fischer 1986:vii; Shanks and Tilley 1987a:34–35, 55). This semi-sacred status of humanity, separate from animals, is similar to the notion of the Great Chain of Being, especially as manifest in the sixteenth and seventeenth centuries, in which man (and especially a nobleman) was a semi-sacred being (Collins 1989:11; Lovejoy 1936:186, 198, 206).

Analysts of postmodern thought have pointed out that, despite their advocacy of extreme relativism, they are united by certain ethics. Rabinow notes that politically active postmodernists have an ethic in which the "guiding value is the constitution of a community-based political subjectivity" (1986:257). D'Andrade points out that postmodern ethics make "strong claims to upper middle-class sensibility in esthetic matters" (1995a:407) and is therefore ethnocentric in its own right. I will treat the religious nature of critical anthropology in the next chapter, but I wish here only to point out that these critics' notion that they know better and need to fix morally wrong situations betrays the fact that they have made some very heavily valued decisions in their research.

In addition to this religious perspective, a properly critical anthropology should be a gentler and kinder anthropology. Tyler notes that postmodern ethnography "founds in the receptivity of 'listening to' and in the mutuality of 'talking with'" (1986:139–140). Scheper-Hughes calls for a "more womanly-hearted anthropology [that] might be concerned not only with how humans think but with how they behave toward each other, thus engaging directly with questions of ethics and power" (1995:409). I am glad that I did not make these totalizing statements.

All attacks upon anthropological scientific knowledge share a religious appeal to higher morals and see a proper anthropology explicitly and directly serving ethical agendas, despite the divergent morals and ethics held by anthropology's critics. Each critique, to borrow a term from postmodernism, has its own grand narrative. For creationists, it is the Bible. The racialists appeal to the organic conservative, grand narrative of biological determinism and justice seen as Natural Law. Finally, postmodernists and critical anthropologists both appeal to an essentially similar grand narrative that might be considered Marxist Enlightenment social democracy, the very culprits they often attack. This irony has not been lost on some analysts (D'Andrade 1995a:405; Nader 1995:427), and others note that the postmodern grand narrative is more hegemonic, essentializing, and totalizing than those they criticize (D'Andrade 1995a; Rubel and Rosman 1994:337; Sangren 1988).

THE SILVER LINING: WHAT CRITICISM CAN DO FOR ANTHROPOLOGICAL SCIENCE

I have certainly been critical of the critics, but this should not be construed as a total dismissal of their arguments. People rarely complain with no reason; an initial problem is usually at the root, and science is not wholly innocent of the charges levied by each of the critics described in this book. If scientists are guilty of some of these charges, they had better re-examine their own assumptions, rhetoric, and practice.

Creationist charges are a reminder that scientists are in the business of science, not of providing a new religion. The creationists aid scientists by pointing out where scientists are trying to be theologians, and not empirical scientists. It is O.K. for a scientist to wax philosophically, but he or she should clearly differentiate this from testing theories and generating data. Scientists should heed Phillip Johnson's remark that, "Falsification is not a defeat for science, but a liberation. It removes the dead weight of prejudice, and thereby frees us" (1991:154).

Those researchers concerned with racial differences in IQ also can help keep anthropologists on their toes. Anthropology, with its long, extensive, and intimate familiarity with people from around the globe has been the primary scientific body that has presented data to counter racialist claims of Western European superiority. Anyone who asserts that there has been a monolithic scientific conspiracy to cast certain races as inferior obviously knows little about anthropology's history—anthropologists have opposed racism with empirical data, refuting racist theories as they have arisen (D'Andrade 1995a:402). I do not think that anthropologists, postmodern or scientific, would want to jettison the very scientific basis that they have used to refute racist claims. Less biased IQ researchers nonetheless point out that some of those advocating social theories of IQ difference have not exactly held themselves up to scientific standards either (MacKenzie 1984; Plomin, et al. 1994; Turkeimer 1991), and this is something against which social scientists must guard if they want to keep the scientific high ground.

Postmodern critiques also hold much promise for those scientists willing to scrutinize their own practice and improve upon it. Indeed, the early anthropological postmodern writings used a rhetoric of support for anthropology's scientific mission.

> An awareness of a text's rhetorical dimension by its writer or reader is finally not at all subversive to sophisticated rather than absolutist standards of objective knowledge, but is an integral part of both generating and evaluating claims to objectivity. (Marcus and Cushman 1982:58–59)

The notion of reflexivity should be essential to doing good science; anthropologists should continually ask whether or not personal biases, cultural backgrounds, or institutional/social positions are unduly biasing research. Laura Nader (1995:426) uses an analogy with the physicist's recalibration of his or her instruments, and this is an apt way of looking at how scientists should use reflexivity, to recalibrate and recenter (not decenter) observations. Some of science's anthropological advocates have duly noted that science is the ultimate in revisionism for this reason (D'Andrade 1995b; Harris 1994; O'Meara 1989:358).

I already have advocated that postmodernists operationalize their concepts and then more systematically examine whether or not cultural biases have had a notable effect on anthropological science. If such systematic biases are not falsified, then scientists should consider how they might change their practices so as to be less biased. Are scientists simply providing elite Western male capitalists with the representations that they want to hear in order to justify the exploitation of Third World others? Can these representations be refuted? If so, how can scientists alter their science so that they not produce such biased accounts? These are the questions that scientifically minded anthropologists could address by heeding the postmodern criticism. In fact, social scientists already have developed methods of analysis appropriate to test these hypotheses, including the citation analysis of library scientists (Borgman 1990), and the graph theory and network analysis developed in sociology (Knoke 1982; Scott 1991). An investigation combining citation analysis with concerns over male bias in anthropology already has been done (Lutz 1990). Certainly there is room for more of this research, and room for scientists to learn from it. This situation easily extends to a consideration of minorities, the exclusion of Third World peoples, and other issues.

Scientific anthropologists have long engaged in such revision; just look at the revision of Neandertal humanity (Trinkaus and Shipman 1992), or the exposure of the Piltdown hoax. Adam Kuper similarly notes that in the context of the debate over the origin of the !Kung bushmen, "All the ethnographers with whom I corresponded were open to alternative interpretations of their material, eager to ensure that the record was accurate" (1992:67), despite the fact that these researchers came from very diverse perspectives. The point was not to push a political agenda, or to see who could produce the more inspiring text—the point was to get it right. Scientific anthropologists should not fear and certainly should not dismiss challenges. If scientific knowledge and methods are as powerful as scientific anthropologists claim, they should have little to fear and much to gain by being open to scrutiny. After all, scrutiny, healthy skepticism, and doubt are the moorings of science, not certainty, intolerance, and absolute truths.

Chapter 9

The Case Against
Crusading Anthropology

The Wise Man, when abroad,
Impartial to the world,
Does not divide or judge.

The Tao

There is no truth existing which I fear, or would wish unknown to the
whole world.

Thomas Jefferson

Whoever combats monsters should contrive that in doing so he does not
himself become a monster.

Friedreich Nietzsche

I do not wish to indict all advocacy or applied anthropology. To the extent that many in our society hold empirically incorrect stereotypes about the situations and people anthropologists study, and to the extent that through publications and teaching anthropologists argue against these empirically incorrect views, all anthropology can be considered advocacy; advocacy on the behalf of truth is not my target. The goal for most applied anthropologists is getting people (whether in governments, development agencies, or in society at large) to accept a more truthful version of either peoples' lives or the effect of policy decisions (Fluehr-Lobban, ed. 1991; Paine, ed. 1985).

I am not targeting this reality-seeking applied anthropology, although I will raise a few general concerns about how well anthropologists can engage in both scientific and policy-oriented research. My main concern is with the strident, moralistic calls-to-action that emanate from critical and postmodern anthropologists. This crusading approach is shared with other critics of scientific anthropology such as creationists and racialist conservatives.

Critical anthropologists would have anthropology serve their ethical, emancipatory goals (Scheper-Hughes 1995:410). Postmodern anthropologists argue that advocacy is a logical result of anthropological theorizing (Harries-Jones 1985). Creationists would have biological science employed in the spreading of their Christian morality (Morris, ed. 1976). Eugenicists would have bioanthropology directed toward breeding a superior human race (Ingle 1973; Carter 1972). All of these are cases of employing anthropology or pseudo-anthropology to advocate certain ethical claims and social programs. I argue that anthropologists should avoid these political/moral projects, both in the interest of generating sound knowledge and, ironically, in the interests of the projects themselves. The difficulties center around the biases inherent in any ethical/political/moral project and the role those biases play in subverting the testing of theories and assumptions. Without testing, people are free to make up and support any cherished theory. Support is easy to find; the world is a complex place and one can almost always find a study that agrees with a particular point of view. It is only when people admit the potential for fault and evaluate ideas with all relevant data that they can advance sound empirical knowledge upon which policy decisions may be made.

Since promoters of strident advocacy use the specter of an unfeeling and malicious science to attack scientific accounts, I will begin by debunking this myth. I will then provide an example of how applied researchers with apparently benign intentions easily subvert their own goals. Finally, in light of the history of applied research and its current ethical debates, I provide a discussion of ethics in the discipline, pointing out several ethical positions that involve minimal moralizing and maximal freedom of scientific research and scrutiny.

ANTHROPOLOGY AS WESTERN CAPITALIST PROPAGANDA—THE MYTH

Pels and Nencel assert that "classical anthropology hid its political projects: the responsibility for the creation and legitimization of professional anthropology and for the support of colonialism was covered with the cloak of the neutral and value-free study of cultural difference" (1991:8). Rosaldo (1991:169) likewise accuses scientific impartiality of being a mask that covers up the actual complicity of the anthropologist with imperial powers. This typification (may I call it a totalization?) of the entire discipline is simply untrue. Anthropologists, including scientific anthropologists, are usually on the vanguard of social critique. Marcus and Fischer (1986:128–131) offer a litany of cultural critiques in anthropology, including James Frazer's *Golden Bough*, Boas's critique of racism, and Mead's feminism. Harris notes that,

> Promoters of "critical anthropology" seem unaware of the fact that their ballyhooed substitute for an imagined morally neutral positivism has roots that go back at least as far as E. B. Tylor and his identification of anthropology as "essentially a reformer's science."...They seem unaware that science-minded anthropologists have a long history of contributing to the struggle against racism, anti-Semitism, colonialism, and, yes, even sexism...and all this before the generation of critical anthropologists had gotten out of grad school. (1995b:424)

I would add to this list the archaeological research of Cyrus Thomas that established a Native American connection to the Ohio Hopewell mounds, thereby challenging the view that Native Americans were incapable of such feats of civilization.

In reality, relationships between anthropologists and government agencies have been much more characterized by tension because anthropologists were out actually recording what goes on in colonized regions. Pels and Nencel's (1991:3–4) discussion of Malinowski's marketing of anthropology to colonial administrators is a good example of this tension; it is not complicity, as they suggest. Malinowski had the unenviable task of locating support from the Rockefeller Foundation for anthropology, and he had to appeal directly to those that anthropologists most often criticize. So, he delivered a selling job that would be the envy of most used-car salesmen. He asserted the scientific thrust of anthropology in describing reality and lamented that the romantic elements of anthropology must be subordinated to this scientific mission. He promised that the science of anthropology would yield laws of human behavior of practical utility to colonial administrators. Pels and Nencel (1991:21) note, however, that the Rockefeller Foundation was convinced by the promise of esoteric scientific knowledge, not by colonial utility. So where is the complicity here? Even evil capitalists seemed more interested in objective knowledge regarding the human condition than they were in the practical usefulness of anthropological knowledge in oppressing others. Furthermore, nowhere in Pels and Nencel's discussion do they indicate that Malinowski is promising colonial administrators a certain party line; he is just promising sound knowledge. Sound knowledge, as little tainted with bias as possible, can be used by anyone for their own purposes; or are we to think that non-Western Others are somehow incapable of using scientific knowledge for their own advocacy?

Adam Kuper has the following to say after reviewing the involvement of British anthropologists in African colonial affairs. While there were a few exceptions, he concludes,

> One characteristic of British functionalist social anthropology should be stressed. After Malinowski, the anthropologists based their methods upon participant-observation, which required intimate and free contact with the peoples they studied. They therefore had to break down the barriers of the colour bar, which existed in most colonies, and they had to challenge the basic, unspoken assumptions of all colonial régimes. Their individual examples of how sophisticated Europeans could happily adopt many tribal habits and live on a basis of friendship with illiterate and poor peoples constituted a constant irritation to settlers and many colonial officers. (1973:148-149)

Johan Helland (1985), Peter Harries-Jones (1985:230–233), and Eliot Fratkin (1991) provide examples of current anthropologist/government relations, indicating that the tension between neo-colonial governments and anthropologists has hardly gone away. These examples amply illustrate that anthropology has been anything but complicitous with capitalism and colonialism—related yes, but not its puppet. The relationship of anthropology to Western establishments resembles more the relationship of an eccentric aunt or uncle to an otherwise upstanding family than it resembles a favorite son; the family certainly has often been embarrassed by our comportment, and not infrequently disturbed. I will elaborate further the familial tensions, difficulties, and ambiguities of applied work in this next example.

THE INDIAN NEW DEAL: NAVAJO STOCK REDUCTION

The Navajo stock reduction is an example of a situation where people's ostensibly best intentions to "do good" subverted a plan to aid a people and an environment. The Navajo people (Diné) had been herding sheep, horses, and cattle on the Colorado Plateau for about three hundred years; and by the 1920s, they had become successful stockherders, fulfilling their expectations for a good standard of living, meeting their religious and social obligations with their economy, and socializing their young in the proper Diné ways of living (Dyk 1938; Bailey and Bailey 1986; Fanale 1982:103; Kelley and Whitely 1989; Schoepfle, et al. 1984a,b; Witherspoon 1973). Throughout history, Navajo stock numbers fluctuated widely in response to disruptions such as drought and snow, epidemics, and market influences (Bailey and Bailey 1986:101–102, 118, 120). During times of stock accumulation, non-Navajos often leveled the charge that Navajos were overgrazing the land, a trend that allegedly would spell environmental disaster for the Southwest in general and economic collapse for the Navajo themselves.

An engineering survey connected with the Boulder Dam in 1928 noted severe erosional effects from overgrazing and called for stock reduction to alleviate this ecological stress (Kelley and Whitley 1989:101). Government officials worried that if the western Navajo lands were overgrazed, this would lead to silting in the Colorado River that in turn would threaten the dam and therefore the electricity supply for growing western cities (Aberle 1966:55; Kelley and Whitley 1989:74). Consequently, officials in the federal government decided that the herds of the Navajo must be reduced in order to avoid this tragedy.

Aberle (1966) provides perhaps the most detailed summary of the events surrounding stock reduction, while Fanale (1982) provides important additional information. Stock reduction related to federal worries about Boulder Dam, as well as to the concerns of an emerging environmentalist movement whose members wanted to help the Navajo both govern and support themselves (Fanale 1982:330; Aberle 1966:55). The objectives of Navajo self-government and environmental conservation came together in the policies of Commissioner of Indian Affairs John Collier. Overgrazing and erosion were seen as threatening to the very existence of the Navajo people by these administrators, and they felt that it had to be stopped (Fanale 1982:330). The actual data regarding overgrazing upon which stock-reduction policies were based appears to be slim. "The basis for the report [on range conditions] was probably a two-week trip to limited areas of the reservation at the height of summer (when things tend to look worst)" (Fanale 1982:220). Furthermore, this view had its opponents, on the range and in the BIA, whose objections and pleas for involving local Navajo herders went unheeded (Fanale 1982:333).

Throughout the 1930s the federal government implemented several voluntary and forced reduction plans, and by 1940, stock levels were reduced by about half, the original goal of the program (Aberle 1966:70; Kluckhohn and Leighton 1962:75; Kelley and Whitley 1989:111). Stock reduction involved more than simply removing excess animals. In order to administrate and control Navajo herding, a series of grazing districts was established for the Navajo reservation, with the stipulation that herds could not move from one district to another (Fanale 1982:229).

These changes during the 1930s, the rapid elimination of one half of the Navajo's wealth in animals and the restriction of mobility, both made sense based on the knowledge possessed by conservationists about the range and Navajo land use. What, however, was the state of that knowledge? Officials conducted range surveys, some sociological surveys, and cartography of the reservation by 1936. However, all of this basic information gathering took place well after government officials had made the decision to reduce stock, and well after the initial stock reductions (Fanale 1982:227).

Government officials blamed Navajo herding practices for the decreased range capacity, while many Navajo herders noted that they were experiencing a temporary drought (Aberle 1966:87; Fanale 1982:310). Fanale (1982) presents data that strongly suggest that drought was the primary cause of range degradation. She combined long-term analyses of climate change using, archaeological research and nineteenth- and twentieth-century climate statistics, to establish that a drying trend began around 1920 (Fanale 1982:177). This cause, independent of Navajo grazing practice, was ignored by conservationists in 1928.

The knowledge held by Navajo herders, a knowledge base accumulated over three hundred years of experience with the range, also was ignored. Recent research among elderly Navajos and a renewed appreciation for Navajo autobiographies (Dyk 1938; Fanale 1982; Newcomb 1964) has uncovered both the character of traditional land use and its relationship to range ecology. Traditional Navajos based their land use for the most part on seasonal and local movements of livestock (Fanale 1982:106). However, long-distance movements were possible and easily made because of the complex system of kinship affiliation used by the Navajo, which guaranteed that one would have some kind of kin in nearly every part of the reservation. These kin were obligated to accept visitors (Fanale 1982:139). What emerges as traditional Navajo land use is a basically local system of mobility with a failsafe of regional movement based on clan kinship. Navajo Frank Goldtooth spelled out how this system worked.

> A homesite is not good when a family lives in the same place too long. The vegetation is tramped on too much, and it never gets a chance to grow again. Long ago, moving with the stock from one place to another was much better than what we do now. It gave the vegetation time to grow again. (Roessel and Johnson 1974:106)

Federal planners and ecologists ignored these ecologically sound practices of traditional Navajos. It is clear that, before understanding the dynamics of erosion and with no regard whatsoever for understanding what traditional Navajo land use was or how it operated, federal officials made their decision and implemented a regional fix to alleged Navajo problems. As Fanale states,

In the zeal and energy with which often well-intentioned conservationists and range technicians took to solving the problem of Navajo range degradation they acted quickly, taking few steps to listen to or come to understand the local point of view. (1982:217)

The establishment of grazing districts destroyed the system of mobility that permitted overgrazed range to rebound (Kuznar 1995b). With restricted mobility, people were forced to graze their herds on dry, gray, and unhealthy vegetation whether they wanted to or not. In this way, stock reduction led to a further degradation of the range (Fanale 1982: 218), a degradation that seems to have persisted since stock reduction, despite the fact that livestock never regained pre-1930 levels (Kelley and Whitley 1989:168).

Stock reduction appears to have had little or no effect on the range, but it had profound effects on the Navajo people. Almost overnight, half of their wealth was eliminated, and wage labor failed to replace the loss in wealth and income (Bailey and Bailey 1986:220). The Navajo economic system was radically transformed from one based on self-sufficient family herd production for markets to a system based on wage labor and public assistance (Kelley and Whitley 1989:115). Unfortunately, combined Navajo income from these sources is not enough to sustain a family, and the Navajo remain for the most part impoverished. Arguably, this grand, and at the time reasonable, experiment in social engineering was a failure from both a Navajo and an environmentalist perspective. This is a good example of why science must be maximally open to alternative theories while maintaining limits on the biases that come with agendas—even benevolent agendas. One may level the charge that this represents a by-gone era of social engineering, although Elliot Fratkin's (1991) research on development among East African cattle herders details a strikingly similar story. When people allow their ethics to guide their research, they stand a greater than normal chance of finding simply what they already suppose to exist; and what they have decided to find may not correspond very closely to reality. The remedy to such examples of poor research is not to abandon scientific skepticism, explicitness, and testing, but to embrace these principles more tightly.

DISCUSSION: ETHICS AND ANTHROPOLOGY

Rosaldo (1991:182) argues that before one can critique a social system, one must be involved (presumably in some political role) in it. He and others (Harries-Jones 1985:233; Marcus 1994:50; Sangren 1988:418) feel that the point of anthropology is culture critique. Hodder (1991a,b) and Shanks and Tilley (1987a,b) call for an activist archaeology. Even anthropologists who are not necessarily in the critical camp sometimes have utopian social goals for their science (Rappoport 1994; Vayda 1994), lending some credence to the notion of Enlightenment grand narratives in anthropological research. The question now before anthropology is most boldly asked by Scheper-Hughes when she calls for a

> new cadre of "barefoot anthropologists" that I envision must become alarmists and shock troopers—the producers of politically complicated and morally demanding texts and images capable of sinking through the layers of acceptance, complicity, and bad faith that allow the suffering and the deaths to continue.... (1995:417)

But should we? Whose side should we take? Furthermore, why are insiders any more honest than outsiders?

I am not arguing for a naive anthropology in which knowledge has no moral, ethical, or political consequences. That kind of naivete leads to involvement in governmental boondoggles and intrigues like the Navajo stock reduction or operations such as the CIA's Project Camelot in the 1960s (see Fluehr-Lobban 1991a), and it reduces anthropology to nothing more than the mere pawn of the politically engaged. The politically driven do not care for reality; they are ultimately driven by their own utopian visions, which include a peaceful world, efficient capitalist economies, environmental salvation, equitable wealth redistribution (capitalistic or socialistic), the assertion of the voices of the oppressed, or perhaps the elimination of those deemed evil. Utopias are not the object of science—the natural, experiential world is—and that is where anthropologists should concentrate their efforts. It is what we do best (Chioni Moore 1994:359; Marcus and Fischer 1986:117).

I also am not suggesting that applied anthropology is impossible, or that anthropologists should never become involved in politics. However, there are some serious problems with conducting such research, problems that most applied researchers fully realize (see Fluehr-Lobban, ed. 1991; Paine 1985). D'Andrade summarizes four problems with activist research, what he calls moral models, and they are:

> The difficulty in getting reliable identifications for basic terms, the tendency toward all-or-none thinking, the tendency toward monocausality and evaluative contagion, and the difficulty of changing a moral model. (1995a:407)

His first problem refers to the ambiguities of labeling many behaviors as either good or bad in the moral sense. This is not to suggest a radical moral relativism, but to point out that often one person's oppression is another's liberation. Generally speaking, applied researchers make moral pre-judgements that scientists cannot evaluate as morally right or wrong. Applied anthropologist Johan Helland (1985:29–30) suggests that moralizing is not an anthropologist's role. Anthropologists should not be as naive as Scheper-Hughes (1995) in taking up sides in political conflicts. Her naivete has led her to condemn some indigenous South African groups for actions that her very own beloved African National Congress commits (Kuper 1995). Is her Marxist fervor so strong that she is blind to what "her people" (note the paternalism, or should I say maternalism here) are doing? D'Andrade's second problem concerns the moral shades of grey that we encounter in our everyday lives. What if someone only oppresses a little? Are they only half bad? His third problem is discussed by Hammersley (1992) and involves the naivete of moral models, and the assumption that if only people would "do the right thing," everything will work out for the better. However, as the Navajo stock reduction example demonstrates, even those with the best of intentions are capable of creating much destruction and misery as experienced by the environments and the people they claim to help.

D'Andrade's fourth problem is the most scientifically troublesome—moral models are difficult to change. He notes that the essentials of Marxism as a moral model were first set down in the late eighteenth century, and these dictums have remained pretty much unchanged since. Proponents of the models credit support when they encounter friendly data and deny or discount contradictory data. This is very logical, given the sanctity of moral models; they are models to be believed and employed in practice, not to be scrutinized and heretically challenged in the scientific tradition. My point here is that anthropologists, already self-critical and reflexive, cannot allow moral models to dominate their discourse. When such moral models blind scientists and overly guide their research, the scientists commit blunders like Lysekoism and Piltdown. I am surprised that the postmodern authors, who so aptly (if not presumptively) identify others' grand narrative moralism, are so blind to how their own grand narratives predetermine their knowledge.

David Hakken (1991) provides a thoughtful reflection upon moralizing in anthropology in which he charges the discipline with "ethical confusion." He (1991:80) notes that many anthropologists have opted for moralistic codes based on a "categorical imperative" to act and think in certain given ways. He points out that this inevitably leads to moralisms, ethnocentrism, and biases that are "philosophical chimera." Far from arguing against ethics, Hakken (1991:90) argues that anthropologists must develop an "ethical culture" in the discipline where ethical concerns can be debated and considered, rather than ignored in favor of dogmas. Robert Paine (1985) noted a similar professional confusion over ethics in his review of an anthropological advocacy workshop. The moralisms of postmodern and critical anthropology are symptomatic of such ethical confusion and moralistic chimera.

Most anthropologists do think that anthropology provides useful information for making peoples' lives better. For example, H. Russell Bernard asserts that "We need to turn our skills in the production of effective knowledge—knowledge for control—to important problems: hunger, disease, poverty, war, environmental pollution, family and intergroup violence, and racism, among others" (1994a:25). So far, this is a standard, value-laden Enlightenment grand narrative, although Bernard goes on with an important qualification. "Social science can play an important role in social change by predicting the consequences of ethically mandated programs, and by refuting false notions (such as various forms of racism) that are inherent in most popular ethical systems." Note here the falsifying role performed by science in Bernard's scheme—science is not used for telling people how to live their lives, it is used to correct misconceptions about how the real world works, or how valued moral directives are likely to fail in the real world. Similar sentiments surfaced in Paine's advocacy workshop (Paine 1985:250, 252). "What, then, is the expertise that the anthropologist brings to these jobs? I imagine most of us agree that it is in the fields of cultural translation and social analysis (explaining behaviour, tracing the ramifications of decisions and the like)" (Helland 1985:29). Scientists here only inform, they do not dictate.

I am suggesting that anthropologists should aim to shed light upon societies and explain phenomena within them. It may often be the case that shedding light is not desirable for those who wish to oppress others. I am sure that Adolph Hitler would not have appreciated an anthropologist shedding light upon his machinations for the Holocaust. Here is the scientific anthropologist's dilemma—advocate and perhaps cover up, lie, and twist, or report as accurately and as honestly as possible (see Paine 1985:256)? D'Andrade (1995:405) notes that "What damages people is the way power is *used* and the way generalizations are *used*. And what helps people is the way power is *used* and the way generalizations are *used*." Scientific generalizations in and of themselves are neither good nor bad, just the way people choose to employ them. It seems to me that for the purposes of lasting critique, knowledge with scientific and objective backing would be much more persuasive than the rantings of a moralistic source. Is our aim the edification of others and ourselves, or preaching to the choir?

Any archaeologist could point out that today's powerful are almost certainly going to be tomorrow's oppressed (see Tainter 1988 for examples). What do we do if our oppressed others of today actually win their struggles? Are they then disqualified from being on the side of the "right." Today, much of the world community is appalled at Serbian depredations in the recent Balkan war, and Serbs are portrayed as barbaric, rapacious pigs. What happens, though, if they become the losers? They probably will not receive any better treatment at the hands of their victims, as Croats and Bosnian Muslims also have been implicated in massacres, mass rapes, and ethnic cleansing (Stiglmayer 1994). What if an anthropologist does an anthropological history and describes Serbs during the fifteenth century, when Ottoman rulers exacted a boy tax on Christian Serb families, taking their sons, converting them to Islam, then turning them into the feared Janissaries (Shaw 1976:113) who in turn massacred thousands of Serbs and ravaged their lands? Are the Serbs O.K. during that period of history?

One of anthropology's more divisive debates of the past decade has been over the ethics of covert and proprietary research. Carolyn Fluehr-Lobban (1991) edited a series of thoughtful essays that emerged from this debate. Reviewing some of the basic positions in this controversy will clarify where many anthropologists stand, and where my argument stands in relation. The turmoil of the 1960s resulted in two ethical/political controversies when anthropologists became involved in actual or planned CIA and U.S. military projects. Outrage at these covert operations resulted in the drafting of the American Anthropological Association's Principles for Professional Responsibility (PPR), which expressly prohibited clandestine and secret research and stressed that the anthropologist's first responsibility is to those studied (Fluehr-Lobban 1991a:29). This statement was weakened in the mid-1980s, and almost entirely removed (Fluehr-Lobban 1991a,b; Berreman 1991). Contributors to Fluehr-Lobban's volume generally agree that the emergence of a large, vigorous non-academic body of applied researchers in the 1970s and 1980s led to these proposed revisions (Fluehr-Lobban 1991b; Berreman 1991; Hakken 1991; Gilbert, et al. 1991). I want to focus on the two ethical principles that have aroused the most controversy: responsibility to people studied, and clandestine research.

One could argue that anthropologists' primary responsibility to those they study is for humanistic reasons (Fluehr-Lobban 1991b:221; Berreman 1991:58), or for practical reasons (i.e., without their trust, they will not cooperate; Gilbert, et al. 1991:202). Personally, I generally adhere to the ethic and the reasoning. However, there are potential pitfalls in this ethic. I already noted the first; if an anthropologist's responsibility is to a "people" and that people becomes powerful and oppressive, then does the anthropologist retract his or her responsibilities to those people? Strictly enforced, and Scheper-Hughes (1995) seems to advocate such a principle, this would limit anthropologists to studying only "downtrodden," or "good" people. However, should we not also understand the culture of the oppressors, as recommended by Laura Nader's (1974) "studying up"? What about groups that are not generally received as "good," like white supremacists? Are anthropologists not allowed to understand them? It seems to me that buying into this ethical principle limits who anthropologists can study, thereby limiting information that would be important in an applied project and potentially harming those for whom anthropologists advocate. Moralistic codes of conduct and crusades are not flexible enough to deal with life's realities, and they nearly always subvert their original intended doctrines. This is a very good reason, *from the perspective of the advocate and advocated*, not to advocate while collecting information and evaluating theories.

The other contentious issue is over clandestine or secret research. Berreman (1991) is very much upset that there no longer is a professional prohibition against clandestine research in anthropology—he saw this as a major reason for the original PPR and is concerned over the potential for anthropologists once again to become involved in covert government operations. I would supply a purely scientific objection that is guided not by an ethic of governmental distrust, but by the ethic of what seems to be good for producing sound empirical scientific information. Since science proceeds by the scrutiny of data and theories, it is imperative that science be a public endeavor, as stressed by scientific anthropologists (see Chapter 1). Public does not mean democratic; scientists are concerned with who is wrong and who is not; no vote should determine what stands as scientific knowledge. But if anthropologists are to scrutinize theories adequately, then they must first know what these theories are, and second, they must be able to bring to bear all relevant data to these theories. This requires that scientists be as public as possible in communicating their theories, data, and results. James Bell prescribes the following social situation for a maximally effective science.

> The importance of a social framework in which ideas can be asserted boldly, but also criticized severely, is best guarded by attitudes implied by refutationist method, attitudes that encourage people to assert bold ideas and yet be open to criticism of those ideas. (1994:292)

Any institutional approval of secrecy in research violates the scientific principle of open, public debate. Fluehr-Lobban (1991b:227) tries to circumvent this problem by differentiating clandestine (i.e., CIA spy research) from proprietary research (i.e., contractual research with social programs, tribal entities, etc.). I have to reject this dichotomy. Any body, whether it be the Federal Government, Alcoholics Anonymous, minority rights groups, or a drug intervention program, has proprietary rights over data; it owns the data and can keep it secret. Anyway you cut it, this hinders scientific practice.

The only consistent ethic that I could see with regard to this issue is one curiously uninformed by the ethics of emancipation or profitmaking. Anthropologists must support the scientific principle of free, public discourse, and we must support our practitioners in approving only of such research, since it is the only type of research that can contribute to a scientific understanding of the human condition. Fluehr-Lobban (1991:224–227) provides examples of rhetoric from various ethics documents in anthropology that suggest this ethical principle. Also, Gilbert, et al. (1991) stress that anthropologists must be upfront with clients about their desires to share data with colleagues; they advocate a "don't sign on the dotted line" approach in which anthropologists should avoid taking on contracts that will violate their professional ethics. Following these guidelines would eliminate the double bind in which anthropologists (academic a well as applied) find themselves.

Another issue in applied research is our social scientific prowess. Hammersley (1992) cautions that we may be overselling our abilities as social scientists. Auguste Comte called sociology the Queen of the Sciences, and noted that it would be the hardest of the scientific disciplines. I have to agree. The complexities of the social world are only beginning to be understood, and anthropologists' competing paradigms and lack of agreement upon basic terms indicate that anthropology does not have a normal science state of knowledge (Lakatos 1970). All of this uncertainty should give anthropologists pause in either claiming that they possess knowledge that clearly defines who is and is not to blame for society's ills, or that anthropological knowledge can surely lead to their resolution. This state of affairs is somewhat depressing, although anthropologists may take solace in that scientific understandings of human phenomena are the best empirical understandings going, and so anthropologists should assume the aspect of experts and authorities, albeit humble ones.

What is anthropology's role to be in all of this? I agree with Scheper-Hughes that anthropology should have plenty of "barefoot" anthropologists who are busy "witnessing." However, that witnessing should be as objective and as thorough as possible. Marcus and Fischer give anthropologists such a guideline and emphasize the unique qualities of anthropology when they suggest that,

> as ethnographers for whom human variety is a principal interest and any subjects are fair game, we are acutely sensitive to the ambivalence, irony, and contradictions in which values, and the opportunities for their realization, find expression in the everyday life of diverse social contexts. Thus the statement and assertion of values are *not* the aim of ethnographic cultural critique; rather, the empirical exploration of the historical and cultural conditions for the articulation and implementation of different values is. (1986:167; emphasis added)

To which I would add, this empirical exploration should be subject to scientific scrutiny. It is encouraging that scientific applied anthropology and the cultural critique of Marcus and Fischer differ little, indicating that there is room to resolve this division in anthropology today.

By providing the most balanced and representative and accurate accounts possible, anthropologists provide the world with sound knowledge upon which to base moral judgements. Harris asserts, "Moral decisions need to be based on the best available knowledge of what the world is like" (1995b:423), and Bernard adjures, "being right about what causes a problem is still the best contribution anyone can make to solving it" (1994b:176). This is not just a scientific point, but one that any person concerned with reality should adopt, since moral decisions ultimately must be enacted in a real world.

Scheper-Hughes asks, "To what end are we given and do we represent these images as long as the misery and the suffering continue unabated?" (1995:416). I would reply that the end to which we are given is science as outlined by anthropologists; that includes collecting representative and accurate data and testing theories that could potentially explain that data. The suffering that she laments (and that I find personally disturbing as well) *is* the human condition. Someone with her field experience among the poor in Brazil and South Africa should realize that the normal state of human affairs is not peaceful harmony. If we are to understand people (maybe even so we can inform effective interventions), then we need to record (represent) these images. This is the tough work of the anthropologist. Hopefully, if anthropologists do their work well, then people engaged in moral decision making will at least have good data and sound theory with which to make their policy decisions. Anthropologists must avoid moral chimera. In this way, we begin with the scientifically valid, and we may end with the politically (ethically) valid. If we begin with the political, all we ever will have are Nietzsche's metaphorical lies, and we will assume the aspect of his monsters.

Chapter 10

Where Do We Go From Here?
A Future for Scientific Anthropology

> *Dust as we are, the immortal spirit grows*
> *Like harmony in music; there is a dark*
> *Inscrutable workmanship that reconciles*
> *Discordant elements, makes them cling together*
> *In one society.*
>
> William Wordsworth

Anthropology must seem to be thoroughly rent at this point, with its own practitioners deconstructing it in an intellectual civil war that threatens to balkanize, if not totally destroy, the discipline forever. I have taken great pains to outline a scientific method now rejected by many, if not most, anthropologists. Scientific anthropologists seem holed-up in defensive citadels, while postmodern and critical factions have taken the field and are now beginning to snipe at one another. I hope, in this chapter, to outline a possible future for anthropology in which competing sides admit their respective faults and rhetorical atrocities, and begin to co-exist for one another's benefit. Chioni Moore, a literary critic, points out that,

> What anthropology must realize is that somewhere in *its* heterogeneity of historical practices must lurk *also* a more or less essential core, distinctive and massively productive....what anthropologists do extraordinarily—with

> a history, on-site tenacity, and physical commitment no other discipline
> can match—is watch, live, measure, interpret...not "text," but, well, life.
> (1994:359)

These are flattering words, respectful of anthropology's strengths. Perhaps
we have degenerated in our civil wars, and become too engaged with ourselves to be objective, to the point where outsiders are the only ones who
can see value in what we do; and ironically, those outsiders hail from the
literary camps that some anthropologists have chosen for dismantling the
discipline.

I suggest that anthropologists adopt, or better, reclaim, their actual scientific heritage and reconstruct the discipline around its tenets. The science
I advocate is not naive positivism, but a "neopositivism" (Harris 1994), that
benefits from a century of anthropological practice, as well as from philosophical debates on the role of evaluation, paradigms, research programs,
and sociological forces on scientific activity. This is a science in which anthropologists strive, although never fully succeed, to remain politically and
morally detached; it is a science in which anthropologists generate sounder
representations of reality that can be used for edification or for the application of policy; it is a science in which anthropologists sagely regard its genesis in modern industrial society and remain respectful of its knowledge
accordingly, neither worshipping it as Truth, nor nihilistically denying its
existence.

This chapter begins with a restatement of the tenets of scientific anthropology. It continues with a consideration of how social and cultural influences affect scientific practice. I suggest several hypotheses regarding these
influences that some ethnographer of science should test. I then will tackle
the thorny issue of ethics and advocacy again; the role of criticism within
the discipline also is reviewed. Finally, I suggest ways in which science and
non-science can complement one another for the overall benefit of the discipline. This may sound awfully hopeful and idealistic, even naive, or perhaps too late. I am sure some will accuse me of projecting my own utopian
grand narrative; if so, then in this narrow way, in my myopic concern for
what this discipline has to offer the human quest for knowledge, I am guilty.

WHAT WE SHOULD DO: A REALLY SCIENTIFIC ANTHROPOLOGY

Anthropologists have rarely made scientific standards explicit and have never agreed upon what those standards should be. This is, perhaps, because when the American Anthropological Association first stated a scientific goal at the turn of this century, philosophers were still developing what would become modern scientific epistemology, and also because there has always been a debate over whether or not science is a primary objective in anthropology. I propose that the following scientific method be the guideline for scientific anthropological research.

The first point upon which anthropologists must be clear is that we assume that, or at least act as if, there is a reality independent of us. Without this assumption, no research, whether it be a quest for truth or a culture critique, makes sense. Even though some postmodern anthropologists adopt an extreme relativist stance, I sincerely do not think that they mean it. Otherwise they would cease doing anthropology. Anthropologists act as though there is something external to themselves, so we should just admit that we assume it and get on with our work. An anthropologist's job is to understand the world as best as possible given cultural biases, perceptual peculiarities, and intellectual limitations. Assuming a reality, anthropologists must be clear about demarcation; they should differentiate scientific research from metaphysics, which includes ethics, moral issues, politics, and religion. Once again, this is crucial because scientific methods of evaluation are not useful for deciding metaphysical issues. So what issues can anthropologists address scientifically? First, any issue that is amenable to empirical study, and second, any issue that anthropologists can and are willing to find false. This excludes many ethical and political issues upon which people have already decided, as well as supernatural issues not amenable to an empirical test. Does this mean that anthropologists can only study physical phenomena? Of course not! Any phenomenon that can somehow be defined empirically, including people's religious ideas, social relationships, statuses, emotions, cognitive abilities, even altered states of consciousness, can be studied scientifically (Bernard 1994a,b; Furst 1990 [1972]; Hammersley 1992; Harner 1972; Harris 1979; Hunt 1995; Sandstrom and Sandstrom 1995).

Anthropologists must insist that theories deal with empirical phenomena, are explanatory and causal, and testable. I have already noted that *empirical* encompasses a wide range of phenomena, including everything from dietary requirements, birth rates, projectile points, economic exchanges, pyramids, altered states of consciousness, religious ecstacy, and feelings of rage in grief. Anthropologists should remember that scientists seek to understand the causal relationships of empirical variables to one another; otherwise there are only empirical generalizations, and anyone with a paper and pencil can come up with these. This involves positing theories in which certain variables are antecedent to others and to which the subsequent variables are dependent for their existence.

Finally, anthropologists must be able to deduce specific hypotheses from theories that predict specific states of nature so that they can then do further research to test the hypotheses and in turn the theories. This testing is absolutely crucial and represents, more than anything else, the hallmark of scientific research.

A scientist is not naive about this process from observation through testing. Positivists introduced the notion of operationalization, making explicit the theory-laden nature of data. Anthropologists use research questions to indicate what they should observe, and how and with what instruments. These research questions even may determine how researchers make instruments of observation. There is no way around this situation, and an informed scientist knows to be aware of the potential biases inherent in the operationalization of variables. Operationalizations and definitions need also to be treated as hypotheses that can be tested and revised, leading to even more appropriate instruments and observations (Bernard 1994a:31).

Another area in which a scientific anthropologist cannot afford naivete concerns the paradigms, or research programs that guide research. Paradigm has been used in a very general manner ever since Kuhn (1970) to incorporate everything from the general worldview of a group of scientists to the specific theories they seek to test. Research program, as used by Lakatos (1970), is more specific and refers to the sets of theories that guide scientific research upon some phenomenon. For instance, sociobiological research is guided by a research program aimed at testing theories of how animals compete for reproductive success. Lakatos (1970) offers further insights into how research programs are (and should be) evaluated.

The core theories of a research program are protected by a negative and positive heuristic, according to Lakatos (1970). The negative heuristic simply maintains that the core theories themselves are not directly tested. This is because they often are too all-encompassing to be refuted easily in some simple experiment. The positive heuristic indicates how the theories deduced from these core theories can be altered so as still to conform to the basic core. All of this may sound like a lot of gerrymandering to preserve some cherished theory or core belief, but an example will illustrate that this is not the case.

Animals compete for reproductive success, and male animals generally have much more potential for reproduction than do female animals. Such is a basic concept from evolutionary theory. However, what does one do if one finds an example where this prediction is violated? Lee Cronk's (1991, 1993) research on reproductive strategies is such an example. He found that among the Mukogodo of East Africa, females have higher expected reproductive success than males, and that mothers physically do not care for their male offspring as well as they do their female offspring. Does this falsify Darwinian theory? Hardly. Ethnographic examination of Mukogodo society demonstrates that the Mukogodo are a poor minority among more wealthy and economically powerful Masai. Both societies require bridewealth, making marriage a difficult if not impossible prospect for Mukogodo males. In polygynous Masai society, however, there is always a demand for wives, giving Mukogodo females the opportunity to marry up into Masai society and thereby secure greater wealth and security for themselves and their offspring. This is reflected in the higher reproductive success of Mukogodo females. Parents faced with the dilemma of choosing which children to invest in with their scarce resources (such as health care), focus on the children who will have the highest reproductive success (thereby enhancing the parents' reproductive success). So, parents are behaving in a manner entirely consistent with evolutionary theory, and a simplistic "males are better" theory needs to be replaced with a more sophisticated theory concerning parental investment. Such repeated tests will eventually challenge core concepts of evolutionary theory, as has already happened with respect to the pace of evolution, the role of chance in evolution, and the role of the individual vs. the group in evolutionary theory (see Gould and Eldridge 1977; King and Jukes 1969; Wilson 1975).

Adopting Lakatos's scheme, grand narratives such as Marxism can reasonably be tested provided that the teleology of historicism be abandoned. The most central ideas of Marx (constant value of labor, capital accumulation, existence of contradictions in capitalistic production) would not be tested directly. However, more specific theories could, using the positive and negative heuristic, be adjusted in concordance with general Marxist theory. In fact, this is what Marxist anthropologists largely have been doing. Eventually, as Marxist scientists generate a body of knowledge, they can then evaluate the limits of the core concepts. Such a use of explicitly scientific methods for evaluating Marxist theories of capital accumulation has been suggested in sociology (Sylvester, et al. 1981).

The important thing to note here is that should anthropologists find no way of resolving the data with the research program, then the program itself comes into jeopardy. If this happens consistently, then it is time for a new research program or paradigm. Lakatos (1970) provides a guideline for replacing a research program that logically guarantees progress—progress in the sense that theories will explain an ever-increasing amount of the real world in a theoretical manner. His guideline is that one does not replace a failing program until one has found a program that not only explains what the old one does, but that also holds the promise of explaining what the old program found problematic.

The scientific anthropology I have just outlined is a science in which anthropologists are sensitive to the issues raised by postmodern writers and critical theorists. It allows for diversity in paradigmatic approach since eventually, through its application, it would become apparent which paradigms are more fruitful than others. One should not expect any such unitary melding of anthropological science soon, however. Lakatos (1970) described the conditions under which mature sciences develop, and anthropological knowledge, with its eclectic mix of biological, historical, economic, Marxist, psychological, and other perspectives is clearly in his pre-scientific stage. We have a lot to work out, but then again, Comte did recognize social science as the hardest of all.

WE ARE ONLY HUMAN TOO: PRACTICING A SCIENTIFIC ANTHROPOLOGY

Should scientists be absolutely dispassionate and disinterested as they glibly witness and describe human sufferings and agonies, or the machinations of powerful groups extracting the products of the weak's labor? Anyone who advocates such a science should bear in mind two things: Weber's notion of rationalization and the humanity of scientists. Max Weber (1978 [1921]) criticized rationalization, the notion that problems will be solved by employing rules of decision making in formulaic and automatic fashion. Weber noted that this total rationality carried with it an irony—the irrationality of rationality (Ritzer 1993:22). Basically, the more institutions are rationalized, the less efficient they are at accomplishing the tasks for which they were designed. George Ritzer (1993) provides an amusing if not enlightening analysis of the many ways in which rationalization is manifest in modern society, from suburban planning to phone sex. Obviously, the concerns of scientists incorporate some elements of rationalization, such as the standardization of observations, the quantification of data when possible and appropriate, the ability to predict phenomena, and the denial of intuitive evaluation. Scientific anthropologists also realize that there are limits to rationalizing even the scientific process. Philosophers like Popper (1959 [1934]:31) and Bell (1994:259) do not discount the importance of intuition and inspiration in the discovery of ideas and data, and psychologists of science research the topic extensively (Tweney, et al. 1981). However, there are some areas of the scientific process for which rational principles appear to be the soundest, and this is in the evaluation of theories, regardless of their origin. The anthropological advocate of science Bernard maintains that "poetry that generates ideas and science that tests ideas are mutually supportive and compatible" (1994a:21).

Scientists are human too, despite their demonization by critics. Being human, scientists' lives are influenced by ethical, moral, and religious concerns. These concerns make up Habermas's (1968) human interest, and they do exert an influence upon scientific enquiry. The point I make is that anthropologists do not have to mandate that their science be relegated to the position of supporting interests. If one studies penal behavior in South Africa because one is disturbed by violent retribution, one must do two things to stand up to scientific muster: one must make observations as honestly, accurately, and objectively as possible, and one must hold one's theories up to the most rigorous scrutiny. Objectivity in anthropological science is never complete and is a difficult endeavor. It takes extreme discipline to be objective about any issue, let alone one about which a person is emotionally engaged.

This is a discipline called for by Max Weber in his support for the vocation of social science. Weber's (1958 [1922]) main point is that science must be approached with a devotion to the discipline, as a vocation, but he noted the irony that if people wish for a science that will address human concerns, they must pursue it in a most dour, professional, and disinterested manner. He (1958 [1922]:155) stated that attempts, all at once, to create great movements and to institute great changes, in a sense to prophesy, usually produce "miserable monstrosities....And academic prophesy, finally, will create only fanatical sects but never genuine community" (note Hammersley's 1992 doubts as well). This is why he urges scientists to put their noses to the grindstone, "to set to work and meet the 'demands of the day'" (Weber 1958 [1922]:156). These demands are scientific.

There also is the issue of the human conduct of anthropological science. Anthropology is unique among the sciences in many ways, one of which is the intimacy with which anthropologists study and come to know their subjects. Researchers in other disciplines at times attempt this intimacy, but as some point out, anthropologists do it best (Chioni Moore 1994). A scientific argument for such intimacy, through long periods of fieldwork, participant-observation, and living with subjects, is that it provides for more valid data. Sanjek asserts, "Anthropology speaks in the language of validity" (1990:395). This is a strength that also carries a special burden. Anthropologists are aware that their presence in small-scale societies influences their operation (Bernard 1994a:150; Pelto and Pelto 1978:177–192; Whiting and Whiting 1970:291). However, I want to focus on the influence of societies upon anthropologists.

We come to know, sympathize, and—through participant-observation—empathize with the conditions of our subject's lives. It is easy to remain detached while administering a mail or phone interview, as is common in many other social sciences. Typical anthropological research does not afford anthropologists such luxuries, and we should be thankful for that. Anthropologists come to know their subjects not as subjects, not as data points (with occasional outliers), but as real people. There are individuals that we come to like and love; there are others that we come to dislike decidedly. We have fights, disputes, controversies, joy, relaxation, sadness, and contentment with those we study. Anthropological fieldwork is, indeed, an emotional roller coaster for many anthropologists, something that demands its own discipline to survive. Given this intimacy, anthropologists are very susceptible not only to their own cultural biases, but to biases that crop up during fieldwork. These biases can be negative, as in the notion that amorality in peasant Italian villages makes them backward (Banfield 1958), or positive and romantic, such as Mead's (1961 [1928]) portrayal of Samoan adolescence. Our job as professionals is to be aware of these biases and to work toward minimizing their influence upon our work; when that is not possible, we must admit our biases openly. Anthropologists' emotions also can lead to insights, although these insights should then be subjected to rigorous scrutiny; they may lead to new explanatory theories, as in Rosaldo's (1991) rage in grief. This emotional closeness with subjects should make anthropologists all the more sensitive to their own biases, and the postmodern call for reflexivity, used judiciously, is a useful tool for honest, scientific fieldwork.

LIVING TOGETHER: ALLOWING TEXT, IDEA, AND SCIENCE TO WORK TOGETHER

I have presented a framework by which anthropologists could practice research that does not violate, and optimally utilizes, scientific methodology. Scientific anthropologists are not naive, but recognize the role of human interest, and they are skeptical about their own roles in professional networks. Hopefully, anthropologists will be able to identify and avoid biases in anthropology that emanate from these social influences. I also have noted that scientific research of an applied nature, or research designed to advocate some position, while very difficult, is not impossible if anthropologists keep in mind that evaluation is the key scientific principle to which they must adhere. Many of these notions are not new to social science, as citations from Comte and Weber clearly indicate, although many of these notions are advocated forcefully by recent critics of science. This is hopeful; perhaps we have been singing the same song all along, just in different keys.

One of the watchwords of postmodernism is reflexivity, and I argue that anthropologists should make this, and in fact have made this, a central part of their science as well. A reflexive scientist would recognize his or her role in constituting a representation of a culture. This involves careful evaluation of the influence researchers have on the people they study, and the influence that our personal and social relationships with those people have on the data we gather. All of these concerns are ultimately concerns with data quality. Since science is an empirical enterprise, concern with the quality of data is no trivial matter.

Another form of reflexivity that benefits scientific anthropology is reflection upon how biases have preconceived anthropologists' impression of a society and perhaps biased observations. The question anthropologists need to ask is, "Are the observations objective?" Ironically, the postmodern attack upon science for lack of reflexivity is an attack on the lack of validity (i.e., objectivity) of some scientific research. The ironic postmodern concern with objectivity is one that should (and generally does) consume science. Comte (1974 [1855]:474) first recognized that facts are theory-laden, and knowing scientists have ever since heeded the dangers inherent in this situation. One means of limiting the biasing effects of facts being theory-laden is to treat all theories, hypotheses, definitions, and even observations as hypotheses that must be tested, and that, surviving scrutiny, need further corroboration before provisionally being accepted as scientific fact. Of course, with improved (i.e., more objective) perspectives, or instruments of observation, the facts can change, but only if their improved accuracy and objectivity is ultimately empirically demonstrable. In the end, a scientific use of reflexivity will provide for more valid data, a condition for robust theory testing.

Postmodern and critical anthropology likewise reinforce a recognition that anthropologists practice science in a social and cultural context that potentially influences what they do and how they do it. Some of these influences can be very general and ideological, such as the notion of male superiority, the assumption of universal subjugation of women, the value of liberal democracy, or the all-pervasiveness of capitalistic hegemony. My criticism of postmodern and critical uses of these notions and other grand narratives like them is that they are uncritical and not operationalized. These concepts, as ideological as they are, are amenable to scientific scrutiny; and to the extent that they seem reasonable, they should be investigated scientifically. This would involve operationally defining the concepts in some manner; it also would involve monitoring them in some way. Given that they are ideological entities, anthropological methods of open-ended questioning and appreciation for context make anthropology the one discipline best situated to study these phenomena scientifically. Finally, and most importantly, the postmodernists and critical anthropologists have postulated a number of ways that grand narratives may influence anthropological work, from the male ignorance of women's lives (Harding 1991; Morgen 1990; Zimbalist-Rosaldo and Lamphere 1974) to the justification of capitalism and colonialism (Asad 1973; Marcus and Fischer 1986; Rabinow 1986; Said 1978; Shanks and Tilley 1987a,b; Tyler 1991). The presence and effect of these postulated grand narratives should be tested.

The role of social relationships and networks is an area developed by the critic Bruno Latour (1987), and discussed by others (Harding 1991; Rabinow 1991; Vincent 1991). This is an area very amenable to scientific research, if critics so choose. Latour notes that his six general principles of scientific practice should be "debated, falsified, replaced by other summaries" (1987:17). The tools for such research have been developed by sociologists (Knoke and Kuklinski 1982), and have even begun to be applied to anthropology (Lutz 1990). I would suggest also that we apply a little old-fashioned ethology to ourselves. I always have been impressed at the baboon-like posturing (verbal and physical) of anthropologists. Primatologists have traveled to far-flung jungles and savannas around the world to observe behaviors that appear to me to be regularly manifest among our very own kind—Homo anthropologicus. We should investigate seriously how rhetorical devices are used to shut off discussion, or to avoid dispute, or to tweak a rival into an emotional retort. Perhaps we have learned more than we suspect by studying our nearest relatives.

Postmodern concerns with the crisis of representation also can benefit a scientific anthropology tremendously, and I would argue these concerns are not as routinely ignored as science's critics suggest. Anthropologists always have agonized over how to represent other societies. Much research has been conducted on what data anthropologists should record (Geertz 1973; Harris 1979; Levi-Strauss 1963), how anthropologists should record data (Joukowsky 1980; Pelto and Pelto 1978; Spradley 1979, 1980; Werner and Schoepfle 1987), and how they should analyze and interpret data (Bernard 1994a; Geertz 1973; Harris 1979; Levi-Strauss 1963; Watson, et al. 1984). These are concerns with representation. While not new, the postmodern and critical concerns are worthy of consideration. Part of any scientific discipline's vigilance involves constant questioning of the validity of its concepts, how it measures them, and whether or not its data is representative. Certainly, feminist concerns over the lack of women and women's views in anthropological science (Friedl 1984 [1975]; Harding 1991; Martin and Voorhies 1975; Morgen 1990; Zimbalist-Rosaldo and Lamphere 1974) are concerns over the representativeness of data on the human condition. Once again, these issues are amenable to scientific scrutiny, and some of us should heed the call of critics for a science of our science (Harding 1991:15), test whether or not such biases exist, and elucidate their effects on our discipline's science.

Finally, all critics of scientific anthropology benefit it by circumscribing and defining what science is. This includes serving as negative or flawed examples of science, or by pointing out science's logical and empirical limits. Negative examples include the racialist researchers who attempt to screen their moralistic and political agenda with a cloak of scientism. Also, the simplistic view of science held by some creationists as an inductive truth-seeking endeavor helps scientists to see what they should not do. Creationists also, through their attacks on scientific anthropology, point out the logical limits of scientific enquiry. Namely, these involve the notion that science, creationist or evolutionary, cannot logically be used to advocate or refute metaphysics. Postmodernists also aid this demarcation by pointing out that science should not be involved in the advocacy of utopian grand narratives.

This discussion so far may have seemed rather narcissistic since I have concentrated on what critics can do for science. But this is a two-way street, a hermeneutic if you will, and science can reciprocate these benefits by providing its critics with more than just a target for their criticism.

I am not sure that creationists have much to gain from science. This is because they are explicitly religious and faith-based in their enquiry. Respecting that, I would suggest that they do not need any science at all. They have a set of beliefs and a text that embodies that set of beliefs. I see the creationist attempt at engaging science as a distraction from their essentially moral crusade. Racialist researchers have much to gain from science, provided they are willing to suspend their political agenda and honestly test their theories and scrutinize the operationalization of their variables. Indeed, some researchers in race and IQ are attempting to do this (Hunt 1995; MacKenzie 1984; Plomin et al. 1994; Turkeimer 1991).

Many postmodern and critical theory criticisms are nearly testable hypotheses in and of themselves. If postmodernists and critical theorists are concerned with their ethical agendas, then I would hope that they would accept some realism (and some do), and with it the notion of testing their hypotheses. Some critics (Harding 1991; Latour 1987; Sangren 1988) have already called for such studies. I would hope that careful and reflective scientific analysis of postmodernists' own grand narratives would be welcome, and that they would accept the alteration of views that are not consistent with reality in favor of more powerful explanations. I think that this sense of criticism is desirable, and indeed is advocated by anthropology's critics of scientism such as Clifford Geertz. Geertz suggests that the "disarray [of anthropology] may not be permanent, because the anxieties that provoke it may prove masterable with a clearer recognition of their proper origin;" anthropology must "adjust itself to a situation in which its goals, its relevance, and its procedures are all questioned" (1988a:138–139). My assertion in this book is that scientific anthropologists have always done this to an extent, and furthermore that scientists are eminently capable of conducting such revisions.

I have endeavored in this chapter to provide a view of the future, an admittedly optimistic, although not very utopian view. I have pointed out numerous flaws in the arguments of scientific anthropology's critics, and I have labored to evaluate their arguments in context. At the same time, I have tried to "absorb what is useful," not to arrive at a mediocre compromise that satisfies no one's arguments, but to evaluate their arguments fairly and to admit when science has failed in its actual objectives or practice. I hope that this chapter has demonstrated that there is something useful to absorb from scientific anthropology's critics. Furthermore, I have pointed out that many criticisms are not novel, and that scientists already have debated, discussed, and regarded many of these issues. In this way, debating anthropologists have been singing the same tune, just in different keys and in different tempos. It is time that anthropologists orchestrate their rhetoric and practice, and look for harmonies that do exist. The future anthropology for which I argue would overcome these debates as much as possible. There will remain some arguments that are not reconcilable, some discordant phrases here and there; and anthropologists will have to live with them. As computer simulators have discovered, tonally perfect music is boring—it is the slight imperfections in tone and timbre that make a piece of music rich and pleasing to the ear, and beautiful music lies between cacophony and perfection. Anthropology should center, and orchestrate around a principal theme, the quest for understanding the human condition using scientific principles, yet be tolerant of the discordance that will, in the end, make it rich and meaningful. I wish the best of luck to us all.

References Cited

Aberle, David F.
  1966 The Peyote Religion among the Navajo. Chicago: University of
    Chicago Press.
  1987 What Kind of Science is Anthropology? American Anthropolo-
    gist 89:551–566.

Aiello, Leslie C., and Peter Wheeler
  1995 The Expensive-Tissue Hypothesis: The Brain and the Digestive
    System in Human and Primate Evolution. Current Anthropology
    36:199–222.

Arnold, Dean
  1993 Ecology and Ceramic Production in an Andean Community.
    Cambridge: Cambridge University Press.

Asad, Talal
  1973a Introduction. *In* Anthropology and the Colonial Encounter.
    Talal Asad, ed. Pp. 9–19. Atlantic Highlands, NJ: Humanities
    Press.
  1973b Two European Images of Non-European Rule. *In* Anthropol-
    ogy and the Colonial Encounter. Talal Asad, ed. Pp. 103–118.
    Atlantic Highlands, NJ: Humanities Press.

Asad, Talal, ed.
    1973 Anthropology and the Colonial Encounter. Atlantic Highlands, NJ: Humanities Press.

Asch, David L., Kenneth B. Farnsworth, and Nancy B. Asch
    1979 Woodland Subsistence and Settlement in West Central Illinois. *In* Hopewell Archaeology: The Chillicothe Conference. D. Brose and N. Greber, eds. Pp. 80–85. Kent, OH: Kent State University Press.

Ayer, A. J.
    1959 [1936–37] Verification and Experience. *In* Logical Positivism. A. J. Ayer, ed. Pp. 228–243. New York: The Free Press.

Ayer, A.J. ed.
    1959 Logical Positivism. New York: The Free Press.

Bacon, Sir Francis
    1960 [1620] The New Organon and Related Writings. Fulton H. Anderson, ed. Indianapolis: Bobbs-Merrill Company, Inc.

Bailey, F. G.
    1991 The Prevalence of Deceit. Ithaca: Cornell University Press.

Bailey, Garrick, and Roberta Glenn Bailey
    1986 A History of the Navajos. Santa Fe: School of American Research Press.

Banfield, Edward C.
    1958 The Moral Basis of a Backward Society. New York: The Free Press.

Baudrillard, J.
    1983a In the Shadow of the Silent Majority. New York: Semiotext(e).
    1983b Simulations. New York: Semiotext(e).
    1987 Forget Foucault, Forget Baudrillard. New York: Semiotext(e).

Bell, James

>   1982 Archaeological Explanation: Progress through Criticism. *In*
>   Theory and Explanation in Archaeology: The Southampton
>   Conference. C. Renfrew, M. Rowlands, and B. Segraves, eds. Pp.
>   65–72. New York: Academic Press.

>   1987 Rationality Versus Relativism: A Review of 'Reading the Past'
>   by Ian Hodder. Archaeological Review of Cambridge 6:75–86.

>   1994 Reconstructing Prehistory. Philadelphia: Temple University
>   Press.

Bender, Barbara, and Brian Morris

>   1991 Twenty Years of History, Evolution, and Social Change in
>   Hunter-Gatherer Studies. *In* Hunters and Gatherers, Vol. 1:
>   History, Evolution and Social Change. Tim Ingold, David Riches,
>   and James Woodburn, eds. Pp. 4–14. New York: Berg.

Bernard, H. Russell

>   1994a Research Methods in Anthropology, Second Edition: Qualita-
>   tive and Quantitative Methods. Thousand Oaks, CA: Sage.

>   1994b Methods Belong to All of Us. *In* Assessing Cultural Anthro-
>   pology. R. Borofsky, ed. Pp. 168–179. New York: McGraw-Hill,
>   Inc.

Berreman, Gerald D.

>   1991 Ethics versus "Realism" in Anthropology. *In* Ethics and the
>   Profession of Anthropology. Carolyn Fleuhr-Lobban, ed. Pp. 38–
>   71. Philadelphia: University of Pennsylvania Press.

Bicchieri, M. G.

>   1972 Preface. *In* Hunters and Gatherers Today. M. G. Bicchieri, ed.
>   Pp. iii–vii. New York: Holt, Rinehart and Winston.

Bicchieri, M. G., ed.

>   1972 Hunters and Gatherers Today. New York: Holt, Rinehart and
>   Winston.

Binet, A., and T. Simon
    1911 A Method of Measuring the Development of the Intelligence of
        Young Children. Lincoln, IL: Courier.

Binford, Lewis R.
    1967 Smudge Pits and Smoking Pots: The Use of Analogy in Ar-
        chaeological Reasoning. American Antiquity 32:1–12.
    1971 Mortuary Practices: Their Study and Their Potential. In Ap-
        proaches to the Social Dimensions of Mortuary Practices. James
        A. Brown, ed. Pp. 6–29. Society for American Archaeology
        Memoir 24.
    1977 Introduction. In For Theory Building in Archaeology. New
        York: Academic Press.
    1978 Nunamiut Ethnoarchaeology. New York: Academic Press.
    1982 Objectivity-Explanation-Archaeology 1981. In Theory and
        Explanation in Archaeology: The Southampton Conference. C.
        Renfrew, M. Rowlands, and B. Segraves, ed. Pp. 125–138. New
        York: Academic Press.
    1983 Working at Archaeology. New York: Academic Press.

Binford, Lewis R., and Jeremy Sabloff
    1982 Paradigms, Systematics, and Archaeology. Journal of Anthropo-
        logical Research 38:137–153.

Bloor, David
    1977 Knowledge and Social Imagery. London: Routledge and Kegan
        Paul.

Blum, Jeffrey M.
    1978 Pseudoscience and Mental Ability: The Origins and Fallacies of
        the IQ Controversy. New York: Monthly Review Press.

Boas, Franz
    1940 Race, Language and Culture. New York: Macmillan and
        Company.

Borgman, Christine L., ed.
   1990 Scholarly Communication and Bibliometrics. Newbury Park,
       CA: Sage.

Bourdieu, Pierre
   1977 Outline of a Theory of Practice. Cambridge: Cambridge
       University Press.
   1990 In Other Words: Essays Toward a Reflexive Sociology.
       Stanford: Stanford University Press.
   1991 Language and Symbolic Power. Cambridge: Harvard Univer-
       sity Press.

Boyd, Robert, and Peter J. Richerson
   1985 Culture and Evolutionary Process. Chicago: University of
       Chicago Press.

Bridgman, Percy
   1961 [1927] The Logic of Modern Physics. New York: Macmillan.

Broad, C. D.
   1972 [1914] Perception, Physics, and Reality. New York: Russell and
       Russell.

Brose, David S.
   1979 An Interpretation of the Hopewellian Traits in Florida. *In*
       Hopewell Archaeology: The Chillicothe Conference. D. Brose
       and N. Greber, eds. Pp. 141–149. Kent, OH: Kent State Univer-
       sity Press.

Brose, David S., and N'omi Greber, eds.
   1979 Hopewell Archaeology: The Chillicothe Conference. Kent, OH:
       Kent State University Press.

Brown, James A.
    1979 Charnel Houses and Mortuary Crypts: Disposal of the Dead in
        the Middle Woodland Period. *In* Hopewell Archaeology: The
        Chillicothe Conference. D. Brose and N. Greber, eds. Pp. 211–
        219. Kent, OH: Kent State University Press.

Brown, Judith K.
    1970. A Note on the Division of Labor by Sex. American Anthro-
        pologist 72:1073–1078.

Buckley, Thomas, and Anna Gottlieb
    1988. A Critical Appraisal of Theories of Menstrual Symbolism. *In*
        Blood Magic: The Anthropology of Menstruation. Thomas
        Buckley and Anna Gottlieb, ed. Pp. 1–50. Berkeley: University
        of California Press.

Buikstra, Jane
    1979. Contributions of Physical Anthropologists to the Concept of
        Hopewell: A Historical Perspective. *In* Hopewell Archaeology:
        The Chillicothe Conference. D. Brose and N. Greber, eds. Pp.
        220–233. Kent, OH: Kent State University Press.

Burch, Ernest S., Jr.
    1991. Modes of Exchange in North-west Alaska. *In* Hunters and
        Gatherers, Vol. 2: Property, Power and Ideology. Tim Ingold,
        David Riches, and James Woodburn, eds. Pp. 95–109. New York:
        Berg.

Carnap, Rudolf
    1959 [1932] The Elimination of Metaphysics through Logical
        Analysis of Language. *In* Logical Positivism. A. J. Ayer, ed. Pp.
        60–81. New York: The Free Press.
    1974. An Introduction to the Philosophy of Science. M. Gardner, ed.
        New York: Basic Books.

Carrithers, Michael
   1990. Is Anthropology Art or Science? Current Anthropology
      31:263–282.

Carroni-Long, E. L.
   1996. Human Science. Anthropology Newsletter 37(1):52.

Carter, C.
   1972 The Galton Lecture 1971: The New Eugenics? *In* Population
      and Pollution, Proceedings of the Eighth Annual Symposium of
      the Eugenics Society London 1971. London: Academic Press.

Cashdan, Elizabeth
   1985 Coping with Risk: Reciprocity among the Basarwa of Northern
      Botswana. Man 20:454–474.

Cavalli–Sforza, L. Luca, Paolo Menozzi, and Alberto Piazza
   1994 The History and Geography of Human Genes. Princeton:
      Princeton University Press.

Chagnon, Napoleon, and William Irons, eds.
   1979 Evolutionary Biology and Human Behavior: An Anthropologi-
      cal Perspective. North Scituate, MA: Duxbury Press.

Chamberlain, T. C.
   1904 The Methods of the Earth Sciences. Popular Science Monthly
      66:66–75.

Chang, Claudia
   1984 The Ethnoarchaeology of Herding Sites in Greece. MASCA
      Journal 3:44–48.

Charles, Douglas
   1992 Woodland Demographic and Social Dynamics in the American
      Midwest: Analysis of a Burial Mound Survey. World Archaeology
      24:175–197.

Chioni Moore, David
1994 Anthropology is Dead, Long Live Anthro(a)pology:
Poststructuralism, Literary Studies, and Anthropology's "Nervous
Present." Journal of Anthropological Research 50:345–366.

Clastres, Pierre
1972 The Guayaki. *In* Hunters and Gatherers Today. M. G. Bicchieri,
ed. Pp.138–174. New York: Holt, Rinehart and Winston.

Clifford, James
1983 On Ethnographic Authority. Representations 1:118–146.
1986a Introduction: Partial Truths. *In* Writing Culture: The Poetics
and Politics of Ethnography. James Clifford and George E.
Marcus, eds. Pp. 1–26, Berkeley: University of California Press.
1986b On Ethnographic Allegory. *In* Writing Culture: The Poetics
and Politics of Ethnography. James Clifford and George E.
Marcus, eds. Pp. 98–121, Berkeley: University of California
Press.

Clifford, James, and George E. Marcus, eds.
1986 Writing Culture: The Poetics and Politics of Ethnography.
Berkeley: University of California Press.

Collins, Stephen L.
1989 From Divine Cosmos to Sovereign State. Oxford: Oxford
University Press.

Comte, Auguste
1974 [1855] The Positive Philosophy of Auguste Comte. New York:
AMS Press, Inc.
1957 [1857] A General View of Positivism. New York: Robert
Speller and Sons.

Coon, Carelton S.
1965 The Living Races of Man. New York: Alfred A. Knopf.

Cronk, Lee
  1991 Intention Versus Behavior in Parental Sex Preferences among
    the Mukogodo of Kenya. Journal of Biosocial Science 23:229–
    240.
  1993 Parental Favoritism toward Daughters. American Scientist
    81:272–279.

D'Andrade, Roy
  1995a Moral Models in Anthropology. Current Anthropology
    36:399–408.
  1995b What Do You Think You're Doing? Anthropology Newsletter
    36:1, 4.

Dahlberg, Frances
  1981a Preface. *In* Woman the Gatherer. F. Dahlberg, ed. Pp. ix–xi.
    New Haven: Yale University Press.
  1981b Introduction. *In* Woman the Gatherer. F. Dahlberg, ed. Pp. 1–
    33. New Haven: Yale University Press.

Dahlberg, Frances, ed.
  1981 Woman the Gatherer. New Haven: Yale University Press.

Damatta, Robert
  1994 Some Biased Remarks on Interpretivism: A View from Brazil.
    In Assessing Cultural Anthropology. R. Borofsky, ed. Pp. 119–
    132. New York: McGraw-Hill, Inc.

Dawkins, Richard
  1976 The Selfish Gene. New York: Oxford University Press.

Deloria, Vine
  1969 Custer Died for Your Sins: An Indian Manifesto. New York:
    Macmillan.

Derrida, Jaques
  1976 Of Grammatology. G. C. Spivak, trans. Baltimore: Johns
    Hopkins University Press.

Deuel, Thorne
   1952 The Hopewellian Community. *In* Hopewellian Communities in
      Illinois. T. Deuel, ed. Pp. 253–265. Springfield: Illinois State
      Museum Scientific Papers Volume 5.

Deuel, Thorne, ed.
   1952 Hopewellian Communities in Illinois. Springfield: Illinois State
      Museum Scientific Papers Volume 5.

Deutscher, I., ed.
   1973 What We Say/What We Do: Sentiments and Acts. Glenview, IL:
      Scott Foresman and Co.

Diamond, Jared
   1994 Race without Color. Discover 15:83–91.

Duhem, Pierre
   1976 [1906] Physical Theory and Experiment. *In* Can Theories be
      Refuted?: Essays on the Duhem–Quine Thesis. Sandra Harding,
      ed. Pp. 1–40. Dordrecht: D. Reidel Publishing Co.

Dyk, Walter
   1938 Son of Old Man Hat. New York: Harcourt, Brace, Janovich.

Earle, Timothy K., and Robert W. Preucel
   1987 Processual Archaeology and the Radical Critique. Current
      Anthropology 28:501–538.

Ember, Carol
   1978 Myths about Hunter-Gatherers. Ethnology 18:439–448.

Endicott, Kirk
   1991 Property, Power and Conflict among the Batek of Malaysia. *In*
      Hunters and Gatherers, Vol. 2: Property, Power and Ideology.
      Tim Ingold, David Riches, and James Woodburn, eds. Pp. 110–
      127. New York: Berg.

Fanale, Rosalie
  1982 Navajo Land and Land Management: A Century of Change.
    Ann Arbor: University Microfilms.

Feder, Kenneth L.
  1990 Frauds, Myths and Mysteries: Science and Pseudoscience in
    Archaeology. Mountain View, CA: Mayfield.

Feyerabend, Paul
  1978. Against Method. London: Verso.

Fitting, James E.
  1979 Middle Woodland Cultural Development in the Straits of
    Mackinac Region: Beyond the Hopewell Frontier. *In* Hopewell
    Archaeology: The Chillicothe Conference. D. Brose and N.
    Greber, eds. Pp. 109–112. Kent, OH: Kent State University
    Press.

Fluehr-Lobban, Carolyn
  1991a The Present Crisis and Its Historical Antecedents. *In* Ethics
    and the Profession of Anthropology. Carolyn Fluehr-Lobban, ed.
    Pp. 15–35. Philadelphia: University of Pennsylvania Press.
  1991b Ethics and Anthropology in the 1990s and Beyond. *In* Ethics
    and the Profession of Anthropology. Carolyn Fluehr-Lobban, ed.
    Pp. 213–236. Philadelphia: University of Pennsylvania Press.

Fluehr-Lobban, Carolyn, ed.
  1991 Ethics and the Profession of Anthropology. Philadelphia:
    University of Pennsylvania Press.

Ford, Richard I.
  1979 Gathering and Gardening: Trends and Consequences of
    Hopewell Subsistence Strategies. *In* Hopewell Archaeology: The
    Chillicothe Conference. D. Brose and N. Greber, eds. Pp. 234–
    238. Kent, OH: Kent State University Press.

Foucault, Michel
    1972 The Archaeology of Knowledge. New York: Pantheon Books.
    1977 Discipline and Punish: The Birth of the Prison. New York:
        Pantheon.
    1978 The History of Sexuality, Volume I: An Introduction. New
        York: Vintage Books.
    1980 Power/Knowledge. Colin Gordon, ed. New York: Pantheon
        Books.
    1984 Foucault Reader. Paul Rabinow, ed. New York: Pantheon
        Books.

Fox, Richard, G.
    1991a Introduction: Working in the Present. *In* Recapturing Anthro-
        pology: Working in the Present. Richard Fox, ed. Pp. 1–16. Santa
        Fe: School of American Research.
    1991b For a Nearly New Culture History. *In* Recapturing Anthropol-
        ogy: Working in the Present. Richard Fox, ed. Pp. 93–114. Santa
        Fe: School of American Research.

Fox, Richard G., ed.
    1991 Recapturing Anthropology: Working in the Present. Santa Fe:
        School of American Research.

Fratkin, Eliot
    1991 Surviving Drought and Development: Ariaal Pastoralists of
        Northern Kenya. Boulder, CO: Westview Press.

Friedl, Ernestine
    1984 [1975] Women and Men: An Anthropologist's View. Prospect
        Heights, IL: Waveland Press.

Frison, George
    1989 Experimental Use of Clovis Weaponry and Tools on African
        Elephants. American Antiquity 54:766–784.

Fritz, John M., and Fred T. Plog
    1970 The Nature of Explanation in Archaeology. American Antiquity 35:405–412.

Furst, Peter
    1990 [1972] Flesh of the Gods: The Ritual Use of Hallucinogens. Prospect Heights, IL: Waveland Press.

Futuyma, Douglas J.
    1983 Science on Trial: The Case for Evolution. Sunderland, MA: Sinauer Associates.

Gardner, H.
    1983 Frames of Mind: The Theory of Multiple Intelligences. New York: Basic Books.

Geertz, Clifford
    1973 The Interpretation of Cultures. New York: Basic Books.
    1988 Works and Lives: The Anthropologist as Author. Stanford: Stanford University Press.

Gellner, Ernest
    1992 Postmodernism, Reason and Religion. London: Routledge.

Gibson, Thomas
    1991 Meat Sharing as a Political Ritual: Forms of Transaction Versus Modes of Subsistence. *In* Hunters and Gatherers, Vol. 2: Property, Power and Ideology. Tim Ingold, David Riches, and James Woodburn, eds. Pp. 165–179. New York: Berg.

Gifford, Diane
    1978 Ethnoarchaeological Observations of Natural Processes Affecting Cultural Materials. *In* Explorations in Ethnoarchaeology. Richard Gould, ed. Pp. 127–179. Albuquerque: University of New Mexico Press.

Gilbert, M. Jean, Nathaniel Tashima, and Claudia C. Fishman
    1991 Ethics and Practicing Anthropologists' Dialogue with the
        Larger World. *In* Ethics and the Profession of Anthropology.
        Carolyn Fluehr-Lobban, ed. Pp. 200–210. Philadelphia: Univer-
        sity of Pennsylvania Press.

Gould, Richard A.
    1980 Living Archaeology. Cambridge: Cambridge University Press.
    1982 To Have and Have Not: The Ecology of Sharing among Hunter-
        Gatherers. *In* Resource Managers: North American and Australian
        Hunter-Gatherers. Nancy M. Williams and Eugene S. Hunn, eds.
        Pp. 69–91. Boulder, CO: Westview Press.

Gould, Stephen J.
    1981 The Mismeasure of Man. New York: W. W. Norton and Co.
    1994 The Geometer of Race. Discover 15:64–69.

Gould, Stephen J., and N. Eldredge.
    1977 Punctuated Equilibria: The Tempo and Mode of Evolution
        Reconsidered. Paleobiology 3:115–151.

Gragson, Ted L.
    1989 Allocation of Time to Subsistence and Settlement in a Ciri
        Khonome Pume Village of the Llanos of Apure, Venezuela. Ph.D.
        Dissertation, Department of Anthropology, The Pennsylvania
        State University.

Graham, Elspeth, Joe Dougherty, and Mo Malek
    1992 Introduction: The Context and Language of Postmodernism. *In*
        Postmodernism and the Social Sciences, Joe Dougherty, Elspeth
        Graham, and Mo Malek, eds. Pp. 1–24. New York: St. Martin's
        Press.

Griffin, James B.
1952a Culture Periods in Eastern United States Archeology. *In* Archaeology of Eastern United States. J. Griffin, ed. Pp. 352–364. Chicago: University of Chicago Press.
1952b Radiocarbon Dates for the Eastern United States. *In* Archaeology of Eastern United States. J. Griffin, ed. Pp. 365–370. Chicago: University of Chicago Press.

Gross, Paul R., and Norman Levitt
1994 Higher Superstition: The Academic Left and Its Quarrels with Science. Baltimore: Johns Hopkins University Press.

Grünbaum, Adolf
1976 [1960] The Duhemian Argument. *In* Can Theories be Refuted?: Essays on the Duhem-Quine Thesis. Sandra Harding, ed. Pp. 116–131. Dordrecht: D. Reidel Publishing Co.

Habermas, Jürgen
1968 Knowledge and Human Interests. Boston: Beacon Press.

Hakken, David
1991 Anthropological Ethics in the 1990s. *In* Ethics and the Profession of Anthropology. Carolyn Fluehr-Lobban, ed. Pp. 74–94. Philadelphia: University of Pennsylvania Press.

Hammersley, Martyn
1992 What's Wrong with Ethnography? Methodological Explorations. London: Routledge.

Harding, Sandra
1976 Introduction. *In* Can Theories Be Refuted? Essays on the Duhem-Quine Thesis. Sandra Harding, ed. Pp. ix–xxi. Dordrecht: D. Reidel Publishing co.
1991 Whose Science? Whose Knowledge? Thinking from Women's Lives. Ithaca: Cornell University Press.

Harner, Michael
    1972 Common Themes in South American Indian Yagé Experiences.
        In Hallucinogens and Shamanism. Michael J. Harner, ed. Pp.
        155–175. Oxford: Oxford University Press.

Harries-Jones, Peter
    1985 From Cultural Translator to Advocate—Changing Circles of
        Interpretation. *In* Advocacy and Anthropology, First Encounters.
        R. Paine, ed. Pp. 224–248. St. Johns: Institute of Social and
        Economic Research, Memorial University of Newfoundland.

Harris, Marvin
    1968 The Rise of Anthropological Theory: A History of Theories of
        Culture. New York: Thomas Y. Crowell Co.
    1975 Why a Perfect Knowledge of All the Rules that One Must
        Know in Order to Act Like a Native Cannot Lead to a Knowledge
        of How Natives Act. Journal of Anthropological Research
        30:242–251.
    1979 Cultural Materialism. New York: Random House.
    1994 Cultural Materialism Is Alive and Well and Won't Go Away
        Until Something Better Comes Along. *In* Assessing Cultural
        Anthropology. R. Borofsky, ed. Pp. 62–76. New York: McGraw-
        Hill, Inc.
    1995a Anthropology and Postmodernism. *In* Science, Materialism,
        and the Study of Culture. Martin F. Murphy and Maxine L.
        Margolis, ed. Pp. 62–77. Gainesville: University Press of Florida.
    1995b Comment: On Objectivity and Militancy: A Debate Current
        Anthropology 36:423–424.

Hawkes, Kristen
    1990 Why Do Men Hunt? Benefits for Risky Choices. *In* Risk and
        Uncertainty in Tribal and Peasant Economies. Elizabeth Cashdan,
        ed. Pp. 145–166. Boulder, CO: Westview Press.
    993a Why Hunter-Gatherers Work. Current Anthropology 34:341–
        361.
    1993b Reply to Hill and Kaplan. Current Anthropology 34:706–710.

Hawkes, Kristen, J. F. O'Connell, and N. G. Blurton Jones
1995 Hadza Children's Foraging: Juvenile Dependency, Social Arrangements, and Mobility among Hunter-Gatherers. Current Anthropology 36:688–700.

Heidegger, Martin
1962 Being and Time. J. Macquarrie and E. Robinson, trans. New York: Harper.

Helland, Johan
1985 Development Agencies and Anthropology. *In* Advocacy and Anthropology, First Encounters. R. Paine, ed. Pp. 28–30. St. Johns: Institute of Social and Economic Research, Memorial University of Newfoundland.

Hempel, Carl G.
1965 Aspects of Scientific Explanation and Essays in the Philosophy of Science. New York: The Free Press.

Herrnstein, Richard J.
1973 I.Q. in the Meritocracy. Boston: Atlantic-Little Brown.

Herrnstein, Richard J., and Charles Murray
1994 The Bell Curve: Intelligence and Class Structure in American Life. New York: Free Press.

Hill, Kim, and Kristen Hawkes
1983 Neotropical Hunting among the Aché of Eastern Paraguay. In Adaptive Responses of Native Amazonians. Raymond B. Hames and William T. Vickers, eds. Pp. 139–188. New York: Academic Press.

Hill, Kim, and Hillard Kaplan
1993 On Why Male Foragers Hunt and Share Food. Current Anthropology 34:701–710.

Hobbes, Thomas
 1962 [1651] Leviathon: Or the Matter, Forme and Power of a Commonwealth Ecclesiastical and Civil. New York: Collier Macmillan.

Hodder, Ian
 1982 Symbols in Action: Ethnoarchaeological Studies of Material Culture. Cambridge: Cambridge University Press.
 1991a Reading the Past: Current Approaches to Interpretation in Archaeology, Second Edition. Cambridge: Cambridge University Press.
 1991b. Interpretive Archaeology and Its Role. American Antiquity 56:7–18.

Hollinger, Robert
 1994 Postmodernism and the Social Sciences: A Thematic Approach. Thousand Oaks, CA: Sage.

Holmberg, Allan R.
 1985 [1950] Nomads of the Long Bow: The Siriono of Eastern Bolivia. Prospect Heights, IL: Waveland Press.

Hume, David
 1956 [1735] A Treatise of Human Nature. In The Age of Enlightenment, Isaiah Berlin ed., New York: Mentor.

Hunt, Earl
 1995 The Role of Intelligence in Modern Society. American Scientist 83:356–368.

Hurtado, Ana Magdalena, Kristen Hawkes, Kim Hill, and Hillard Kaplan
 1985 Female Subsistence Strategies among Ache Hunter-Gatherers of Eastern Paraguay. Human Ecology 13:1–28.

Hymes, Dell
 1974 The Use of Anthropology: Critical, Political, Personal. In Reinventing Anthropology. Dell Hymes, ed. Pp. 1–79. New York: Vintage Books.

Hymes, Dell, ed.
    1974 Reinventing Anthropology. New York: Vintage Books.

Ingle, Dwight J.
    1973 Who Should Have Children: An Environmental and Genetic
        Approach. Indianapolis: Bobbs-Merrill Co.

Ingold, Tim, David Riches, and James Woodburn, eds.
    1991a Hunters and Gatherers, Vol. 1: History, Evolution and Social
        Change. New York: Berg.
    1991b Hunters and Gatherers, Vol. 2: Property, Power and Ideology.
        New York: Berg.

Jacoby, Russell, and Naomi Glauberman
    1995 The Bell Curve Debate: History, Documents, Opinions. New
        York: Random House.

Jaimes, M. Annette, with Theresa Halsey
    1992 American Indian Women: At the Center of Indigenous Resis-
        tance in Contemporary North America. *In* The State of Native
        America. M. Annette Jaimes, ed. Pp. 311–344. Boston: South End
        Press.

Jensen, A.R.
    1969 How Much Can We Boost IQ and Scholastic Achievement?
        Havard Educational Review 39:1–123.

Jeske, Robert
    1989 Economies in Raw Material Use by Prehistoric Hunter-Gather-
        ers. *In* Time, Energy and Stone Tools. Robin Torrence, ed. Pp.
        34–45. Cambridge: Cambridge University Press.
    1992 Who Owns the Past? Paper presented at the Indiana University
        Cornelius O'Brien Conference on Historic Preservation, French
        Lick, Indiana, October 1992.
    1996 World Systems Theory, Core-Periphery Interactions and Elite
        Economic Exchange in Mississippian Societies. Journal of World
        Systems Research 2(10):1–30. http://csf.colorado.edu/wsystems/
        jwsr.html

Johnson, Alfred E.
 1979 Kansas City Hopewell. *In* Hopewell Archaeology: The
 Chillicothe Conference. D. Brose and N. Greber, eds. Pp. 86–93.
 Kent, OH: Kent State University Press.

Johnson, Phillip E.
 1991 Darwin on Trial. Washington D.C.: Regnery Press.
 1994 Shouting 'Heresy' in the Temple of Darwin. Christianity Today,
 October 24, 1994:22–26.

Jones, W. T.
 1969 A History of Western Philosophy: Kant to Wittgenstein and
 Sartre, Second Edition. New York: Harcourt Brace.

Joukowsky, Martha
 1980 Field Archaeology: Tools and Techniques of Field Work for
 Archaeologists. Englewood Cliffs, New Jersey: Prentice-Hall,
 Inc.

Kaplan, Hillard, and Kim Hill
 1985 Hunting Ability and Reproductive Success among Male Ache
 Foragers: Preliminary Results. Current Anthropology 26:131–
 133.

Kaplan, Hillard, Kim Hill, and A. Magdalena Hurtado
 1990 Risk, Foraging and Food Sharing among the Ache. *In* Risk and
 Uncertainty in Tribal and Peasant Economies. Elizabeth Cashdan,
 ed. Pp. 107–144. Boulder, CO: Westview Press.

Kay, Marvin
 1979 On the Periphery: Hopewell Settlement of Central Missouri. *In*
 Hopewell Archaeology: The Chillicothe Conference. D. Brose
 and N. Greber, eds. Pp. 94–99. Kent, OH: Kent State University
 Press.

Keeley, Lawrence H.
1980 Experimental Determination of Stone Tool Uses: A Microwear Analysis. Chicago: University of Chicago Press.
1996 War Before Civilization. New York: Oxford University Press.

Kelley, Klara B., and Peter M. Whitley
1989 Navajoland: Family and Settlement and Land Use. Tsaile, AZ: Navajo Community College Press.

Kelly, Robert L.
1995 The Foraging Spectrum: Diversity in Hunter-Gatherer Lifeways. Washington D C: Smithsonian Institution Press.

King, J. L., and T. H. Jukes
1969 Non-Darwinian Evolution. Science 164:788–798.

Kleindienst, Maxine and Patty Jo Watson
1956 Action Archaeology: The Archaeological Inventory of a Living Community. Anthropology Tomorrow 5:75–78.

Kluckhohn, Clyde, and Dorothea Leighton
1962 The Navajo. Garden City, New York: Anchor Books and Doubleday & Co., Inc.

Knoke, David, and James Kuklinski
1982 Network Analysis. Beverly Hills, CA: Sage.

Kosso, Peter
1991 Method in Archaeology: Middle-Range Theory as Hermeneutics. American Antiquity 56:621–627.

Kühl, Stefan
1994 The Nazi Connection: Eugenics, American Racism and German National Socialism. Oxford: Oxford University Press.

Kuhn, Thomas
> 1970 The Structure of Scientific Revolutions, Second Edition, Enlarged. Chicago: University of Chicago Press.

Kuper, Adam
> 1973 Anthropologists and Anthropology: The British School 1922–1972. New York: Pica Press.
> 1992 Post-Modernism, Cambridge and the Great Kalahari Debate. Social Anthropology 1:57–71.
> 1995 Comment on Objectivity and Militancy: A Debate. Current Anthropology 36:424–426.

Kuznar, Lawrence A.
> 1995a Awatimarka: The Ethnoarchaeology of an Andean Herding Community. Fort Worth: Harcourt Brace.
> 1995b Aymara Herding Practices in Peru and Their Effects on the Environment: The Interaction of Perception, Politics, and the Land. Proceedings of the Indiana Academy of the Social Sciences 26:62–69.
> 1996 What People Say and What People Do: A Central Dilemma for Anthropology—Or, Archaeology to the Rescue. Paper presented at the 61st Annual Meetings of the Society for American Archaeology, New Orleans, April 1996.

Lakatos, Imre
> 1970 Falsification and the Methodology of Scientific Programmes. *In* Criticism and the Growth of Knowledge. Imre Lakatos and Alan Musgrave, ed. Pp. 91–196. Cambridge: Cambridge University Press.
> 1978 The Methodology of Scientific Research Programmes. Cambridge: Cambridge University Press.

Lane, Charles
> 1994 The Tainted Sources of 'The Bell Curve.' New York Review of Books 41:14–19.

Latour, Bruno
  1987 Science in Action: How to Follow Scientists and Engineers
    through Society. Cambridge: Harvard University Press.

Laughlin, William S.
  1957 Blood Groups of the Anaktuvuk Eskimos, Alaska. Anthropo-
    logical Papers of the University of Alaska 6:2–15.
  1968 Hunting: An Integrated Biobehavior System and Its Evolution-
    ary Importance. *In* Man the Hunter. Richard B. Lee and Irven
    DeVore, eds. Pp. 304–320. Chicago: Aldine.

Lebar, Frank M.
  1970 Coding Ethnographic materials. *In* A Handbook of Method in
    Cultural Anthropology. Raoul Naroll and Ronald Cohen, eds. Pp.
    707–720. New York: Columbia University Press.

Lee, Richard B.
  1968 What Hunters Do for a Living, or, How to Make Out on Scarce
    Resources. *In* Man the Hunter. Richard B. Lee and Irven Devore,
    eds. Pp. 30–48. Chicago: Aldine.
  1972 The !Kung Bushmen of Botswana. *In* Hunters and Gatherers
    Today. M. G. Bicchieri, ed. Pp. 326–368. New York: Holt,
    Rinehart and Winston.
  1979 The !Kung San: Men, Women, and Work in a Foraging Society.
    Cambridge: Cambridge University Press.

Lee, Richard B., and Irven Devore
  1968 Problems in the Study of Hunters and Gatherers. *In* Man the
    Hunter. Richard B. Lee and Irven Devore, eds. Pp. 3–12. Chi-
    cago: Aldine.

Levi-Strauss, Claude
  1963 Structural Anthropology. Garden City, NY: Doubleday and
    Company.

Lewontin, R. C.
    1972 The Apportionment of Human Diversity. Evolutionary Biology
          6:381–398.

Livingstone, Frank B.
    1958 Anthropological Implications of the Sickle Cell Gene Distribu-
          tion in Africa. American Anthropologist 60:533–557.

Losee, John
    1972 A Historical Introduction to the Philosophy of Science. London:
          Oxford University Press.

Lovejoy, Arthur O.
    1936 The Great Chain of Being: A Study of the History of an Idea.
          Cambridge: Havard University Press.

Lutz, Catherine
    1990 The Erasure of Women's Writing in Sociocultural Anthropol-
          ogy. American Ethnologist 17:611–627.

Lyotard, Jaques
    1984 The Postmodern Condition: A Report on Knowledge. G.
          Bennington and B. Massumi, trans., Minneapolis: University of
          Minnesota Press, Minneapolis.

Mackenzie, Brian
    1984 Explaining Race Differences in IQ. American Psychologist
          39:1214–1233.

MacNeish, Robert S.
    1978 The Science of Archaeology? North Scituate, MA: Duxbury
          Press.

Malinowski, Bronislaw
    1984 [1922] Argonauts of the Western Pacific. Prospect Heights, IL:
          Waveland Press.

Marcus, George E.
   1994 After the Critique of Ethnography: Faith, Hope and Charity,
       But the Greatest of These is Charity. *In* Assessing Cultural
       Anthropology R. Borofsky, ed. Pp. 40–54. New York: McGraw-
       Hill, Inc.

Marcus, George E., and Dick Cushman
   1982 Ethnographies as Texts. Annual Review of Anthropology
       11:25–69.

Marcus, George E., and Michael M. J. Fisher
   1986 Anthropology as Cultural Critique: An Experimental Moment
       in the Human Sciences. Chicago: University of Chicago Press.

Marshall, Lorna
   1976 Sharing, Talking and Giving: Relief of Social Tensions among
       the !Kung. *In* Kalahari Hunter-Gatherers. Richard B. Lee and
       Irven DeVore, eds. Pp. 349–371. Cambridge: Harvard University
       Press.

Martin, M. Kay, and Barbara Voorhies
   1975 Female of the Species. New York: Columbia University Press.

Mascia-Lees, F., P. Sharpe, and C. Ballerino Cohen.
   1989 The Postmodernist Turn in Anthropology: Cautions from a
       Feminist Perspective. Signs 15:7-33.

Mauss, Marcel
   1967 [1925] The Gift: Forms and Functions of Exchange in Archaic
       Societies. New York: W. W. Norton & Co.

Mead, Margaret
   1961 [1928]. Coming of Age in Samoa. New York: William Morrow
       & Company.

Medvedev, Zhores
   1969 The Rise and Fall of T. D. Lysenko. Michael Lerner, trans. New
       York: Columbia University Press.

Meiskins Wood, Ellen
    1995 What is the 'Postmodern' Agenda? An Introduction. Monthly
          Review 47:1–12.

Miller, G.A.
    1956 The Magical Number Seven, Plus or Minus Two: Some Limits
          on Our Capacity for Processing Information. Psychological
          Review 63:81–97.

Molino, Fernando
    1962 Existentialism as Philosophy. Englewood Cliffs, NJ: Prentice-
          Hall.

Montagu, Ashley, ed.
    1975 Race and IQ. London: Oxford University Press.

Morgan, Lewis Henry
    1963 [1877] Ancient Society. Cleveland: Meridian.

Morgan, Richard G.
    1952 Outline of Cultures in the Ohio Region. *In* Archeology of
          Eastern United States. James B. Griffin, ed. Pp. 83–98. Chicago:
          University of Chicago Press.

Morgen, Sandra
    1990 Gender and Anthropology: Introductory Essay. *In* Gender and
          Anthropology: Critical Reviews for Research and Teaching. S.
          Morgen, ed. Pp. 1–20. Washington DC: American Anthropologi-
          cal Association.

Morris, Henry M.
    1984 The Biblical Basis for Modern Science. Grand Rapids, MI:
          Baker Book House.

Morris, Henry M., ed.
    1974 Scientific Creationism. San Diego: Creation-Life Publishers.

Mulhern, Francis
1995 The Politics of Cultural Studies. Monthly Review 47:31–40.

Murdock, George P., and Caterina Provost
1973 Factors in the Division of Labor by Sex: A Cross-Cultural Analysis. Ethnology 12:203–235.

Nader, Laura
1974 Up the Anthropologist: Perspectives Gained from Studying Up. *In* Reinventing Anthropology. Dell Hymes, ed. Pp. 285–311. New York: Vintage Books.
1995 Comment on Objectivity and Militancy. Current Anthropology 36:426–427.

Naroll, Raoul
1970 Data Quality Control in Cross-Cultural Surveys. *In* A Handbook of Method in Cultural Anthropology. Raoul Naroll and Ronald Cohen, eds. Pp. 927–945. New York: Columbia University Press.

Naroll, Raoul, and Ronald Cohen, eds.
1970 A Handbook of Method in Cultural Anthropology. New York: Columbia University Press.

Neel, J. V., F. M. Salzano, P. C. Junqueira, F. Keiter, and D. Maybury-Lewis
1964 Studies in the Xavante Indians of the Brazilian Mato Grosso. American Journal of Human Genetics 16:52–140.

Nencel, Lorraine and Peter Pels eds.,
1991 Constructing Knowledge: Authority and Critique in Social Science. London: Sage.

Newcomb, Franc J.
1964 Hosteen Klah: Navajo Medicine Man and Sand Painter. Norman: University of Oklahoma Press.

Nietzsche, Friedrich
    1954 [1873] On Truth and Lie in an Extra-Moral Sense. *In* The
        Portable Nietzsche. W. Kaufmann, ed. trans. Pp. 42–47. New
        York: Penguin.

Nusbaumer, Michael, Judith DiIorio, and Robert Baller
    1994 The Boycott of 'Star Wars' by Academic Scientists: The
        Relative Roles of Political and Technical Judgement. Social
        Science Journal 31:375–388.

O'Meara, J. Tim
    1989 Anthropology as Empirical Science. American Anthropologist
        91:354–369.

Paine, Robert
    1985 Overview. *In* Advocacy and Anthropology, First Encounters. R.
        Paine, ed. Pp. 249–259. St. Johns: Institute of Social and Eco-
        nomic Research, Memorial University of Newfoundland.

Paine, Robert, ed.
    1985 Advocacy and Anthropology, First Encounters. St. Johns:
        Institute of Social and Economic Research, Memorial University
        of Newfoundland.

Pels, Peter, and Lorraine Nencel
    1991 Introduction: Critique and the Deconstruction of Anthropologi-
        cal Authority. Constructing Knowledge: Authority and Critique
        in Social Science. Lorraine Nencel and Peter Pels, eds. Pp. 1–21.
        London: Sage.

Pelto, Pertti J., and Pelto, Gretel H.
    1978 Anthropological Research: The Structure of Inquiry. Cam-
        bridge: Cambridge University Press.

Peregrine, Peter
    1992 Mississippian Evolution: A World-Systems Perspective.
        Madison, WI: Prehistory Press.

Perkins, David
   1995 Outsmarting IQ: The Emerging Science of Learnable Intelli-
      gence. New York: The Free Press.

Platt, John R.
   1964 Strong Inference. Science 146:347–353.

Plomin, Robert, Michael J. Owen, and Peter McGuffin
   1994 The Genetic Basis of Complex Human Behaviors. Science
      264:1733–1739.

Popper, Karl R.
   1959 [1934] The Logic of Scientific Discovery. New York: Harper &
      Row.
   1972 Objective Knowledge: An Evolutionary Approach, Revised
      Edition. Oxford: Oxford University Press.

Powdermaker, Hortense
   1966 Stranger and Friend: The Way of an Anthropologist. New York:
      W. W. Norton & Co.

Preucel, Robert W.
   1991 Comment on R. Watson's 'What the New Archaeology Has
      Accomplished.' Current Anthropology 32:287–288.

Price, T. Douglas, and James A. Brown
   1985 Aspects of Hunter-Gatherer Complexity. *In* Prehistoric Hunter-
      Gatherers: The Emergence of Cultural Complexity. T. Douglas
      Price and James A. Brown, eds. Pp. 3–20. Orlando: Academic
      Press.

Prufer, Olaf H.
   1964 The Hopewell Complex of Ohio. *In* Hopewellian Studies. J.
      Caldwell and R. Hall, eds. Pp. 35–83, Springfield: Illinois State
      Museum Scientific Papers Volume 12.

Quine, Willard Van Orman
  1976 [1953] Two Dogmas of Empiricism. *In* Can Theories be
    Refuted?: Essays on the Duhem-Quine Thesis. Sandra Harding,
    ed. Pp. 41–63. Dordrecht: D. Reidel Publishing Co.

Rabinow, Paul
  1977 Reflections on Fieldwork in Morocco. Berkeley: University of
    California Press.
  1986 Representations Are Social Facts: Modernity and Post-Moder-
    nity in Anthropology. *In* Writing Culture: The Poetics and
    Politics of Ethnography. James Clifford and George E. Marcus,
    eds. Pp. 234–261. Berkeley: University of California Press.
  1991 For Hire: Resolutely Late Modern. *In* Recapturing Anthropol-
    ogy: Working in the Present. Richard G. Fox, ed. Pp. 59–72.
    Santa Fe: School of American Research.

Radcliffe-Brown, A. R.
  1964 [1932] The Andaman Islanders. Glencoe: Free Press.
  1965 [1924] Structure and Function in Primitive Society. New York:
    The Free Press.

Rappaport, Roy A.
  1994 Humanity's Evolution and Anthropology's Future. *In* Assessing
    Cultural Anthropology R. Borofsky, ed. Pp. 153–167. New York:
    McGraw-Hill, Inc.

Rathje, William A.
  1973 The Tuscon Garbage Project. Tuscon: University of Arizona
    Press.

Redman, Charles
  1974 Archaeological Sampling Strategies. Reading, MA: Addison-
    Wesley Module in Anthropology.

Riley, Thomas J.
  1991 On "Explicitly Scientific Archaeology" and the Radical Cri-
    tique. Current Anthropology 32:590–592.

Riley, Thomas J., Gregory R. Waltz, Charles J. Bareis, Andrew C. Fortier, and Kathryn E. Parker
1994 Accelerator Mass Spectrometry (AMS) Dates Confirm Early *Zea mays* in the Mississippi River Valley. American Antiquity 59:490–498.

Rimmer, Harry
1945 Modern Science and the Genesis Record. Berne, IN: Berne Witness Company.

Rindos, D.
1984 The Origins of Agriculture: An Evolutionary Perspective. New York: Academic Press.

Ritzer, George
1993 The McDonaldization of Society. Newbury Park, CA: Pine Forge Press.

Roessel, R., and B. Johnson, compilers
1974 Navajo Livestock Reduction: A National Disgrace. Chinle, AZ: Navajo Community College Press.

Rogers, Edward S.
1972 The Mistassini Cree. *In* Hunters and Gatherers Today. M. G. Bicchieri, ed. Pp. 90–137. New York: Holt, Rinehart and Winston.

Rorty, Richard
1979 Philosophy and the Mirror of Nature. Princeton: Princeton University Press.

Rosaldo, Renato
1991 Culture and Truth: The Remaking of Social Analysis. Boston: Beacon Press.

Roscoe, Paul B.
1995 The Perils of "Positivism" in Cultural Anthropology. American Anthropologist 97:49–504.

Rosenau, Pauline
1992 Post-Modernism and the Social Sciences: Insights, Inroads, and Intrusions. Princeton: Princeton University Press.

Rosman, Abraham, and Paula Rubel
1986 [1971] Feasting with Mine Enemy: Rank and Exchange among Northwest Coast Societies. Prospect Heights, IL: Waveland Press.

Rousseau, Jean Jaques
1954 [1762] The Social Contract. Chicago: Regnery Gateway.

Rubel, Paula, and Abraham Rosman
1994 The Past and Future of Anthropology. Journal of Anthropological Research 50:335–344.

Rummel, Rudolph J.
1970 Dimensions of Error in Cross-National Data. *In* A Handbook of Method in Cultural Anthropology. Raoul Naroll and Ronald Cohen, eds. Pp. 946-961. New York: Columbia University Press.

Rushton, J. Philippe
1995 Race, Evolution, and Behavior. New Brunswick, NJ: Transaction Publishers.

Russell, Bertrand
1959 [1931] The Scientific Outlook. New York: W. W. Norton & Co.
1972 [1945] A History of Western Philosophy. New York: Simon and Schuster.

Sahlins, Marshall
1972 Stone Age Economics. Chicago: Aldine.

Said, Edward
1978 Orientalism. New York: Pantheon Books.

Salmon, Merrilee H.
  1982a Philosophy and Archaeology. New York: Academic Press.
  1982b Models of Explanation: Two Views. *In* Theory and Explanation in Archaeology: The Southampton Conference. C. Renfrew, M. Rowlands, and B. Segraves, eds. Pp. 35–44. New York: Academic Press.
  1992 Philosophical Models for Postprocessual Archaeology. *In* Metaarchaeology. L. Embree, ed. Pp. 227–241. Dordrecht: Kluwer Academic Publishers.

Salmon, Wesley C.
  1982 Causality in Archaeological Explanation. *In* Theory and Explanation in Archaeology: The Southampton Conference. C. Renfrew, M. Rowlands, and B. Segraves, eds. Pp. 45–55. New York: Academic Press.
  1992 Explanation in Archaeology: An Update. *In* Metaarchaeology. L. Embree, ed. Pp. 243–253. Dordrecht: Kluwer Academic Publishers.

Sandstrom, Pamela Effraim, and Alan Sandstrom
  1995 The Use and Misuse of Anthropological Methods in Library and Information Science Research. Library Quarterly 65(2):161–199.

Sangren, P. Steven
  1988 Rhetoric and the Authority of Ethnography: "Postmodernism" and the Social Reproduction of Texts. Current Anthropology 29:405–436.

Sanjek, Roger
  1990 On Ethnographic Validity. *In* Fieldnotes: The Makings of Anthropology. Roger Sanjek, ed. Pp. 385–417. Ithaca:Cornell University Press.

Sanjek, Roger, ed.
  1990 Fieldnotes: The Makings of Anthropology. Ithaca:Cornell University Press.

Saxe, Arthur A.
    1970 Social Dimensions of Mortuary Practices. Ph.D. Dissertation, University of Michigan, Ann Arbor. University Microfilms International.

Scheper-Hughes, Nancy
    1995 The Primacy of the Ethical: Propositions for a Militant Anthropology. Current Anthropology 36:409–420.

Schiffer, Michael B.
    1976 Behavioral Archaeology. New York: Academic Press.

Schlick, Moritz
    1959 Positivism and Realism. *In* Logical Positivism. A. J. Ayer, ed. Pp. 82–107. New York: Free Press.

Schoepfle, M., M. Burton, and K. Begishe
    1984a Navajo Attitudes toward Development and Change: A Unified Ethnographic and Survey Approach to an Understanding of Their Future. American Anthropologist 86:885–905.

Schoepfle, M., M. Burton, and F. Morgan
    1984b Navajos and Energy Development: Economic Decision Making Under Political Uncertainty. Human Organization 3:265–276.

Scott, John
    1991 Social Network Analysis: A Handbook. Newbury Park, CA: Sage.

Segall, Marshall H.
    1979 Cross-Cultural Psychology: Human Behavior in a Global Perspective. Monterey, CA: Wadsworth, Inc.

Service, Elman R.
    1966 The Hunters. Englewood Cliffs, NJ: Prentice-Hall, Inc.
    1971 [1962] Primitive Social Organization. New York: Random House.

Shanks, Michael, and Christopher Tilley
  1987a Re-Constructing Archaeology: Theory and Practice. Cambridge: Cambridge University Press.
  1987b Social Theory and Archaeology. Cambridge: Polity Press.

Sharp, Henry S.
  1981 The Null Case: The Chipewyan. *In* Woman the Gatherer. F. Dahlberg, ed. Pp. 221–244. New Haven: Yale University Press.

Shaw, Stanford
  1976 History of the Ottoman Empire and Modern Turkey, Volume I. Cambridge: Cambridge University Press.

Shipman, Pat
  1994 The Evolution of Racism: Human Differences and the Use and Abuse of Science. New York: Simon and Schuster.

Shostak, Marjorie
  1981 Nisa: The Life and Words of a !Kung Woman. New York: Vintage.

Silverberg, Robert
  1970 The Mound Builders. New York: Ballantine.

Simpson, G. Gaylord
  1949 The Meaning of Evolution. New Haven: Yale University Press.

Simpson, J. A., and E. S. C. Weiner
  1989 Oxford English Dictionary, 2nd Edition. New York: Oxford University Press.

Siskind, Janet
  1973 To Hunt in the Morning. London: Oxford University Press.

Smart, Barry
  1993 Postmodernity: Key Ideas. New York: Routledge.

Smith, Eric Alden

    1991 Risk and Uncertainty in the "Original Affluent Society":
         Evolutionary Ecology of Resource-Sharing and Land Tenure. *In*
         Hunters and Gatherers, Vol. 1: History, Evolution and Social
         Change. Tim Ingold, David Riches, and James Woodburn, eds.
         Pp. 222–251. New York: Berg.

Solway, J., and R. B. Lee

    1990 Forgers, Genuine or Spurious? Current Anthropology 31:109–
         146.

Spearman, Charles

    1904 "General Intelligence," Objectively Determined and Measured.
         American Journal of Psychology 15:201–209.

Spence, M.W., W. Finlayson, and R. Pihl

    1979 Hopewellian Influences on Middle Woodland Cultures in
         Southern Ontario. *In* Hopewell Archaeology: The Chillicothe
         Conference. D. Brose and N. Greber, eds. Pp. 115–121. Kent,
         OH: Kent State University Press.

Spradley, James P.

    1979 Participant Observation. New York: Holt, Rinehart and Win-
         ston.
    1980 The Ethnographic Interview. New York: Holt, Rinehart and
         Winston.

Stanford, Craig B.

    1995 Chimpanzee Hunting Behavior. American Scientist 83:56–261.
    1996 The Hunting Ecology of Wild Chimpanzees: Implications for
         the Evolutionary Ecology of Pliocene Hominids. American
         Anthropologist 98:96–113.

Stearman, Allyn Maclean

    1989 Yuquí: Forest Nomads in a Changing World. New York: Holt,
         Rinehart and Winston.

Steward, Julian
    1955 Theory of Culture Change: The Methodology of Multilinear
        Evolution. Urbana: University of Illinois Press.

Stiglmayer, Alexandra
    1994 The War in the Former Yugoslavia. *In* Mass Rape: The War
        against Women in Bosnia-Herzegovina. Pp. 1–34. Lincoln:
        University of Nebraska Press.

Strathern, Andrew
    1971 The Rope of Moka: Big-Men and Ceremonial Exchange in
        Mount Hagen, New Guinea. Cambridge: Cambridge University
        Press.

Struever, Stuart
    1964 The Hopewell Interaction Sphere in Riverine-Western Great
        Lakes Culture History. *In* Hopewellian Studies. J. Caldwell and
        R. Hall, ed. Pp. 85–106, Springfield, IL: Illinois State Museum
        Scientific Papers No. 12.

Struever, Stuart, and Gail L. Houart
    1972 An Analysis of the Hopewell Interaction Sphere. *In* Social
        Exchange and Interaction. E. N. Wilmsen, ed. Pp. 47–79. Ann
        Arbor: University of Michigan Museum of Anthropology Anthro-
        pological Papers No. 46.

Suttles, Wayne
    1968 Coping with Abundance: Subsistence on the Northwest Coast.
        In Man the Hunter. Richard B. Lee, and Irven Devore, eds. Pp.
        56–68. Chicago: Aldine.

Sylvester, Joan, Patrick Ashton, and Peter Iadicola
    1981 Methodological Problems in Marxist Sociology. A Paper
        Presented at the Annual Meeting of the Southern Sociological
        Society, Louisville, Kentucky, April 9–11, 1981.

Tainter, Joseph
    1988 The Collapse of Complex Societies. New York: Cambridge
        University Press.

Taylor, Walter
    1948 A Study of Archaeology. Menasha, WI: American Anthropo-
        logical Association.

Thomas, Cyrus
    1985 [1894] Report on the Mound Explorations of the Bureau of
        Ethnology. Washington, DC: Smithsonian Institution Press.

Trinkaus, Erik
    1978 Hard Times among the Neanderthals. Natural History 87:58–
        63.

Trinkaus, Erik, and Pat Shipman
    1992 The Neandertals: Changing the Image of Mankind. New York:
        Alfred A. Knopf.

Truswell, A. Stewart, and John D. L. Hansen.
    1976 Medical Research among the !Kung. *In* Kalahari Hunter-
        Gatherers. Richard B. Lee and Irven Devore, eds. Pp. 166–194.
        Cambridge: Harvard University Press.

Turkeimer, Eric
    1991 Individual and Group Differences in Adoption Studies of IQ.
        Psychological Bulletin 110:392–405.

Tweney, Ryan D., Michael E. Dougherty, and Clifford R. Mynatt, eds.
    1981 On Scientific Thinking. New York: Columbia University Press.

Tyler, Stephen A.
  1986 Post-Modern Ethnography: From Document of the Occult to Occult Document. Writing Culture: The Poetics and Politics of Ethnography. James Clifford and George E. Marcus, eds. Pp. 122–140. Berkeley: University of California Press.
  1991 A Post-modern In-stance. *In* Constructing Knowledge: Authority and Critique in Social Science. Lorraine Nencel and Peter Pels, eds. Pp. 78–94. London: Sage.

Tylor, E. B.
  1960 [1881] Anthropology. Ann Arbor: University of Michigan Press.

Vayda, Andrew P.
  1994 Actions, Variations, and Change: The Emerging Anti-Essentialist View in Anthropology. *In* Assessing Cultural Anthropology. R. Borofsky, ed. Pp. 320–330. New York: McGraw-Hill, Inc.

Vincent, Joan
  1991 Engaging Historicism. *In* Recapturing Anthropology: Working in the Present. Richard Fox, ed. Pp. 45–58. Santa Fe: School of American Research.

Washburn, Sherwood, and C. S. Lancaster
  1968 The Evolution of Hunting. *In* Man the Hunter. Richard B. Lee, and Irven Devore, eds. Pp. 293–303. Chicago: Aldine.

Watson, Graham
  1991 Rewriting Culture. *In* Recapturing Anthropology: Working in the Present. Richard Fox, ed. Pp. 73–92. Santa Fe: School of American Research.

Watson, Patty Jo
  1992 Explanation in Archaeology: Reactions and Rebuttals. *In* Metaarchaeology. L. Embree, ed. Pp. 121–140. Dordrecht: Kluwer Academic Publishers.

Watson, P. J., S. A. LeBlanc, and C. L. Redman
    1971 Explanation in Archaeology. New York: Columbia University
        Press.
    1984 Archaeological Explanation: The Scientific Method in Archae-
        ology. New York: Columbia University Press.

Watson, Richard A.
    1976 Inference in Archaeology. American Antiquity 41:58–66.
    1990 Ozymandius, King of Kings: Postprocessual Radical Archaeol-
        ogy as Critique. American Antiquity 55:673–689.
    1991 What the New Archaeology Has Accomplished. Current
        Anthropology 32:275–291.
    1992 The Place of Archaeology in Science. *In* Metaarchaeology. L.
        Embree, ed. Pp. 255–267. Dordrecht: Kluwer Academic Pub-
        lishers.

Weatherford, Jack
    1991 Native Roots: How the Indians Enriched America. New York:
        Fawcett Columbine.

Weber, Max
    1958 [1922] Science as Vocation. *In* From Max Weber: Essays in
        Sociology. H. H. Gerth and C. Wright Mills, eds. Pp. 129–156.
        New York: Oxford University Press.
    1978 [1921] Economy and Society. Guenther Roth and Claus
        Wittich, eds. Berkeley: University of California Press.

Weiner, Annette B.
    1976 Women of Value, Men of Renown: New Perspectives in
        Trobriand Exchange. Austin: University of Texas Press.

Werner, Dennis
    1990 Amazon Journey: An Anthropologist's Year among Brazil's
        Mekranoti Indians. Englewood Cliffs, NJ: Prentice-Hall, Inc.

Werner, Oswald, and G. Mark Schoepfle
    1987 Systematic Fieldwork, Volume 1: Foundations of Ethnography
        and Interviewing. Newbury Park, CA: Sage Publications.

Whiting, Beatrice, and John Whiting
  1970 Methods for Observing and Recording Behavior. *In* A Handbook of Method in Cultural Anthropology. Raoul Naroll and Ronald Cohen, eds. Pp. 282–315. New York: Columbia University Press.

Wiessner, Polly
  1982 Risk, Reciprocity and Social Influences on !Kung San Economics. *In* Politics and History in Band Societies. E. Leacock and Richard B. Lee, eds. Pp. 61–83. Cambridge: Cambridge University Press.

Willey, Gordon R. and Phillip Phillips
  1958 Method and Theory in American Archaeology. Chicago: University of Chicago Press.

Williamson, John B., Linda Evans, and Anne Munley, eds.
  1985 Social Problems: Contemporary Debates. Boston: Little and Brown.

Wilmsen, E., and J. Denbow
  1990 Paradigmatic History of San-Speaking Peoples and Current Attempts at Revision. Current Anthropology 31:489–524.

Wilson, E. O.
  1975 Sociobiology: The New Synthesis. Cambridge: Havard University Press.

Winterhalder, Bruce
  1981 Optimal Foraging Strategies and Hunter-Gatherer Research in Anthropology: Theory and Models. *In* Hunter-Gatherer Foraging Strategies: Archaeological and Ethnographic Analyses. B. Winterhalder and E. A. Smith, eds. Pp. 13–35. Chicago: University of Chicago Press.
  1986 Optimal Foraging: Simulation Studies of Diet Choice in a Stochastic Environment. Journal of Ethnobiology 6:205–223.

Witherspoon, Gary
1973 Sheep in Navajo Culture and Social Organization. American Anthropologist 75:1441–1448.

Wittgenstein, Ludwig
1953 Philosophical Investigations. New York: Macmillan and Company
1972 [1921] Tractatus Logico-philosophicus. D. F. Pears and B. F. McGuiness, trans. New York: Humanities Press.

Woodburn, James
1968 An Introduction to Hadza Ecology. In Man the Hunter. Richard B. Lee and Irven Devore, eds. Pp. 49–55. Chicago: Aldine.

Wylie, Alison
1992a On "Heavily Decomposing Red Herrings": Scientific Method in Archaeology and the Ladening of Evidence with Theory. In Metaarchaeology. L. Embree, ed. Pp. 269–288. Dordrecht: Kluwer Academic Publishers.
1992b The Interplay of Evidential Constraints and Political Interests: Recent Archaeological Research on Gender. American Antiquity 57:5–35.

Wysong, R. L.
1976 The Creation-Evolution Controversy. Midland, MI: Inquiry Press.

Yellen, John
1977 Archaeological Approaches to the Present: Models for Reconstructing the Past. New York: Academic Press.

Yellen, John, and Richard B. Lee
1976 The Dobe-/Du/da Environment: Background to a Hunting and Gathering Way of Life. In Kalahari Hunter-Gatherers. Richard B. Lee and Irven Devore, eds. Pp. 27–46. Cambridge: Harvard University Press.

Zimbalist-Rosaldo, Michelle, and Louise Lamphere
    1974 Introduction. *In* Woman Culture & Society. M. Zimbalist-
        Rosaldo and L. Lamphere, eds. Pp. 1–15. Stanford: Stanford
        University Press.

Zimbalist-Rosaldo, Michelle, and Louise Lamphere, eds.
    1974 Woman Culture & Society. Stanford: Stanford University Press.

Index

X